# THE UNIVERSITY
## A PLACE OF SLAVERY

# THE UNIVERSITY
## A PLACE OF SLAVERY

A Glimpse into the Role of the
Academia in the Capitalist Order

GEORGE HAJJAR PH.D

Library of Congress Control Number:        2015915366
ISBN:            Hardcover              978-1-5144-0858-2
                 Softcover              978-1-5144-0857-5
                 eBook                  978-1-5144-0856-8

Print information available on the last page.

Rev. date: 09/17/2015

**To order additional copies of this book, contact:**
Xlibris
1-888-795-4274
www.Xlibris.com
Orders@Xlibris.com
721240

# Contents

Preface........................................................................................................ vii
Introduction ............................................................................................... ix

## PART 1: HUBRIS

Chapter 1   Robotry and Rebellion in the Social System........................3
Chapter 2   Man, Caliban, Clerk................................................... 22
Chapter 3   Student Radicalism:
            Copulation, Co-Optation, Liberation ............................... 29
Chapter 4   Academic Unfreedom................................................ 38
Chapter 5   Hierarchy and Dissent in Academe ................................. 43

## PART 2: SPARTICIST: BLACK AND WHITE

Chapter 6   Lutheran Fossil................................................... 53
            Sparticist I: Open Letter to Lutheran CAUT .......................... 71
            Sparticist II: Note on Scholarship and Humanism..................... 74
            Sparticist II: The Politics of Politics............................... 77
            Sparticist III: Open letter to Professor Milner............................ 87
            Sparticist IV: Intellectual Masturbation: Faculty Style ................ 92

Chapter 7   The Suno Upheaval:
            The Birth Pangs of Black Freedom.............................. 99

## PART 3: ACADEMIC ODYSSEY

Chapter 8   The Treason of the Clerks ...................................... 137
Chapter 9   Student Protest................................................. 144
Chapter 10  The University: Liberty or Servility?................................154

Chapter 11   The University Game ................................................ 161

Chapter 12   The Thoughts of Comrade Bissell.................................. 167

Chapter 13   The American Model ................................................ 175

## PART 4

Chapter 14   Rousseau's Emile: Education for Enlightenment............. 183

Appendix ................................................................................ 211

Index.................................................................................... 239

# Preface

Over forty years ago, I wrote a memo for the sixties, *The University: A Place of Slavery*, in the heat of the battle. I did not alter or revise the text so that the reader of the second decade of the twenty-first century can capture the temper and the spirit of the exciting sixties.

The memo is self-explanatory; it is hubris and upheavals with a Sparticist touch, and it includes the literature of the epoch with its divergent perspectives. Moreover, it embraces Rousseau's *Emile* in the age of Enlightenment, the forerunner to the French Revolution and the education for liberation and the rediscovery of the humankind.

The appendix is indeed as illustrations for the contents of the memo, and it adds what is relevant to the context I wrote in. Besides, some of the press reports under struggle I engaged in with the autocracies of the university system, which I faced with its arrogance and futilitarian nonsense. To the students and professors of this era, I say: it is time to revive the spirit of humanism and human integrity and to move the world from the kingdom of necessity to the kingdom of revolutionary change and to inscribe under the sun that never sets that freedom is our lodestar that teaches us to paint wings of freedom on our shackles.

Finally, I am deeply indebted to Elias Bacas in helping me have this book published.

# Introduction

Stability is a goddess the Western man worships. *Dissent* is a word he utters to demonstrate his liberality, but he means it not. Revolution to him is either a term of opprobrium to intimidate critics and silence them or a public relations slogan to disseminate the revolutionary discoveries recently made in dog food or deodorants. The high priests of stability propound it incessantly and make certain that their victims share their perceptions of reality, their conceptions of themselves and their destiny, their world view. The pivot for all these misconceptions is bourgeois private property, a system of property relations that dictates the character of man's social being, his place in the universe, and the kind of functions he has to perform to subsist in a property-ridden environment. Now among the most important loci of psychic power in bourgeois society is the university, not only because its employees manufacture the mental constructs that undergird their rulers but also because it pretends to be a transcending institution in but outside society—an autonomous and objective republic of learning. The university, however, has never been, is not, and can never be anything but an ideological center that prepares cadres to serve the social system under which it exists and trains rhetoricians and orators to expound its virtues. That is, the university cannot be non-ideological. It is by definition ideological. It can at best play the role of the "loyal opposition" in a secure and technologically advanced system, but on the whole, it is always a subservient institution. Therefore, in choosing to attack the bourgeois university, the radicals have selected the most important ideological prop of capitalism; and by contributing to the erosion of its influence, they are undermining the mental maelstrom of the social order that oppresses them.

Power and justice are an abiding theme in Western thought. Justice, however, has only been a frail feminine phenomenon. Power—sacerdotal, regal, bureaucratic, and corporate—has always held sway in a totalitarian manner. Its wielders have always regarded it as a possession and a relationship among themselves. How much power was exercised and what kind of power was to be called upon depended largely on the stage of social evolution the rulers were in, the power of potential opposition, the nature of an impending crisis. The power holders sought to retain their powers forever, and the struggle against them had to be waged and mounted in the name of justice. But the moment justice triumphed, she was abandoned and sacrificed on the altar of power. Justice, however, is rearing her head again in our age; but this time, it must abolish power forever—abolish not only bourgeois private property but also bourgeois social relations and habits of thought. At any rate, this is how I see the mission of contemporary radicalism, and it is to help clarify this mission that I wrote these essays. In part one of this booklet, I try to clarify the stages of social systems and explain how that university and its constituents behave and react toward each other. In part two, I focus on the issues of power and justice as they affected me and cite two case studies in which I was involved—part autobiographical, part social criticism. In part three, I illustrate how some university constituents conceive of their roles and offer critiques of their views. In part four, some documents are reproduced to give credence to the meaning of power and by implication to show how the self-professed guardians of justice are asleep at their post while she lies slain.

These essays were not written for the intellectual edification of pseudo-colleagues or in humble gratitude to foundation-assigned tasks. They were written in the hope that a few people will read them and learn how to discern the hypocrisy and fraudulence of the university and to expose the political harlots that maintain the ramparts of capitalism. Therefore, I have to acknowledge no one or express ostentatious indebtedness to chairmen, deans, and other underlings. Those ideologues and their sponsors will only be confirmed in their beliefs should these essays fall into their hands. Should they decide that I constitute a danger, they will do their utmost to banish me completely from Canadian society. But in all probability, they will remain silent and take notice of these essays and ignore them. Whatever they do, their actions will have no bearing on the future of history. Those ideologues of capitalism are doomed, and the dustbin of history awaits them for permanent consignment.

Lastly, a word to my radical friends: Your bourgeois professors and news media commentators and perhaps your parents and neighbors are currently celebrating the "defection" of Mr. Kuznetsov as they celebrated those of Stalin's daughter and Fidel's sister. Do not let such "defections" affect, neutralize, or silence you. Those people have abdicated; they have not defected, and in coming to Britain or America, those "defectors" will sooner or later discover how temporary their celebrity is and how little they are indeed. Giants defect by fighting against injustice and unconscionable power. They stand up to bureaucratic control and manipulatory democracy. They say no to oppression everywhere. They do not flee the barricades. Dwarfs, on the other hand, defect for personal safety and lucrative markets. They do not "defect" for or to freedom. They "defect" for false fame and popularity. They come to sell their empty souls for silver and to display their flossy wares in the marketplace of greed and avarice. They are non-people. They have rejected both revolution and counterrevolution, the only possibilities that honest men can embrace. They have opted for sodomy, the choice of the imbecile and sterile. Heed them not for these, and your professors are the barriers to liberty, and only by overcoming them will you be free!

Cold warriors and their opponents contend that their particular social system is superior to that of the enemy on the basis of its freedom, effluence, productivity. Each antagonist purports to live under the most virtuous system ever conceived of by the mind of man; each flaunts his system as being universally valid, desires to make the world safe for it, and aims at extending its fruits to every corner of the globe; each proponent assumes that his system is either divinely or naturally revealed, and therefore, it ought to be and must be actualized. In this chapter, it will be asserted that all socioeconomic systems are totalitarian; that all systems undergo the same birth pangs and the natural disintegration of all bio-physical phenomena; that in spite of the long-recorded history of man, he has lived only under four orientations (religion, technology, poetry, science); and, finally, that though there are literally dozens of legal sovereignties and dependencies with enormous varieties and peculiar forms of governments, there are, in fact, only seven genera combinations of government. Having classified governments in general categories, we are able to prescribe what type of action is required of revolutionaries, particularly in North America.

# PART 1

# Hubris

# Chapter 1

## Robotry and Rebellion in the Social System

All socioeconomic systems irrespective of the *isms* they avow are totalitarian. Social systems, however libertarian they may be at the outset, become totalitarian as their original truth is metamorphosed into superstition, ritual, and pervasive, unreasoning orthodoxy. Under such dispensation, power wielding becomes empirically compartmentalized but psychic ally unified by the conditions of mental despotism, which conduces an immanently stultifying uniformity that brooks no dissent, no divergence of opinion, no liberty of thought or action. Indeed, the order of mental and social servitude through the mechanisms of psychological terrorism, social ostracism, and economic proscription is capable, depending upon what stage of the political life cycle of the political system it is in, of reaching every department of life from child rearing to methods of burial; from religious rectitude to the annihilation of radical opposition; from styles of life and taste to the performance of the sexual act; from economic planning for private or communal benefit to bureaucratic implementation of decisions; from governing "kingly" to governing autocratically. Therefore, totalitarianism is an all-embracing, all-encompassing social phenomenon; and no liberal or moralistic incantation, ideology, or apology can wish it away or absolutely excuse it. Totalitarianism is an ineluctable law of life, reality and being everywhere in organized society, particularly in this age of technology.

We in the West deceive ourselves when we think we are free, independent, and autonomous people who have constructed societies that make it possible for man to be free and to develop his creative intellect. Factually, the West is much more totalitarian than the Soviet Union or its satrapies where people know clearly that to oppose the regime violently or critically is to incur self-destruction. In the West, we live under the illusion that we are free and rest content with that knowledge. But if we were to test this proposition, we should discover much to our dismay its falsity. Indeed, we are programmed to think of ourselves as free when we are not. However, if the naive among us were to resolve to exercise their freedom, they would soon discover the difference between the rhetoric of freedom and the fact of unfreedom: suppression. We therefore live under a mental slavery that is doubly pernicious, doubly destructive, doubly dehumanizing. The only difference, therefore, between a Kennedy and his American Green Berets, on the one hand, and Mussolini and his Fascist Brown Shirts, on the other, is that the latter unabashedly called themselves totalitarian while the former under the pretext of anti-Communism and American "freedom" are prepared to put an end to the human story every time their world hegemony is contested or someone resists their encroachments or blandishments. This American freedom is universal totalitarianism, world soldiery, the vampiring of mankind. From U.S.-Soviet posturing and past history, we deduce that totalitarianism is preponderant everywhere, and the difference between one and another is not a difference of kind but of degree, not of humanness but of competence, not of barbarity or freedom but between systematic and efficient liquidation of opposition and haphazard and periodic dissipation of its forces. Let our reader not only be reminded of Budapest and Prague but also of Beirut, Santo Domingo, and others in addition to Saigon and Chicago.

In the chronology of war, folly, progress, and human adventure, no truly free society ever existed or is likely ever to come into being in our epoch. Only free individuals have lived and live today, and our hope is their multiplication. Therefore, our focus is the characteristically free man who is free of illusions or lives with a modicum of illusions. His only article of faith is the scientific method and the belief in man's ability to perfect himself, to progress indefinitely, to expand his consciousness. A free man, moreover, is one who knows the premise or starting point of the totalitarianism he expounds. He is aware of the implications, consequences, and requirements of his totalitarianism and is prepared to pay the price for actualizing it. He does not obfuscate his position or confounds his stances; his aim is clear; his method is discernible; his approach is open— the marketplace or assembly are the temples of his science. The only justification his totalitarianism has is its superior method, its love of collision, its tentativeness, its openness, its eternal flux, its perpetual truth. It follows, therefore, that the kind of totalitarianism we espouse is empirical teleology, not transcendental or material totalitarianism. It is a totalitarianism of sciences, not of religion, party, state, group, or class—a totalitarianism of self-transcendence, humanization, communitarianism. It is not the MKVD terrorism, CIA counter-insurgency, or the trampling of Vietnam underfoot to free it. It is a totalitarianism of man for man. Only hermits, idiots, and gods are immunized against it. It is a totalitarianism whose starting points, ramifications, and gyrations can be grasped by only a few, are denounced by most, and denied by many. Our foes are a race of charlatans, of ideologues, and fetish worshipers who are capable of infinite self-deception, and their outrage against us will be enhanced by the reigning totalitarianism of the age and the invidiousness of its clerical proponents. We are guilty of destroying their cherished illusions and of unmasking their sophistication, urbanity, civility. We are immoral, impious blasphemers whose god is man, whose altar is humanity, whose inspiration is the love of life.

Translated into the stream of history, our scientific totalitarianism declares that all hitherto recorded history was not the by-product of multiple-party systems, two-party systems, or single-party dominance systems. All emerging political systems have been and will be violent, intolerant of opposition, self-righteous, well-knit groups with cohesive and dedicated leadership. All political parties are closed corporations, whether or not they admit it, reflect the trends of the socioeconomic milieu and, however masked, represent class interests. Only an ascendant class pretends to be representative of the totality of society; and only a revolutionary party claims to represent mankind, the future, the coming kingdom. Thus, it behooves us to sketch a typology of the life cycle of the system of the world, which seems to consist of the following stages (1) threshold and birth (2) growth and acculturation, (3) acme and maturity, (4) decline and decay, and (5) disintegration and dissolution.

1. **Threshold and Birth:** The stages of birth and dissolution of every political organism are inextricably intertwined and are almost indistinguishable. The only index that enables us to determine that the preceding system has finally broken down, and a new crystallization has been consummated—that of the conquest of political power by the revolutionary party. A period

of great agitation, fermentation, and radicalism preceded the event; and a period of exhilaration, relief and repression ensued. However, the organism itself is never annihilated—never completely extinguished. It survives in part, and the children of the revolution carry its genes, not its torches; its habits of action, not its freedom, thoughts and rituals; its skills and achievements, not its lackeys and hangers-on. In sum, what survives of the political system is its physical attainment, not its political culture, and it is this combination we call the self-transcending and self-perpetuating mechanism of all systems in history. This phenomenon can be discerned in the universalist propensity of all systems at the time of their birth. It is the aspect that reformers and radicals rediscover when the political system is on the verge of disintegration and appeal—to no avail—to the ruling coteries in the name of its ideals to save Christianity, civilization, morality, Americanism or the "Socialist commonwealth." Reformers, whatever the adopted ideology may be, inevitably plead for the enhancement of system maintenance by regrouping the "moral" elements in hope of penetrating the conscience of the power holders to rescue themselves. Revolutionaries seize the occasion to deepen the revolutionary consciousness of the multitude, organize the cadres to mount the final assault, prepare a charter of freedom to replace the fossil mythology. When the revolution takes place, the counter-elite becomes the governing elite. Therefore, the old elite is smashed, its state machinery shattered, its cultural apparatus destroyed.

2. **Growth and Acculturation:** With the liquidation of the old and the emergence of the new, growth begins in earnest and unhampered. The system takes roots, branches out into other realms of life as new cultural elite, instills the new ideology, and disseminates the "noble lie" of the new science. Lapses will doubtlessly occur, but the revolution is irreversible, and the task of the revolutionaries in the aftermath will be that of revolutionizing their national society and spreading the revolutionary gospel to others.

At the outset, the revolutionary party is not wholly revolutionary. It is both conservative and revolutionary. It conserves the techno-economic achievement and builds on it as a foundation. It builds, however, with much greater enthusiasm, vision, purity, dedication—the sources of the right to rule. The revolutionary party embodies a deeper feeling for humanity, a profound commitment to science, a greater devotion to experimentation, and an unsuspicious faith in the prospects of man— the sources of its clan, vitality, life force. No Constantine conversion of society can be affected or expected; and since the general public abhors abrupt moral radical change and cannot be transformed overnight, physical violence will be employed to defeat the enemies of the new order, neutralize the wavering elements, and galvanize the friends of the revolution into a mighty invincible force within and without the system.

Violence will also be necessary to eradicate intra-party strife and withstand the onslaught of prospective outside aggressors. Therefore, the revolutionary class must be ruthless in the treatment of the enemy, friendly toward its followers, fierce to all challengers. It must become the universally dominant class; the only activity it can condone is a loyal, ineffectual opposition without a power base. As the revolutionary class expands its power and eliminates its enemies, it creates the intellectual environment for technical innovation. It also enlarges its base of support and inculcates its morality, religion, and psychology. The more entrenched the revolutionary virtues and mores become, the less frequently will physical violence be required. The more universal the revolutionary ethos, the more pervasive the psychic violence will become; the more potent the new "social myths," the more "democracy" there will be; the more stable the system, the greater its "repressive tolerance" will be; the more homogenized the system, the greater the diversity of organization will be. In brief, when the new totalitarianism becomes the universal religion and man and god become its altar boys, we will have achieved the new freedom, the new fundamental rights, and will have created the new man. Also, we will have acquired absolute faith in the inherent superiority of our system and its infallibility in its divine or natural ordination, contempt for other inferior systems, the unshaken belief that there is no alternative to our "imperfect order." We will proclaim that the human mind cannot conceive of a better system of liberty, security, and property. The firmness of our belief stems from our unlimited commitment to the justness of the historic process of birth, which was bloody, agonizing, and, at times, appeared abortive. However, the birth of the new order, new life, new potential caused and required violence, "the midwife of progress," which we learn to deem necessary and externally imposed. We will contend that the "founding fathers" had no choice but to resort to force to destroy tyranny, whereas the "rabble" bypass the regular channels for redress of grievance or abolish it.

After the revolution, there was organized chaos; then mushrooming growth followed and enabled life to take roots, germinate the new seeds, hasten the coming of the spring. The sudden burst of life come from the bosom of the old society, which throttled growth and stifled expansion. The revolutionary party triggered the process, and there was new life. Without a revolutionary party, there can be no revolutionary outcome. Without potentiality and an agent to actualize it, no new forms of life can take shape. Without an acorn, no oak tree can be had. Without a prolonged winter, there cannot be a beautiful spring. Without death, there can never be life. Without renewal, there can only be death, stagnation, decay. The revolution is life itself and a life-giving agency. It is man's affirmation of his essence and man's ability to proclaim himself master of his life, creator of gods, author of his history. It is life denying life by becoming life. It is revolution!

The growth and expansion of the revolution and acculturation of its citizenry entail a remodelling of the landscape. To ascend from the nadir to the summit of the mountain is no easy task. At certain intervals, the Sisyphean mythology comes close to be true. But the revolution in its stage of growth develops a momentum of its own, which is most dynamic, most energizing, most exciting and enveloping. As it approaches the stage of some, however, the revolution begins to deteriorate. Indeed, in a way it starts, like all things in nature, to die a little with the birth; but in the stages of birth, growth, and some, life force is mightier than life death. Therefore, the signs of life eclipse and conceal the signs of death, and the blossom of spring and warmth of summer hide the coming autumn and winter. Spring has its heady way of denying other seasons; youth, of its charms of not counting years; counterrevolutionaries, of fighting for life to death.

3. **Acme and Maturity:** When a system reaches the stage of acme, two options are open to it: internal self-development and democratization or external expansion and imperialism. All known systems managers in history selected the latter option because of material thrust and ambitions, because imperialism

requires little or no accountability and enables the elite to maintain a semblance of growth internally while training the citizenry to feel as a world benefactor when, in fact, it is a world exploiter. Therefore, the period of acme as a period of culmination is brief. Only in post-historic society can it endure. That happy era of permanent growth cannot be attained until the nation state is abolished, the level of well-being is almost universally the same, and technology is an evenly distributed accomplishment. Meanwhile, the "revolutionaries" become a self-perpetuating elite who slowly forget the public good and begin to seek their self-advantage. The revolution on the eve of its fulfilment commences to its steep decline, which the governors call maturity. In this process, immorality, cynicism, power, manipulation, and political machinations replace revolutionary asceticism, morality, spontaneity, initiative, enterprise, and human relations. The ideologue becomes a party hack, the revolutionary bureaucrat, the servant and a master the citizen voter, the teacher a wage slave, the prophet a priest, the judge a policeman, the governor an autocrat, the professor a storyteller, the worker a hand, the child a toy, the lover an erotic object— man becomes a monad.

In the stage of maturity, a well-functioning political system uses a modicum of physical violence to maintain itself and its relics heavily on social tyranny, ostracism of critics, the weeding out of potential or actual opposition. The system depends on the internalization of its morality by the generality of the citizenry to cope with stress signals or danger signs; it operates on the automatically responsive reflex psychology of homogenized robots to pulverize dissent, subversion, radicalism.

To maintain itself, a healthy socioeconomic system creates a superstructure commensurate with its requisite morality, psychology, religion, and folkways. It also trains cadres of political brokers and groups to justify, explain, and elaborate upon it. It is a formidable system to overthrow. Indeed, it cannot be overthrown; it can only be exposed. Therefore, in the state of acme, the revolutionary party program must be educational, visionary, poetic. Its deeds by necessity remain individualistic, heroic, exemplary.

Its appeals, to be effective, must be general, diffuse, inchoate, idealistic. Its function deals with the generation of necessary doubt with reference to the validity of the system by demonstrating its injustices, exploitations, inhumanities. However, the impact of these expository manifestations may be cushioning or reinforcing to the system because the ruling elite is not disoriented and divided, and only a small segment of its members have defected to the revolution. To solve this dilemma, the revolutionary party must differentiate between liberal reforms and social revolution, social tinkering and systematic restructuring, moralism and morality. It must constitute itself the sole vanguard of the oppressed.

4. **Decline and Decay:** Because of the imperceptible character of the decline processes, decline is not discerned until it is too late to reverse the trend. With mounting trouble from within and without, and with the diminishing ability of the rulers to manipulate their citizenry, the system enters the stage of decay. The speed, tempo, and extent of this process will be determined by the environmental context of the social system, the stupidity or the enlightenment of contemporary oligarchs in other countries, their preparedness to rescue their kind, and, above all, the daring, intelligence, and vision of the revolutionary party. Decay or disintegration could be a long stage of atrophy in the life cycle of any political system. There is no reason to believe that this period cannot be maintained indefinitely. Indeed, most systems live in this semi-twilight stage. At present, only two polities—China and Cuba—are in periods of vital growth edging toward acme.

The United States and the Soviet Union and their satellites are essentially somewhere between the stages of acme and decay. In other words, these systems have reached their apogee and are in a state of decomposition. This process cannot be reversed; it can be stopped, stalled, damned, especially if the ruling class refurbishes itself by co-option, changes in personnel, or social experimentation.

5. **Disintegration and Dissolution:** On the eve of dissolution, the great industrial, technological, and social attainment of the preceding stages of the social system become highly warped and distorted. Innovation and experimentation are restricted to

certain sectors of the economy, to gadgetry, to the production of superfluity for a ruling class, to the planned obsolescence of American monopoly capitalism, or to the class consumption of Soviet managerialism. This period we identify as disintegration. It commences when the oligarchy is divided, when many citizens doubt the 'justice" of their foreign adventures, when they begin to feel guilty about their possessions, when the children become ungrateful, when the governors become extravagant, when the dispossessed become demanding and assertive. However, objectively speaking, the oligarchy does not perceive these phenomena and continues in its mindless, merry way as if nothing is happening. When pressed for action, it calls critics rebels, rebels foreign agents, opposition treason. It has no answer to all problems: bribery. If bribery fails to obtain the desired result, the police will; and if necessary, the armed forces will join them too. The stage for dissolution is set in motion.

As the system approaches the stage of dissolution, the ruling class remains imbued with a sense of transcendental righteousness and power. Opposition is systematically liquidated, isolated, or co-opted. Some important groups and individuals desert their class, but there is no mass defection to the revolution. Only the careerists join when the revolution becomes an inevitably accomplished fact. Dissolution, in most cases, is hastened by the Marie Antoinettes, the tsarinas, the Madam Chiang-Kai Sheks. Revolution occurs as a result of military defeat, war, general disillusionment, thoroughgoing fatigue, and exhaustion on the part of the ruling class, not because revolutionaries plan it. All the systemic revolutions that have taken place—the French, which ended ancient history; the Soviet, which obliterated tsardom, the Chinese, which ushered in world history—validate the generalization that only in war, on the eve, or in its aftermath do we have thoroughgoing revolution. The periods of rising expectations and rising frustrations we only get bourgeois radical mobocracy, not revolutions. Moreover, the character, scope, intensiveness, and extensiveness of the use of violence determine the extent and depth of the changes that will be effected. In other words, the profundity or the shallowness of change is proportional to the amount of violence used by the ruling and the emerging counter-elites. If the revolution were abortive, counterrevolutionary repression will be mercilessly and indiscriminately inflicted. If the revolution triumphs, revolutionary violence will be more systematic and extensive. An entire class will be eliminated as a class. It is a deadly contest, a war of annihilation. There can be no compromise. Therefore, the mission of the revolutionary party is the complete destruction of the preceding ruling class and its lackeys and its replacement by the revolutionary order and class with its cadres. This course of action is imperative because without periodic revolutionary renewal, no society or people can remain vital, strong, vibrant, or human. If this characterization is true, each society must undergo a revolution approximately every hundred years or every three generations.

In our present stage of world history, systematic revolutions are imperative in America, Africa, Asia (excluding China), and Western Europe. When these revolutions take place, the regions of East Europe, Soviet Union, and China will be in dire need of a revolution.(Until the French Revolution, we only had national or city history, although the impact of empire was transnational. The French Revolution was the first to have had international secular repercussions, and the Soviet revolution was the first to have placed within the purview of history's section of the European working class. The Chinese revolution marked the entry of the human race into history. If the Arab-Afro societies throw off the yoke of imperialism, they will become actors in world history. At the moment, however, they are only entities.)

**4. World Views:** With our analytical schemata, we can proceed to identify the stages occupied by each power cluster in the world. The stages, however, are not neat perspectives. We therefore need to link them with four world views that explain the entire mental history of mankind: (a) religion, (b) poetry, (c) technology, and (d) science.

(a) Religion is as universal as ignorance. Its ascendancy or extirpation depends on the poverty or might of consciousness, rationality, science. As a world view, it explains the primitives, however mysteriously, and, unsatisfactorily, their position in the cosmos vis-à-vis God, nature, men. Its power is pervasive. Priesthood ensures religious dominion. As an overpowering set of dogmas and procedures, religion conditions the moral behavior of the faithful, helps them relate to others "meaningfully," and makes them lead obedient, unexamined lives. Thus, religion has a crippling effect on men especially in his intellectual infancy. His fear of the unknown impels him to deny himself, project himself onto the screen of eternity, and worship it as an objectified external force, which he regards as omniscient, omnipotent, omnipresent. Religion is indeed the "sigh" of the oppressed and the "opium" of man in the ages of faith and autocracy. Absolutism and paternalism are the hallmarks of a religion whose demise will be determined by the persistence or abolition of ignorance and by the vigor of flabbiness of capitalist and feudal orthodoxies the world over. Societies where religion is dominant are the most backward in every way morally, culturally, socioeconomically.

The religious orientation still has a powerful grip on the minds of many people even in "advanced" countries. The roots of this power are to bound, on the one hand, in the alliance between religion and the ruling classes in many countries and, on the other, among the Catholic, Protestant, and Jewish internationals and imperialism. The exposition of this conspiracy in its modern form of "ecumenicism" is an essential task for radicals everywhere.

(b) Technology is the concretization of man's mental growth. It reflects his state of knowledge and his quest for material acquisition. Religion hampers men's endeavor; but technology, since the age of exploration and the discovery of the "new world," has assumed an autonomy of its own, which in due course became science and challenged the religious orthodoxy and undermined its foundation. However, technology, as such, has been and still is governed by some sort of religion, whether in the guise of Catholic Christianity, tribal Judaism, Protestantism, or spiritualized capitalism. The interplay between religion and technology determines the social structures of non-scientific societies: the division of labor, the strata that prevail, the mores, beliefs, and values. Technology, under the auspices of religion, is science in its nascent phase. By and large, it is manipulated in the service of religion. Technology, as gadgetry and frills, is science gone mad in the hands of profiteers, buccaneers, and soothsayers who prey on man and fleece the ignorant who live by suggestion and trust, not reflection and conviction. When technology becomes the accepted religion, it too impedes the growth of knowledge, the expansion of the human spirit, the evolution of life.

(c) Poetry is man's rebellion against religiosity and the instrumental reason. It is an affirmation of man's imagination and his dignity. It is an effort to recover man and elevate him above his sordid creatures: gods, temples, governors, poverty, oppression, war.

Poetry is an endeavor to say yes and no at the same time—a declaration that man cannot be crushed, subjugated; and mutilated forever, that man can transcend himself and his environment; that man can and will achieve self-determination. As an expression of faith in man and hope for a better tomorrow, poetry is revolutionary and cannot be otherwise. "Poets," however, as image makers, intellectual peddlers, or refined critics, can be a herd of sentimental, nostalgic, self-serving "literati" who make the banal litany of orthodoxy seem like the coming of spring and a reflection of the "true" spirit. Such "poets" are most reactionary. They are part of the religious and moral economy of every phantasmagoria. Good poets, on the other hand, are saints, prophets, and apostles of mankind. They possess the moral stamina and sensibilities that compel them to say no to deadening, enervating, emasculating environments. They are hated by bureaucrats, clerics, mythmakers, and religious animals everywhere. They are a standing reminder that other possibilities exist. Therefore, every time a true poet dies—and he dies daily—part of mankind dies and is resurrected with him. His deeds are the songs of human triumph; his words, the expressions of the human heart; his thoughts, the outpouring of our feeble imagination.

A regime solely based on poetry is not probable. It is a thoroughgoing communitarianism that can be had only in post-scientific society. Meanwhile, poetry can be found in pockets in every region of the world. Indeed, poets are in abundance in the most backward of societies and in great scarcity in super-rich America and Western Europe where "poets" are isolated harlots, hipsterish quacks, jingle writers, or storytellers. Poetry is on the eve of return to those arid clines and is casting a shadow on reigning religiosity there. Its unfolding will be the revolutionary drama or our time.

(d) Science is man's emancipation from himself and his environment. It is the conquest of nature, the subjugation of the universe, the construction of new life. Science is a state of technique and a critical cultural outlook; it is a way of viewing reality, essence, and all things with the method of validation, experimentation, skepticism. It is a brake on feelings, erratic imagination, sentimentalism. Happy is the society that combines the scientific and the poetic visions. Degenerate is the society that embraces poetastry and religiosity or instrumentalism and scientism and erects walls that compartmentalize life and stop its process of osmosis.

A scientific society is a society where science is the dominant religion. It is a critical society whose citizens lead the examined life; whose politics are the politics of rationality and humanism; whose economics are designed to serve the community, not the ruling class and its servants; whose social morality is open and style of life experimental; whose architecture, highways, transport, and homes reflect the work of art. A scientific society underpinned by a poetic vision is a true human abode—a paradise on earth. A ruling cabal cannot aspire to this vision, but many individuals do so. It is the minority party of man.

**Classification of Governments:** Without definition of stages of the life cycle of social systems and the identification of world views, which record man's social achievements, we are able to classify the states and the regimes that rule the world. Our criteria are not solely based on GNP, per capita income, steel production, electricity, hardware, mortality rate, or education. These are important indices. But the more important standards are man's relatedness to man, engagement in productive enterprise, social undertaking, communal participation. On the basis of these criteria, we discern the following patterns or combinations in the world. The first is religiosity and poetastery, which predominate in Latin America and the African states. Poetry and religion of the most oppressive kind dominate Latin America. The oligarchies are tribal groupings or families who use man and god to service their bestial and illusory "needs." They have no perspective on life, no thought of man, no conception of anything that is not theirs. They are the world and its possessor. The African states are at a slightly higher stage of development than the Latin banana and coffee republics. Religion is not as pervasive, and the oligarchs who reign there are not as competent and efficient as the Latins. Their geographic position and colonial history make them more susceptible to poetry and less enthralled with religion. Therefore, the prospects for change in Africa are brighter than they are in Latin America. However, the possibilities of revolution are not much greater, thanks to U.S. and European imperialisms and the backwardness of their economies.

The second combination is religiosity and instrumentalism (technology). This pattern is prevalent in the Asian states except China. Religion is unconsciously losing its total grip there, and poetry is slowly emerging. The more technology the modernist face-lifters incorporate, the greater the growth of poetry will be. On the whole, however, the orientation remains religious, and technology is being subordinated to religion. Therefore, technology will not develop autonomously here. It will only assume "modernist" features such as airline fleets, a few monuments to dictators, a number of residential constructions of vulturing real estate. Although religion is the starting point of everything, it does not control life absolutely. Thus, only an external force can precipitate a revolution. The forces of discontent are too feeble to overcome the ruling cliques; they are in a state of disarray. Their growth can only be hastened by fortuitous revolutionary upheavals elsewhere or extremely flagrant aberrations on the part of oligarchs at home.

The third combination consists of poetry and technology, and we find this in the Arab states. Ostensibly, these states are predominantly Moslem anachronistic regimes caught in the web of a medieval world view. Basically, however, religion is both a refuge and a vital force because Islam and Arabism were interchangeable until recently. Poetry is much more characteristic of the Arab even in his most religious period. Technology, of course, was a contribution of his history when Europe was in the age of barbarism, but the Arabs until recently were in the age of darkness and religiosity. Poetry replaced poetastery with the beginnings of the Arab revolution during World War I. Technology started as a European technicism and in developing into a critique of culture in view of the catastrophic defeats suffered by the Arabs at the hands of a few comparatively imperial Zionists. This crystallization placed the Arabs on the threshold of revolutionary cataclysms, which will catapult them to the stage of historical renewal. The prospects of revolution are highly promising in the Arab world, and the oligarchies are in an advanced stage of exhaustion and decay. The rolling back of counterinsurgency on a worldwide scale is likely to commence here.

The fourth combination of technology and religion is most characteristic of second-level industrial states excluding the Soviet Union and Japan. Most of such states where prospects for change are pregnant with possibilities are European; but the historic ossifications of Europe, the competence and moral authority of the oligarchies, make revolution a possibility, not a probability, contingent on the preoccupations, readiness, and ability of Europe's respective masters (Soviet and American) to act adversely or favorably to change them. Neither master is likely to abdicate. Therefore, internal and external factors conspire to suppress revolutionism. A certain darkness hangs over Europe, and the convulsion of the spring of '68 may be the last gasp of a dying order. These upheavals and the "moral upsurge" they typify are essentially a nostalgic, pseudo-affluent outburst of a decadent order. The "contestation" is a fete, a grand universal masturbation of outraged middle-class elements who wanted the system to live up to its professed ideals—they did not want to abolish it. Thus, the deadlock between religion and technology and the state of immobilism, which results therefrom, make Europe incapable of self-redemption. The balance, however, will be tipped in favor of technology verging on science as bipolarity disintegration and a true polycentrism replaces it. In brief, no European state can act independently. None can be expected in the near future. At the moment, Western Europe acts in unison under the tutelage of the United States. East Europe wallows and writhes under Soviet mastery.

The fifth combination of technology and science is to be found in the United States, Soviet Union, Japan, and Canada. In these states, imagination is dead. However, a number of individuals and groups retain this faculty, and most people yearn for it. Happily, a few prophets, saints, and poets are slowly crystallizing a poetic vision and integrating it with science. Science in these lands is partly autonomous, though subjected to technologism. Therefore, the prospects for change are highly promising although the autocracies that rule are efficient and well armed in terms of physical and psychic violence. Science as a powerful corrective to technicism provides the necessary doubt and skepticism needed to develop a revolutionary consciousness and detach the multitudes from the maelstrom of the dominant order. Japan, as an advance colonized power with a colonial history of its own and a powerful left-wing movement, is ripe for revolution in this combination. Its distance from the two major loci of power, its scientific achievement and potential, and its internal forces make Japan a possible candidate for radical change. Canada is, on the other hand, a smugly colonized state without history. She has lived her entire life under the imperial and spiritual yokes of England and America within the ambience of counterrevolution and spiritual impoverishment. If revolution breaks out here, the center will be Quebec, an island of people in North America!

The United States' only hope of restructuring itself lies in a Viet Cong victory as a precipitant to world revolution against her hegemony. The Americans on their own are only capable of revolutionary sloganeering and starting new publications. They cannot free themselves unaided.

Their revolutionism is bourgeois radicalism and individual martyrdom, not Socialist humanism and collective freedom. The Soviets as managers of a Socialist economy without a Socialist culture have no hope and no future except for more economism and bureaucratism. The first "Socialist commonwealth" abolished the stranglehold of monopoly capitalism but retained the authoritarian and exploitative structure of bourgeois economics. It has become the most efficient nation-state machine under the guise of proletarian internationalism. It has choked the creative potential of the working people by not going beyond Stalinism. Only a return to Leninism and working-class solidarity can rescue it from the present morass. This is not in the offing.

The sixth combination is that of science and religion. The North European Protestant states and Israel fall into this category. Science is the basic orientation, religion the fundamental impediment to change; and the struggle between the two makes life exciting, experimental, liveable, particularly in Scandinavia. Socially, these states are enlightened. Religiously, they are backward, especially in Israel where atavistic nativism predominates. Thus, in Scandinavia, the prospects for revolution are zero. In Israel, the prospects depend on the outcome of the Arab-Israeli conflict, the Arab revolution, and the exogenous forces that impinge on the region. Israel's fate and future are symbiotically related to American imperialism. Jewish world power or lack of it will determine her continued existence. If its inhabitants transcend their religious bias and ally themselves with the Arab revolution (which I do not think they will), they could replace religion with poetry and thereafter reach a state of human creativity. Meanwhile, they will remain America's advance soldiery in the Mideast.

The seventh combination of science and poetry is to be found in China and Cuba where the "world spirit" has taken residence. Here, man's spiritual essence rules his material existence. The moral, not the material, incentive is the motive and mode of life. Man, not the GNP, is the index of value. Man is the measure of all things, not God, the church, mammon. The deification of an individual or the cultivation of the personality cult is a transitional phenomenon that helps rather than hinders the propagation of science and poetry at the same time. Although material affluence is not abundant and widespread, it is adequate. Superfluity and waste, which dominate America, are not likely to become rules of life when technology reaches its full flowering in Cuba and China. However, there is no absolute guarantee that the poetic and scientific visions may not be perverted or corrupted. What is certain is that these two polities are the first in history of mankind to have attempted thoroughgoing Socialist revolutions. The obstacles they confront are formidable; the handicaps they must surmount are monumental; the tasks ahead are gigantic; the possibilities are infinite; the revolution will triumph.

## The Role of Rebels

In view of our definition of reality and classification of the existing states of the world, what tasks do we assign to carry out the revolution and to whom? Since in our view, all existing institutions are dead by definition and live by the laws of ritual and inertia, we can only look to the emerging forces of life in the world, the composition of its population, the prospects of its science. By this categorization, revolutionaries the world over will basically be colonial subjects, students, and young workers. Intellectuals, irrespective of age, country, sex, education, income, will perform their historic function as guardians of the human spirit, custodians of true knowledge, apostles of the revolution. As revolutionary cadres in non-revolutionary worlds, intellectuals express the present as future, the future as imminent, the present as historic. Therefore, their numbers must be increased, and their message must reach everyone in the West. The university, high school, factory, shop, office, the streets are their best recruiting grounds.

The "revolutions" of weaponry, cybernetics, and colonialism are the momentous changes of our times. The revolution to abolish human and economic bondage will be the task of the next generation. Our task, especially in North America, is basically agitational, and the "global village" will make it possible for us to affect the desired goal, setting the stage for world revolution. Only a catastrophic defeat of America can enable us to topple its ruling oligarchy. Such defeat is not imminent. Moreover, a Soviet-U.S. confrontation is most unlikely in view of the nuclear holocaust. Thus, it is unthinkable to rely on overt external factors to overturn the regime. However, protracted war abroad and radicalism at home will undermine the regime; and in due course, we could possibly engage the autocracy in a prolonged civil war that would usher in a new epoch of history of mankind.

In brief, the essential task of the immediate future is to foment and ferment, to recruit and train, to plan and contemplate, to wait for the right moment to strike a deadly blow—the blow of death and life.

Meanwhile, revolutionaries should head to the campuses, factories, and communications media. They ought to know that white-collar employees are incapable of seeking anything beyond status; therefore, they should be eschewed. Others like technicians, journalists, some dumb rich kids, non-Jewish Jews, and non-Christian Christians are the likeliest and most susceptible targets. Numbers, or percentages, of course, in so far as the revolution is concerned, are important, not paramount. History, we should remember, is the history of minorities. The makers of history have always been the class strugglers, who, at certain junctures in history, detected the nodal point of change and stuck a blow on behalf of man's emancipation. Therefore, it will be incumbent upon revolutionaries to recruit strategic individuals, creative leaders, heroic models, exemplary chiefs, the general staff. If and when the revolution breaks out, the masses will flock to the party, if the party and the leadership are there to perform their historic functions.

On the whole, robotism is the universal order in the stages of "statesmanship and administration" in every social order including the bourgeois formation (these stages parallel the stages of decay and dissolution in the life cycle outlined above). Programs, therefore, must be devised and designed to reach the entire multitude of robots, however unresponsive they may be. In the universities, automatons are more susceptible than other sectors of society. In those cloisters, there is a pretension that man is unique—a doctrine bourgeois psychology reaches. Thus, it is possible through appeals to pride, uniqueness, and scholastic ideals to convert a few individuals; but the world will not be converted by such methods. Confrontation policies on the campus can evoke sympathy if the aim is liberal, legal, "moderate," and the leadership has mastered liberal rhetoric. Such a policy is useful in conservative environments; it is worthless in radical settings or places of liberal consciousness. In these latter milieus, the "social question" at home, the revolutions and wars abroad should be uppermost on the minds of the revolutionaries. In workplaces, the strategy must be part economism, part revolution. The emphasis must be on the identificatory and universal aspects of the struggle and the role of the shop in the political economy of imperialism. The purpose should be the creation of mass movement, not political parties in the ordinary sense. The only party is that of the intellectuals or revolutionaries—an international party with national foot only. The party needs no central committee or executive; it only needs revolutionaries everywhere equipped to carry out the revolution. The union of power and wisdom has become possible in outrage. Persecution, however potent and effective, has failed to annihilate man. Intellectuals of the world, unite. You have a world to inherit!

# Chapter 2

## Man, Caliban, Clerk

The only humanly redeeming feature of contemporary Western society is the revolutionary upheavals that have taken place and are likely to occur in the foreseeable future. These manifestations speak of inner contradictions in the socioeconomic system whose most vulnerable facet at the moment is the educational system—system that in the coming decades will probably be the decisive battleground of the social wars to be waged between the industrial-commercial magnates and their human victims. Moreover, what is unsettling and disturbing from the point of view of "liberal" society is that the revolts of students and young workers are being led by the children of the affluent, who are, by and large, academically brilliant, vocationally well trained, socially and emotionally well adjusted in their nominal settings, but lacking in self-determination in their schools and factories and in productive social interaction in general. This verity alone highlights, if nothing else, the spiritual emptiness of capitalism and demonstrates its inability to respond to human aspirations beyond the cash nexus. In brief, capitalism has given the rebels at Renault, the Sorbonne, and Columbia homes without parents, schools without intellectuals, societies without communities, shops, offices, and factories without people. It has given them intellectual and industrial savages to rule over them arbitrarily in the name of democracy. It has made them slaves to its technology and tried to teach them a morality of indifference and callousness. Fortunately, they are gradually becoming conscious of their slavery and social estrangement. Herein lies the danger to capitalism: the beneficiaries are becoming the Huns—the possible nimble apologists, the gravediggers. Indeed, this is an unprecedented revolution, and no nonsensical generational conflict or other psychologism can explain this profound phenomenon of our epoch: the phenomenon of man versus Caliban and the parties that espouse their diametrically opposed world views.

The party of man is a party that celebrates the human spirit, asserts its authenticity, reverences its dignity. It is a party that deprecates the cult of efficiency, repudiates the malignant fetishes of managerial society, spurns the rhetoric of liberalism, and embraces the deed of the social revolutionary. It is a Promethean party for the emancipation of man, releasing him from the shackles of the past and developing his manhood. It is the party of affirmation!

The party of Caliban is an all-embracing, all-pervasive party. It is the party of strength, wealth, and power. It is the party of the privileged who consider that everyone owes them allegiance and ought to pay homage to their gods and idols. It is the party of callous calculators to whom human brain and brawn, coal and electricity, are mere sources of energy to be harnessed in the conquest of man and nature. It is the party that employs the editors, professors, priests, lawyers, and other symbol manipulators. To justify its misdeeds and defend its spoliations of society, it uses political brokers to ensure the prevalence of "liberty" and the dominance of "virtue." The media are its free and "objective" outlet. The airways are its monopoly, the Gods are its servants, the heavens are its sporting grounds. It is a party whose illusions are law, whose wishes are morality, whose fiats are science. It is the negation of man!

If we are to put the party of Caliban in historical perspective, we must remember that its genesis may be located in the fetus of the human heritage. Its modern dilemma, however, is that it is schizoid: it has created a technology and a technologist mentality that has subjugated man instead of liberating him; it has enthroned the invisible hand of the entrepreneur and deposed the omnipotent hand of God; it has transmuted the catapult into the solid-fueled rocket but has retained a theological-metaphysical-political outlook; it has expropriated the fruits of nature and the genius of man for the benefit of Western European and North American oligarchs while proclaiming liberty, equality, and fraternity for all men. It has sailed the oceans and discovered every river and is reaching for the stars, but it has failed to discover man. Its victories were the by-products of reason and revolution values that have now been rejected and whose exponents are labeled cranks, dupes, and rebels. The party of Caliban has divorced reason from reasoning and assigned it the abject role of marketing, packaging, and determining what human frailties and foibles Caliban can exploit. It has smashed the confined, circumscribed but integrated medieval man, and replaced him by the compartmentalized, fragmented atom of our era. The party of Caliban has substituted consumption for human production, seemingness for essence, the ape or man! At present, however, the harmonious cosmos of Caliban is under attack, and the party's reflexive response has shown its moral bankruptcy and the uncertainty of its certitude. It can no longer rely on psychic violence alone. It has had to supplement it with physical repression and has dispatched vigilantes of liberal totalitarians to smash the temple of liberty. In this dehumanizing enterprise, its love of tyranny and passion for ritual have been exposed, particularly in its pronouncements with reference to opposition and critical groups. It has a simple answer to all questions: force and violence, which are as proudly professed as law and order.

This myopia and public approbation have enabled the moralists of the prevailing order to diagnose the malaise as psychologistic, and they, consequently, have set out to locate its source in the permissiveness of "liberal" society and its espousal of "freedom." On the latter point, they are in part right but for the wrong reasons; on the former, they are absolutely mistaken because bourgeois society, while proclaiming itself free, lives by the laws of servility. The dilemma for capitalism, however, is that its science discovered the gap between the word and the deed—a discovery of which the youth of today are aware. They are saying no to sham dignity. Convinced that their parents, teachers, professors, and other "professionals" who make the system work are frauds, they are forming this "mobster minority" and are resolved to overturn Leviathan, lest they too become victims of that frightening apparatus. It is evident then that the radical movement of students has nothing to do with permissiveness but with alienation—the essential prerequisite for understanding reality. It must be understood that alienation is the product of this "permissiveness," which is, in fact, compulsion, compression, condescension. Although parents of the liberal persuasion thought that they had reared their children in freedom, they had, on the contrary, raised them in accordance with their own image of reality, an image that was a visionless vision, in which the offspring was brought up as a replica of the sterile, the inauthentic, the hypocrite. Thus, the contemporary revolt is not an escape from freedom but from authoritarianism masked as freedom. It's a plea for liberty, a demand to end slavery, a rebellion to rediscover community. Therefore, the young workers and students of today are the harbingers of the coming world, not the world of their elders but the world of the future—the world they will fashion to actualize the greatness of man by incorporating the human achievement of the past without adopting its glacial crusts. It is a movement whose aim is the deification of spontaneity. These fundamental differences between the two antagonists—man versus Caliban—make the conflict irreconcilable. It is a conflict of conscience as the spring of human action and compassion, and its concretization in societal living, on the one hand, and, on the other hand, of greed and pride with their requisite psychology of acquisitiveness. In the contours of this contest, the party of man does not reject the knowledge and wisdom of the past; it merely rejects the idols, amorality, and scientism of bureaucratic, monopoly capitalism, which forced "capitalists" to lead a life without love, without passion, without poetry. It is not that these latter-day saints have no passion. They do. Their passion is for drugs, escape, rationalization—standards by which Caliban society declares its opponents to be rebels, cranks, psychological misfits. The rebels, undoubtedly, plead guilty to these charges since, their standards, they are the party of human redemption, rescue.

If Luddism is not the leitmotif of the movement whose aims are not to expunge the technological accomplishments but rather to repudiate its concomitant capitalist morality, how has such "morality" been maintained and can it be overcome? The university, its administrators, teachers, and students, as a society in microcosm, provide us with the answer. Although literature abounds on this subject, very little is noteworthy except for Farber's article "The Student as Nigger." This article is of value because it underscores the spiritual enslavement of the student and the preparations he undergoes to, the analysis proffered does not undermine graduate to Caliban society. Its popularity stems from its provocative bourgeois appeal to sex and the personalization of the "social question." In this latter aspect, the analysis proffered does not undermine but helps the existing system to perpetuate itself by treating a socioeconomic question as psychological, which, in part, it is, thereby weakening, if not destroying, the revolutionary potential of some students. In this sense, Farber has unwittingly become the accomplice of liberal reformers who understand alienation and know how to cope with it as an individual and temporary phenomenon rather than a permanent feature of capitalist society. This failure, on the part of Farber, to grasp the "social question" has enabled him to abstract the student from his social context and depict him as a slave when the student is, in fact, a relative libertine, an overfed adolescent, a social parasite. His characterization of the university as an Auschwitz is not only inaccurate but also false and is, therefore, inimical to, if not diversionary of, the argument that the university is an essential "plant" in the political economy of bourgeois society. The university, as every observer should know, performs the social function of reproducing the required clerks for the maintenance of the prevailing industrial and commercial systems. These giant corporations dominate North American society and stamp it with an appropriate lifestyle that enhances the well-being and expansion of capitalism. Thus, the student is to be regarded as an apprentice-clerk in a training shop whose character has been determined by the demands of the social system in which he is trained to operate.

What is appalling, however, is that neither student nor teacher has a clear perception of this transactional reality; and the teacher, as chief clerk, is the more deluded party. The illusions of this sacrosanct deity are legion. He thinks of himself as a professor when he has nothing to profess, as a scholar when he remains silent on the great of the age, as an intellectual when he publishes a notice in an obscure "academic" journal on a foundation-approved topic. Nevertheless, his true function is ape training, the inculcation of slave morality, and wage slavery by methods deemed desirable by his superiors. In other words, the professor is no more than the seller of a commodity in a supermarket or a shopping center. However, because of his ability to articulate and elaborate his position by retiring behind a psychic proscenium arch, he sets himself apart from other merchandisers who rely on other techniques to market their goods. Moreover, because of his servile mentality and impoverished socioeconomic conditions, which ensure his continued slavery, he is a highly dependent person who, in order to survive and acquire prestige and power, must become more and more subservient to his chairman, dean, president, and the robber-barons who run the university. To advance his socially induced goals, he plays the game according to established "scholarly" canons of esoteric-exoteric relations. He must also know the politics of his university and pander to the whims of "senior" colleagues who decide who are the scholars and reward them accordingly. He must be in contact with the "right people" elsewhere to move upward to the prestigious universities. He must entertain the students, respect the social and political mores of the status quo, and express any aesthetic criticism of the system in the least offensive language and in a tone replete with deference to the ruling gods and their lesser disciples. Therefore, the classification of the Professor as Kitchen Nigger is the most apt portrayal of his status, mentality, role, and obsequious manners. Because of the unilaterality of relations in university life, which is typical of all social intercourse under capitalism, the professor is not a free, autonomous, self-determining agent but a myrmidon who lives by his tongue, shares the table with his master, nods cheerfully to his orders, and carries out decrees without expressed reservations. Such is the life of the chatterboxes, puppets, and social eunuchs of the universities! The tragedy of the professor is that, in spite of this "learning" and trained "intelligence," he is not conscious of his imprisonment. Indeed, it is no exaggeration to contend that most professors enjoy their slavery and adore their jailers. Therefore, a major task of the student radicals and intellectuals outside the system is to catch the young professors before they "sell out" completely and become "adjusted" to the comfort of the "republic of knowledge" and the feminine manners of aristocratic elites of academe. As for the remainder of the clerks, the most radicals can do is demystify, demythologize, and unmask their complicity, their acquiescence, their fraudulence, their inhumanity, their treason! Hence, in the coming struggle, the supreme target should be the professor, not only because he is system oriented but also because he holds a strategic position as mediator between the proprietors of the system and its prospective victims. If this pivotal link in the chain of slavery is roiled up, the entire system will be in a state of disarray and confusion, and the radicals will be aide in this battle of defoliation by the anti-intellectual environment produced by the system itself. Thus, it becomes necessary to know how the professor evolves from the status of an apprentice clerk to that of chief clerk—a process that consists of kneading and moulding his as a robot to fulfill the functions assigned to such "hands."

Professors are wont of concealing the travails they undergo in order to attain their Delphic positions. They fear a disclosure that would expose their meager resources of intelligence, independence, and individualism as a cultural elite and their morality as a "pack of professionals." However, it is incumbent upon us to point out that merit plays a minor role in the admission to universities and graduate schools, in the awarding of scholarships and appointments of faculty. Moreover, secrecy is facilitated because most professors come from the upper strata of society, share its beliefs, mores and values, and look upon education as a communications medium to perpetuate and enhance what is. They, as a class, accept society, respect hierarchy, and cherish all the intoxicating illusions of king and country. In brief, they are the moral bureaucrats of the established political economy who burn incense and chant hymns for their kin. They are not the arbiters but the servants of society; they are not the interpreters of the good and the sublime but the priests who embody that mystery. They are not the critics but the fawning scribes, not the guerrillas of the new age but the gorillas of the old. They are a civil soldiery guarding the acropolis of capitalism. As clerks who administer the cultural apparatus, the professors are an exclusive tribe, which replenishes its ranks by co-option. They cannot and are incapable of transcending their social milieu. Therefore, the intellectual who, by his choice, carries the burden of mankind cannot be in the university as servant, and he will not be allowed to remain there if he entered the "island of democracy" to restructure it. The intellectual is man, citizen, lover. The professorial clerk is an intellectual minion, a voter, a sex escapist. He is for what is. He lives for others, complies with their will, submits to their commands. He is an administrator working for a wage; he lives for it and abides by its requirements. He is available for sale to any department in the economy that demands his services. He is a commodity to be had by the highest bidder. He is Caliban per excellence! The intellectual is the vehicle of reason, the instrument of the revolution, the messenger of the human spirit. He is for what ought to be; he is for himself and for all men. He is a Man! He knows that the octopus-like system of capitalism cannot be overcome by persuasion but only by a frontal assault. Therefore, to him, the act of negation in our age is the greatest act of affirmation, and the arena for it is the university—the center of indoctrination, dehumanization, debauchery.

Intellectuals of all countries, unite! You must reconstruct world history!

# Chapter 3

# Student Radicalism:
# Copulation, Co-Optation, Liberation

There are only three possible ways of stereotyping the "student radicalism" of the past decade: copulationist, co-optationsist, and liberationist movements. In terms of historical perspective, "student radicalism" has remained an embryonic, inchoate, and incoherent grouping of disenchanted, disgruntled, distraught liberal individualists; self-immolating, guilt-ridden middle-class busybodies; and individual revolutionaries without follower and action-related issues. In this article, it is my intention to identify those psychological types in the hope of aiding "radicals" to discover themselves, thereby reducing the amount of self-deception and clarifying the paths that have, in fact, been pursued and underlining the path that ought to be traversed.

It is my contention that "student radicalism" has been defined by its enemies and critics, not by itself or its advocates. It has not gone beyond the negative stage of definition. It has had therefore to relate to issues and define itself as the opponents wished it and, as a result, has remained trapped in the "society" that it rejected. In brief, radicalism has not converted the dialogue to an argument on its own terms and therefore has remained on the defensive and continues to argue within the context of the "enemy" and under categories conjured up by "establishment" apologists. Indeed, the latter have attacked "radicals" for being "rebels without a program," as if the radical function were the salvaging of the decadent status quo.

Our typology of radicalism-copulation, co-optation, and liberation is not conceived in isolation. It corresponds with political, economic, and ethical manifestations that are evident in society. In the political realm, system-oriented parties lead themselves and their adherents into believing that their approach is a genuine alternative to the chicanery and manipulation of the opponent; that they possess the answer to every malaise and will grapple with it with vigor if given the opportunity though they concede that they live in a world of "imperfections." This in-out or cynical brokerage politics is challenged by Laborist (NDP) or Social democratic parties in terms of the professed ideals of political liberalism. At the outset, the challenge is purist and moralistic; but in due course, the challengers adopt the trappings and theatricalism of in-out politics, its types of organizations, issues, and policies. This will be done in the name of political exigencies, the necessity of broadening the base of political support and giving a chance for the people "to elect us." Meanwhile, this reformist party prides itself on being the "conscience" of the nation and contends that its leaders, as individuals, deserve to be prime ministers (presidents), etc. Thus, we delineate the cycle that begins with social Calvinism and ends with the ethic of middle-class babbitry and the pursuit of power and prestige within the established framework, thereby obtaining a revamped, more viable and vital system cushioned by hide-bound conservatives and undergirded by a multitude of proliferating agencies of obfuscation. In sum, there are three political phenomena: conservatism, liberalism, and NDPism, which correspond with three forms of economic organizations (private entrepreneurship, corporate huckstering, communal and cooperative enterprise) and three psychological ethical types: (1) the personalistic type (copulationist), which is a sort of possessive, pseudo-alienated, pseudo-individualist psychology; (2) the moralistic type of person (co-optionist), who is a pragmatic (opportunistic) or eclectic politically but obsessive compulsive procedurally and ritualistically; and (3) the cybernationist type, the truly human, self-knowing, socially motivated communitarian.

The copulationists, whether they are hedonists, beatniks, hippies, yippies, or known by some other title, are of the same breed and biochemistry of social abdication and individual escapism. They do, however, feel the oppression and destructiveness of the surrounding environment. Indeed, they feel beleaguered by a ring of steel, learn to maneuver within its confines, laugh at it, use it, and get it to sponsor their trips, emotional and physical, and publish their masochistic outpourings and sadistic vaporings. However, they do not understand Leviathan intellectually, and they make no effort to deal with it collectively except as pacifist exhibitionists. They individualize their frustrations, deprivations, and powerlessness and seek to overcome them by drugs, sex, or cults rather than by analysis of the root causes of their malaise and action to uproot it. Therefore, by inclination, emotional and intellectual persuasion, they are apt to seek safety by withdrawal and the creation of privatized communities where they share individually, not socially, thereby failing to develop group consciousness, social identification, and an all-embracing critique of society. Thus, in their subcultures, copulationists merely develop a therapist-patient relationship toward each other rather than an individually transcending ideology of humanism. Some achieve self-knowledge, but few, if any, ever reach the liberationist stage. By and large, most wallow in the copulationist stage forever and move with the dominant currents of the time until they "outgrow" their adolescence and "mature" for co-optation into middle-class society. As a result, the copulationist is incapable of thinking in terms of societal emancipation. He has little or no interest in anything that does not affect his person primarily, although he extols such ambiguous liberal commodities as family, the ethnic group, nation, the West, the world, and mankind. His use of liberal rhetoric is a declaration of his intellectual bankruptcy, on the one hand, and a shield on the other—a situation that reveals his alienated self and schizophrenic condition. There is something, however, which is revolutionary in this levitational psychological type. The copulationist's revolt is cultural, and as an aesthetic revolutionary, he disrupts the apparatus of socialization and indoctrination and exposes its exclusivist close-endedness. His "revolting." His "revolting" existence is a testament to the inadequacy of the system, a reminder of a possible alternative, and a challenge to authority, bureaucracy, and "universal pragmatic happiness." He becomes only a threat because his response to impersonality, anonymity, giganticism is individualistic. He fails to grasp the interrelationships of systems, institutions, and personality structures that are needed to man the institutions, explain and justify and defend them. He understands the ideology, motivation, and machination of a McNamara, a Kennedy, or a Trudeau but not as an essential feature of the system of oppression. However "sincere" the copulationist is as a supporter of the system, a believer in its values, a defender of its "liberties," he is a safety valve to help the system adapt to changing reality—a victim of the McCarthys, Kennedys, and their "cool" replicas.

The co-optationist is an unsettled, ill-adapted middle-class liberal whether he calls himself Socialist, Laborist, non-violent Democrat, left-wing, or practical idealist. He accepts the system and aims at the eradication of its "imperfections." He sees specific wrongs and offers specific remedies to correct them. He conceives of his function and mission in terms of transcendental morality and judges the system's shortcomings from a moralistic point of view. As a non-structuralist, the co-optationist denounces the system for not living up to its professed ideals, for failing to give all a "sense of belonging," for being too slow to accommodate to people's demands. He attacks the system for its lack of democratic procedure, for not extending democracy to the university (the liberal panacea), the economy (the Socialist nostrum), social life (the anarchist utopia of stateslessness), for bureaucratic behavior (the ombudsman syndrome of academic liberalism), for elitist authoritarianism, and organization (the new leftists, CUS and a few NDP teachers and preachers). In brief, the co-optationist is a reformer, not a revolutionary, although his critics and opponents will bludgeon him with such terms as hothead, radical, rebel, self-appointed prophet, self-styled leader or so-called revolutionary. However, if the movement develops roots and gains flowers, it will be honored by such appellations as foreign inspired, directed, controlled, financed. The leaders become foreign agents, conspirators; the followers, the deceived; the admirers, the naive idealists and fellow travelers. Since no such language has been used systematically against the New Left, we feel that the system upholders consider it a minor threat or a mere nuisance at this stage. Although right-wing hysterics have overreacted to the leftist "peril," the "mainstream" has kept its cool and composure and proceeded to buy the leftists out.

The co-optationist's revolt is political and, to some extent, social. The revolt is against the party machine, the incompetent leadership, the ineffective government, the university structure, the bureaucratic red tape, the lack of democracy, the overweening powers of high finance, big labor, gigness. Furthermore, since co-optationists come from the middle class or seek to join it, they have the "objective" media on their side, the gadfly columnists, politicians, writers (those champions of the people need something to talk about or write for to remain distinguished in the public view), and a few maverick professors without consultancies or foundation fellowships. For these reasons, a revolt of cabals is regarded as a revolution, and to casual observers, North America appears to be in a state of permanent revolt when it is a huge stagnant morass of system worshipers who differ on the ways of kneeling, strictly on the ritual and symbolic. The co-optationist's use of language ranges from conventional to liberal, verbal diarrhea—to Maoism and Guevarism. The more "violent" the language, the more radical the proponent is supposed to be. Upon further analysis, it will be discovered that the use of foreign vocabulary in particular is a means of intimidating one's superiors with threats of dire things to come unless they yield to the "democratic" wave of the future. The language of Guevarism and Maoism is particularly frightening to parents, relatives, and friends who will be "alienated" unless Johnny recovers his sanity and returns to the fold. They, therefore, proceed with patience to disabuse him of the ill-conceived notions he has collected in the classroom, or from the "radical" magazines or underground societies. He, in turn, demonstrates his potency and vitality by clubbing them with more incomprehensible verbiage and exhibits his knowledge of "dialectics" in the pubs to impress freshettes and obtain sexual favours. Radicalism to Johnny is a splendid means of exploitation, distinction, self-aggrandizement. Neither he nor his society know the fraudulence of his posturing and the acting out of his neurotic needs as a big joke on himself and his "seniors" who also played the same game in the thirties. Because administrators in the academics are aware of these phenomena, they respond with guarded negativism initially. If the "movement" appears to be "genuine," they try to dam it with "concessions." If, however, administrative dictators are drawn to the vortex of "confrontation" and violence breaks out, the recalcitrant on both sides will be sacrificed (Berkeley, Columbia, Simon Fraser, San Francisco State, etc.); and a more "enlightened" age will dawn for all. It is instructive here to remember that in the aftermath the "agitators" will be drafted or expelled, the administrators pensioned off to a life of luxury or appointed to educational commissions.

From the stages of copulation and co-optation, a few liberationists emerge and form the hard core of the revolution. In North America, few, if any, survive the first two stages. The reasons are not hard to discover: the system is simply too powerful and too viable; the system upholders are united and well equipped with the instruments of system maintenance; neither is exhausted nor defeated, and the true revolutionaries are too few and too feeble to make a successful bid for power.

The liberationists are the incarnation of man's alienated self and his hope for a kingdom of earthly freedom. They embody the accumulated wisdom of the past and articulate man's aspirations for the future. They have developed an ideology that transcends and encompasses the preceding experience. They do not cut the umbilical cord and sever themselves from historic society: they form a higher synthesis. Thus, we have elucidated the stages of intellectual and emotional growth that are required to produce revolutionary individuals and parties. Let us now apply our typology more specifically to student radicalism.

Student power, however democratic its professed aims appear to be, is a co-optationist movement. Its most "radical" demand is "participation" in university government (in Quebec, it advocates student syndicalism or unionism on the Labor model), the sharing of power as an integral constituency of the university community, or the democratization of the university structure. Those in authority have, of course, spurned the offer to help them govern more effectively. Some, however, have recognized the value of student "participation," assigned them to unwieldy, non-functional committees that are virtually powerless, or co-opted one or two "responsible" students to secretive presidential councils or senates. Needless to say, the university administrators and bureaucrats are capable of dealing with student power without losing one iota of their power or prestige. Indeed, they can concede every student demand and find themselves with enhanced, rather than diminished, power and authority because the students are not arguing for the abolition or weakening of the university but for a share in self-government in areas affecting their educational life. However, this minimal demand will not be granted until and unless students revolt en masse, burn down a few buildings, hand a president or two, mug a few deans and professors, and kill a few rightist and leftist students. Student power advocates who dare not even speak this language will certainly not act on it as a policy. They, therefore, will continue the verbal tug-of-war with their deeply entrenched elders. On the other hand, assuming that the university, by a sudden illumination, is converted to the doctrine of student power and recognize the principle of "one-man vote," which will place them along with the professors in a minority position (we are assuming a double miracle here, for if the presidents and deans accept, the professors will not), no permanent restructuring of the university will take place. Even if it does, it will not be transferred to other institutions in society: the corporation, shop, school, ad agency, ministry, civil service, or whatever institution the graduate will work for. Student power is, therefore, doomed to failure not only because of its specificity and circumscribed outlook but also because it is and remains part of the liberal matrix of reality. Even if student federation adopt syndicalism as an ideology (which is not likely, if the CUSites want to have chatters on most campuses), at best, all that can be hoped for is another "autonomous" agency of bureaucracy in this great "pluralist" society. Moreover, if the university itself embraces syndicalism, it will become merely a self-governing guild with master and apprentice working as a parasite collectively to further imprison society in its obscurantist middle classness and hierarchical idiocy. Whatever is done in the university, or for the university, must come and will come from society; and the latter, under the reigning economic order, is not on the verge of democracy. Therefore, the university will remain an authoritarian, bureaucratic showpiece of corporate capitalism and will continue to function as a training center for the production of clerks to maintain, enhance, and expand the industrial machine. It is thus evident from the above account that student power is a liberal co-optationist movement that intelligent administrators will advocate, encourage, and use as a means of extorting money from the legislators and taxpayers to build their "educational empires" and walk in glory as great educators and intellectual beacons of our time. However, since most administrators are selected presidents for their business acumen rather than intellectual integrity, or proclivity, we cannot expect them to comprehend and act to manipulate the co-optationist propensity of student radicalism except marginally. They, therefore, will continue to think of the university in terms of its traditional function as a loco parentis and defend the corporate model as the most efficient, intelligible, unalterable principle of the university government; and the herd of professors will furnish them with arguments and will applaud their firmness, humanity, and business manners. (Some universities like the U of T will always give an eager appearance to restructure itself; but in reality, a change in ruling cliques, names, committees and a bit of democratization are no more than grudging tolerance in terms of style not substance.) It follows, therefore, that even electoral democracy will not be possible in the university—a meaningless and procedural obfuscation that has deceived entire nations, generations and societies.

If student power cannot affect the university structure at the center because most students are en route to other institutions, the professors can do so because of their strategic location and permanency in the system. But as a class, they are incapable of thoroughgoing revolution. However, since they believe in incremental, imperceptible change, they have been using student power as leverage to advance themselves. Like most despicable small-time exploiters who have neither morality nor integrity, they have, without compunction, sided with the administrators and persuaded some of them to committee the student to death. (Some students talk about departmental parallel committees and the sharing of appointive power in chiliastic tones rather than oppose it as an instrument of co-optation and social control and proposed complete equality and openness).

As the educational soldiery of the dominant order, they know the loci of power, its source, and its ramifications; they also know how to exercise power and use it vis-à-vis the student and act petulantly upon him as if he were a mere object of contempt. The teachers—as the middlemen among students, administrators, and society—are the embodiment of society; and as such, they instill its values, defend its mores, and propagate its causes. Therefore, professors, by their vocation and deeds, are a servile breed of people who must be deemed a contemptible lot. As retailers of "conventional wisdom," they are incapable of emancipating themselves and therewith their environment. As central pillars of the university, the professors must change first before structural change becomes conceivable in the university. Without radical change in the profession and the thinking of teachers, all talk of change is chimera, utopian, naive. Thus, the rhetoric of "restructuring" by CUS and counter-CUS reactionaries (the latter are in the process of organizing a right-wing movement to challenge CUS, which will probably ending in the collapse of both) is marginal and peripheral, if not downright deceptive. For these reasons, students who are or want to become radical within the system must eschew hobnobbing with the establishment. They must reject the ethic of "responsibility" and completely shun the working for or within the system. If they do so as individuals, they have ipso facto abdicated in favor of co-optation. Thus, the movement to "reform" the university, "restructure" it, or "participate" in it must be regarded as a co-optationist movement of procedural democracy; and no one must be deluded into believing that students are "redeeming" anyone other than themselves by boring from within. The path of co-optation leads one to the womb of the old society, the path of liberation to the creation of a new one. Marxists, however, must not fear soiling their hand by "participating" in this reformism. Their function is clear: expose and unmask the power structure and organize for its demise. Therefore, let liberation be our guide and let those who seek liberation adopt the liberation of Canada from the clutches of American imperialism as their goal by restoring Canadian sovereignty and rediscovering a true Canadian alternative to the American behemoth.

To achieve Canada's liberation, a coalition of the emerging forces of liberation must be formed on the basis of the third alternative in which Canada's considered appearance is that of a highly advanced colony in the orbit of U.S. imperialism. This alternative rejects Canada's role as it traditionally operates in Britain and the U.S.-contrived alliances and repudiates the defunct "third world" idea of supercilious moralists, bankrupt dictators, and bourgeois nationalists. The Third Alternative is a revolutionary ideology not fully in being but in becoming. Only its outline, direction, and goal are clear. Its strategy, tactics, agents, and details are sketchy and tentative. In this view, Canada is a strategic land mass with great economic potential, if detached from imperialism, can complete the latter's socialistic encirclement. This is the historic role of Canada, and the foremost, the goal of liberation must be liberation of Canada; the Canadian liberation can only be achieved by genuine revolutionary nationalism imbued with a Socialist ideology, not by a kind of branch-plant radicalism that professes a false internationalism and a confessional fundamentalist Marxism. Moreover, the liberation of Canada can only be attained by a revolutionary upheaval led by revolutionary intellectuals grounded in the reality of working-class life and aimed at the abolition of monopoly capitalism. There is no other way.

# Chapter 4

## Academic Unfreedom

(Note: A liberalized version of this chapter and the review of the university game appeared in *Canadian Dimension* in 1968. The editors of *CD* have an amazing capacity for mutilating the works of gratis contributors and for supressing articles that do not corroborate Zionist pretensions and extol the virtues of the NDP.)

Whenever we are on the verge of a crisis, in its midst, or suffering from its aftereffects, we resort to the time-honored escape mechanism of the royal commission. The latest, of course, is the commission on academic freedom headed by Messrs. Rowat and Hurtubise.

It is obvious that the creation of this commission is intended as a brake to diffuse the social contagion of the worldwide student revolt. Certainly, Canadian academia, judging by its official journals and the activities of its liberal and conservative pedants, are not the activities of its liberal and conservative pendants—are not a place of fermentation, stirring intellectual collision. Therefore, it is probable that the organizations (CAUT, AUCC, UUS) that have appointed the commission are hoping to muffle student dissent, stifle radicalism, and silence the coy critics of the ruling university autocracies. The "profession" and its employers are in collusion against radical restructuring of the university system, notwithstanding its liberal posturing.

It is well-known that the university system in this country is run on the model of business corporations with super-ordinate-subordinate relationships and absentee landlordism. The system of education is highly ascriptive and elitist, and the professors who teach in it are not only the children of autocracy but its most faithful practitioners. They have invested interest in perpetuating the system both as a closed shop and as a means to maintain their ego gratification. Therefore, the university system is incapable of any structural change; and no commission, whatever its recommendations, will alter this fact. In the most recent past, we have had several commissions such as the Bladen's Commission (October '65), the Duff Berdahl Report (March '66), and the Spinks Commission (December '66). Their findings are well-known: nice liberal proposals made by nice liberal gentlemen all nicely tucked away for future liberal researchers to uncover and enlarge upon. We trust that the new commission will fulfill this function. The commissions have dealt with finance, university government, post graduate training, and university merger in the report. Mr. Bladen and his associates treated education as a liberal commodity, strongly opposed the abolition of tuition fees, and argued in favor of expanding this commodity in terms of economic growth and what graduates could earn for themselves and how much more they could contribute to our beloved GNP.

Duff-Berdahl, on the other hand, pointed out that the universities "cannot appropriately be governed as if they were either business corporations or medieval dukedoms; that their responsibility is to the republic of knowledge and also to the immediate tax-paying community, in both of which they must exist" (Percy Smith, *University Affairs* vol. 7, no. 4, April 1966, p.2). But to convert "medieval dukedoms" into "the republic of knowledge," the commissioners merely recommended that (1) the senate be recognized as a supreme academic body with the right to "make recommendations to the Board on any matter of interest to the university"; (2) that the supreme authority of the university should rest in a board of governors, most of whom were to be non-academic, and that there be faculty representation on the board; (3) that a "university court" be set up to strengthen relations between the community and university and that joint faculty-student committee be established to give a voice to students.

As to the Spinks Commission, its main recommendation was almost revolutionary; and for this reason, its report is almost unobtainable. The commissioners recommended the amalgamation of Ontario's fourteen provincially assisted universities and made the daring suggestion of eliminating their boards of governors; the rationale is that they have become largely superfluous in a province where the taxpayers and students foot the entire bill. Moreover, the Advisory Committee on Education was to be transformed into an accrediting agency; and quite conceivably, the appointive power of teaching staff was to devolve upon it eventually, thereby undermining the power of local Napoleons. The presidents, deans, and their apologists became enraged; and wrath descended upon the commissioners whose report has been consigned to the dustbin of history. The only meaningful commission with meaningful proposals has been totally ignored.

Doubtless, friends of the establishments can cite some "moderate," considerable, and "significant reforms" such as one or two "senior" professors siting on the boards of two or three universities and will name some "responsible" students who were "elected" to the senates or appointed to some innocuous subsidiary, non-functioning organization in the university system; and in all this parade of liberality, we are supposed to be satisfied by this tokenism, masquerading as the new epoch, the "participatory democracy." It is almost trivial to underscore the fact that the university system is no better or worse than any department of Canadian life, with the example of business, the archetype of Canadian life and action. It is flabby, effeminate, servile, pretentious, self-righteous, professing a mission when it has none beyond the provision of well-trained clerks to serve the industrial, commercial, and banking complexes of this country. Moreover, since the university system attracts less than the second-rate (the first-raters are in business) and condones nothing above mediocrity, it is like every department of life, incapable of self-liberation; and all its agitation is no more than group therapy for oppressor and oppressed alike.

"Academic freedom is as alien a concept to the Canadian university as is liberty as an ethical postulate in the direction of Argus Corporation. If academic freedom means the freedom to teach, the freedom to learn and the freedom to exercise one's civil rights as a citizen, it is as absent in the Canadian university as democracy was absent in the Senates of Nero, Hitler, Mussolini and Stalin, and to a large extent this autocracy must be ascribed to the reaching profession whose latest statement (November '67) on academic freedom reads as follows: Academic freedom includes the right within the university to decide who shall teach, who shall be taught and what shall be studied, taught or published. Because the university's essential concerns are intellectual, academic freedom involves the right of appointment of staff or admission of students regardless of race, sex, religion, or politics. It involves the right to teach, investigate and speculate without deference to prescribed doctrine. It involves the right to criticize the university."

Clause 5 of the preamble, however, qualifies the definition by stating that the faculty member, in exercising his rights, must have "a due regard for responsibility, as he sees fit." Here is the crux of the matter. The profession, first of all, confuses academic freedom and university autonomy; then insists that the professors must act responsible (responsibility is to be defined by presidents, deans, chairmen, and senior colleagues, of course); and, above all, excludes the freedom to learn from its purview. Moreover, the freedom "to teach, investigate and speculate without deference to prescribed doctrine" does not mean that a professor cannot be dismissed if his teaching does not correspond with the "teaching" of his "university." He can be fired, if he has no tenure, irrespective of his competence, integrity, ability, publications, etc.; and he can be fired even if he had tenure for "due cause" however vague it may be, something, of course, to be determined by the university. No matter how we look at the definition of academic freedom, we find that it is designed not to uphold the freedom of teachers and students but to protect and safeguard the freedom (arbitrariness) of presidents, deans, and chairmen. Therefore, our universities are not communities of scholars as they pretend to be but business communities whose aim is to produce the appropriate automatons the industrial machine requires. And the professors in their deeds and verbal diarrhea are the greatest cooperators who sanctify this unholy enterprise. Before I am condemned for my irrationality, emotionalism, etc., I ask my readers to think of a university in this country where the freedom to learn exists, and the students have anything to do with the selection of the curriculum or the appointment and promotion of their teachers and to name me a professor who dares act, in a way, contrary to the accepted ethical norms of the dominant order and still retains his position. Let me pose the crucial question that I face: Who in this country can tell me that a university professor with a PhD from Columbia in Political Science with five years of teaching and over twenty publications can indeed exercise his citizenship rights and find a position in Canada's university system? Would anyone—government, academia or any other group—dare contemplate? The implications of academic freedom, or are we merely to use it as a glittering generality essential for the psychic edification of obsequious professors who dare not imagine, who dare not think, who dare not say no to tyranny?

Lest my reader thinks that this is all imaginary and it could only happen at Lutheran or Southern, I refer them to the 1968 report of the so-called most progressive educator Claude Bissell, president of U of T. Mr. Bissell, the representative of the most minuscule minority of this country categorized the dissent of thousands of students as minority dissent and threatened to resort to police violence should these apostles of the future knock on his doors in the name of liberty. If the most progressive educator can adopt this stance, and not a single professor on the campus of this allegedly greatest of Commonwealth universities utters a word of criticism or challenge, does anyone expect the professors of this country to say no to the local tyrants and usurpers at Maritime, Western, or Quebec universities? That the professors have no moral fiber in their blood is attested to by the non-existence of a self-governing professional body to look after the affairs of the profession and by the fact that more than 10,500 professors subscribe to a civil-service type of association rather than establish an autonomous, self-regulating organ or their own. CAUT in its censure report of Simon Fraser expresses disdain for unions and the exponents of unionism for the profession. If what I am saying is accurate in principle, it follows that the Commission on Academic Freedom, which was financed by a $ 150,000 grant from the Ford Foundation, will not contribute anything significant to the literature of academic freedom but will add more to our moral bewilderment especially since its tasks are the investigation of the role of the financiers of university education, accessibility of student to university, and the utility of research to society. Such terms of reference have nothing to do with academic freedom if the latter is an intellectual attribute and a moral habituation of the mind affecting teachers and students and their intellectual intercourse.

If academic freedom is to become an operative code of university life, not a slogan as it is today, a total severance of relations between business and university must be carried out; a new breed of professors must be educated in the tradition of liberty, not autocracy; and students must come to university not to buy a passport to junior executive positions but to discover man, his potential, his essence, his destiny. To overcome the rhetoric of the liberal age, it will be necessary to build a new university, but Canadian society itself must be rebuilt, and that is a question for royal commissions to examine. It is a question of freedom to resolve!

# Chapter 5

## Hierarchy and Dissent in Academe

E d. Note: Darrol Bryant was a Christian moralist who taught at Lutheran University for two years. Basically, he was dismissed for trying to organize an SDS chapter at Lutheran. This chapter was written as an open letter to him and was published in part in the *Cord*, March 7, 1964.

My Waterloo correspondents tell me that the supervisors of Mr. Hush Puppies (Greb Shoes), acting in the best arbitrary and self-righteous tradition of robber-barons determined to dismiss you on the flimsy ground of "upgrading" their enterprise in order to enhance Christianity, civilization and scholarship—characteristics that are as alien to Lutheran as the love of Russians and East Europeans to Hitlerism, the love of Greeks to Turks, or the admiration of Zionists to the Palestinian Arab freedom-fighters. Lutheran as a microcosm of the institutional cage does its "thing" without subtlety, transparent humanity or refined brutality. All universities, whether great or retarded outposts of learning, act in the same fashion, be they Yales in the case of the pacifist Staughton Lynd, Chicagoes in Dixon's non-renewal of contract or Lutherans in your "terminal contract." The only difference is that at an Ivy League, a few "colleagues" whisper muffled protest to no avail; at Lutheran, the entire faculty as a group of castrated, impotent beasts react silently, indifferently or find justification to uphold or acquiesce in the "new policy." This behaviour can easily be explained by a close look at the structure of each university where we find a clique of sinecurists or tenured faculty at the apex. At Lutheran, the criterion for inclusion in this coterie is a profession of the correct faith and sufficient visible piety to attain that enviable status. Of late, however, non-Lutherans have been accorded sinecures by virtue of their subservient posturing and seniority. At other

43

universities, especially the first-rate schools, the tenured faculties consists of people who have expanded their doctoral dissertations into a book or two and thereafter reshuffled their cards, written a few articles and perhaps some commissioned books. They possess the correct secular faith. Such indeed is the fraudulence practiced throughout the continent in the name of scholarship. Those village notables decide who will be elevated to their ranks, when and how, and they determine the allocation of "scholarships" and the appointments of staffs. In brief, they are a self-perpetuating oligarchy without accountability to anyone, other than the trustees or governors who share their values, practice their beliefs and pray to the same goddess of success and universal happiness. Sinecurists or tenured faculties are essentially the intellectual "executive committee of the bourgeois"—the guardians of the "treasures" of learning, and the instruments of higher immorality and indoctrination. They are the ever-ready servants of the ruling class, who do its bidding, advise it and justify it to the world by their public utterances, publications, secret reports, private missions and research. They and their apprentices are a servile clique in the august garb of medieval monks and lawyers who practise contemporary witchcraft and invent superstitions to deceive the working multitudes and stifle every incipient rebellion of liberty. The so-called "senior" faculty is senior in its submission to authoritarianism, senior in its suppression of innovation, and senior in its profession of "conventional wisdom."

Secondly, there is a crew of professionals or academic entrepreneurs whose only loyalty is to their private empires, personal advantage and self-advancement. At Lutheran, this group of non-people are by and large, marketable types who can move from one academic slum to another; they possess the union card without its requisite morality and professional ethos. Elsewhere, those who move in this orbit become mutual admirers who designate themselves theorists, intellectuals, advisors, whiz kids. They espouse the political values of the dominant culture, set political and social styles in motion, decree the extinction of opponents, and move like gadflies from one centre to another. As a group they are fully assimilated into the system and live like their counterparts in the corporations, the bureaucracy, the military and the polity. In fact, they are the women's auxiliary of these organizations and some of them manage to circulate freely and frequently in the upper echelons of this "liberal society" with its high regard for obedient servants, literary jugglers and fortune tellers.

Thirdly, there is a whole flock of sheep who is better known as careerists or clerks. These scribes form the field corps of the teaching staffs of all colleges and universities. In North America most of them are unimaginative dullards who rely on their scribbled graduate notes in teaching fellow-dullards and bored replicas. They dress neatly and conspicuously; they are beautifully manicured; they are overfed and look "happy" (judging from their smiling faces and manners); and their speeches are qualified and over-footnotes; they attend public lectures by distinguished authorities brought to their "superior" campuses and try to emulate the grade and elucidate their thoughts; they have nothing of their own, other than their monotone voices which occasionally break and become indignant when someone poses a question. Since they rarely read books and must appear to be learned, they read academic reviews or articles in popular journals and augment their intellectual diet by reading *Time*, the weekly fiction magazine. The truly dedicated among them read The *New York Times*, the opium of the "liberal" intelligentsia. Moreover, with their distinctly overwhelming knowledge, a few well-spaced jokes, a dose of sexual allusions, a bit of showmanship, and the use of incomprehensible jargon, we have a herd of satiated learned and learners, and in this world of "communication," this entertaining approach will compensate for the dullness, ineptness and ignorance of deceivers and deceived. That is liberal education today. Because of the precariousness of their positions, academically and emotionally, these clerks are the most obsequious group in every college. They follow bureaucratic procedure without question and apply it literally. They embrace and propagandize the superstitions of their society and transmit them to naïve and ill-tutored students as objective analyses, and the latter in turn socialize themselves "rationally" and reproduce the same effluvia to buy grades from their immediate masters. Little wonder that intelligent students are dropping out or revolting against the "system." Yet their elders are stunned by such "ungrateful" behaviour and the susceptibilities of those maladjusted scions of the middle class to "outside agitators." Meanwhile, reactionaries—academics, professional liberals, politicians and journalists—are calling upon the great "silent," but "responsible" majority to suppress the "dissidents" and "extremists," without of course realizing that their majority of robots and undeveloped minds lack the intellectual capacity and moral stamina to challenge and defeat them. Indeed, the only way by which these cheerful robots can win is by resorting to physical violence and by turning the campuses into local Vietnams—jungles they dare not traverse.

Fourthly, there is a category of corvee labour: the teaching assistants. Generally, they consist of B.A. and J.D. types. Most of the latter infest the entire educational system in North America. They are, in most cases, former Nazis turned American agents, who have received appointments in recognition of the services to the "free world." They are a group of fervent anti-communists who have contributed considerably to the repressive environment by reinforcing the residual right-wing animus against radicalism on the campuses. In some instances, liberal universities employed them to fill positions that remained vacant and unapplied for by Ph.D. holders from distinguished universities. The assistants are either employees of one of the entrepreneurs or graduate students who were unable to obtain scholarships. These, with other academic hands, constitute the immense majority of teachers who are either flunky Ph.D.s or flunky graduate students who teach flunky undergraduates whose supreme aim in life is the purchase of a wife, a job, and a 25-year mortgaged house. Thus it is apparent that the university system of apprenticeship for careerists, priests, bureaucrats and soldiers who man and operate a system of human degradation, exploitation, butchery. The system is alive, long live the system! It is a beehive of interminable activity.

Fifthly, there is an infinitesimal group of "Christians," moralists, and revolutionaries in the university system. At Lutheran, the Siiralas, the Calders, and the Bryants are the ineffectual "Christian" representatives. They are a decent lot of people who still believe in the system, but they and their like are being eliminated. The revolutionaries as a category do not exist in Canada; however, there are a number of isolated radical individuals in B.C. and less than a handful of silent Marxists in Ontario and Quebec. In the entire university system in Canada, there is only one former right-wing Communist. There is not a single person who is an avowed Marxist-Leninist, and what is more surprising is that the bourgeois radicals have failed to honor themselves with exhibit A—is this a sign of fear and insecurity, or is it that such a breed is extinct in Canada? The U.S. is not much better on this score. The only known case is at Bryn Mawr, a Pennsylvania college, that appointed Herbert Aptheker of the Communist party U.S.A. as a "visiting" lecturer of black history in the summer of 1969. The scarcity of Marxists is compensated for by a motley crew of N.D.P. types who populate the system, some of whom are very important at the big universities as a group i.e. the University League for Social Reform at U. of T. In brief, at the secular universities, the academic socialists, radical, and left-wing liberals exist and constitute a strong group that agitate for and obtain procedural reforms—seats on University Senates, positions for "moderate and responsible" students on non-functioning committees, and occasionally get one or two seats on a Board of Governors. Some of them even head commissions. Moreover, in collaboration with right-wing elements and centrists, the "socialists" work to improve the "quality of life" in the "university community" and stimulate the "moral conscience" of institutions to respond to "just" demands. They are an appendage of the system, not an autonomous forces within it, whatever their illusions.

In the United States, Christian and liberal reform elements are prominent at some institutions like Oberlin, San Francisco State, and Berkeley, and one can find a few new left revolutionaries and liberals on other campuses who have spoken out. But basically the Canadian account applies universally and the same arid conditions prevail. The reason one can find a few liberal revolutionaries in America must be attributed to bigness (over seven million students, and approximately 450,000 professors). These as compared with 300,000 students and 20,000 teachers in Canada, to some extent, to the streak of radicalism in America's "progressive tradition." However, on the whole, American radicalism is an industrialized brand of Frontier social consciousness in the city of Babylon. It is totally anachronistic and unimportant.

In spite of this environment of suppression, destruction, and homogenization, a wave of repression is setting in on the continent aided and abetted by the same forces that unleashed the "Liberal impulse" in the Kennedy age. In Canada, the era of Liberal reformism which was supposed to have been ushered in by the overthrow of Diefenbaker by the State Department in Feb., 1963, generated an interest in the "young" people that converted SUPA-types from "revolutionaries" into junior social workers and finally absorbed them into waspish freedom and eliminated the remaining residue of the movement. Canadian universities however, never harbored more than the CUS types as students and the few socialist leaguers that roved throughout the country, were never able to mobilize students massively or seize any campuses. The few outbursts that occurred at Simon Frazer, McGill, U. of T., Sir George Wilhelm or Lutheran were parochial in character, and single-issue oriented in their origins and aspirations. In sum, there is not, and there has not been a student movement of renown or permanent in Canada. On the other hand, the U.S. has a Reformist Student Movement in SDS and a few revolutionary Black groups of the "Third World" variety which have underscored not only the racist reality of America, but also the ethnic suppression of such minorities as Blacks and Mexicans and challenged the authoritarian character of the university and its built-in biases. At the moment, the Blacks are going beyond the "confrontationist" policy of SDS and its exhibitionism—the major attribute of middle classness and Jewish liberalism. And that is precisely what the battle is all about at San Francisco State, Southern and other universities. The battle cry is the abolition of the system of slavery. For this reason, the forces of "law and order" are reasserting their "authorities," abrogating reforms, expelling radical students and hordes of professorial presidents to invoke the dastardly law of depriving students of their government grants and scholarship if they participate in student radical activities. Thus the Hayskawas of the Ky stripe become the prototypes of the new academic soldiery—a soldiery that is shedding the velvet gloves of academe, its refined and sophisticated reasoning, and replacing it with Storm Troop tactics and police riots to frighten and intimidate middle-class children who love status more than authentic life and cherish jobs more than humanity and comradeship.

Although, historically, North American universities were never run other than autocratically by benevolent, white-haired dictators from the corporate world, in the past few years "participatory democracy" by public relations took some roots which became the symbol of the new university liberalism. Currently however, obeisance to such ritualism and tokenism is being jettisoned and a return to "law and order" is being advocated. The old P.R. presidents and fund raisers are slowly being eclipsed by high business, academic and political barbarians to suppress academic freedom and the expansion of consciousness, and the media have turned on their student-sponsored creatures to restrain the "extremists" and restore the era of the moderate and responsible majority—the robots and careerists of all systems and all times. In this atmosphere of fear, counter-revolution, and retrenchments, faculty "radicals" and students are being sacrificed on the altar of "law and order," and very few, if any, are protesting or challenging he latent and overt McCarthyism of this epoch. It is in this context that every dismissal of every radical must be interpreted and understood. And this brings me to the point concerning the actions radicals must undertake to frustrate or undermine this pernicious tide of official violence and repression. Legislators are beginning to see the danger of "independence" and university autonomy. They fear the prospect of the university developing into self-governing agencies of power that could challenge the economic and political hegemony of Canada's client bourgeois and America's imperial masters—the commercial corporate and industrial military complexes. They, therefore, desire to eliminate that possibility in its embryonic growth by containing university expansion and maintaining the university as an agent of "pluralism," rather than allowing it to become the locus of the emerging forces of youthful workers and students whose interests conflict with those of the dominant order. University presidents like Bissell of U. of T. are making their contribution by appointing Commissions on university governments to ratify and propagate their pet projects that are allegedly designed to democratize the system, and streamline and restructure the governing apparatus. Therefore, I see three major enemies on the horizon: the university system, the legislatures, and the teaching profession. The first and second have been somewhat exposed in leftist literature, and we must continue to expose them. The third enemy, the teaching, however, has been scarcely touched and we must focus on him in the new strategy of analysis, not only because of the servility of teachers but also because of their pivotal position in the management, maintenance, and perpetuation of the system. Moreover, since the profession values status and contract more than democracy and the communal compact, our task of exposure of those vulnerable parasites is much simpler and easier, especially in America's environment of anti-intellectualism and pretentious egg-headedness. And since the profession's professionals are the "senior scholars" who decide on appointments, and apply parity system and faculty-student committees are mere facades of the diversity and means of co-optation, it follows that radicals ought to use their resourcefulness not only to cripple and undermine the official juggernaut, but also to highlight the intellectual dishonesty of "academics," their abuse of public funds and power and oligarchic methods of operation. The new target must be the academic rascals!

As to the meaning of a dismissal, radicals must not lose sight of its educative aspects on themselves and on their environment. The only questions are: what impact will a dismissal have on its victims and victimized milieu and how enduring will it be? Briefly, will the "radical," after his expulsion retreat to the family shell, or will he stake all for a new man and a new morality, outlook, mission? Will he indeed achieve a new higher synthesis, that transcending "Christian humanisms," the pathology of "democratic socialism" and the other assorted shadows and make-believe images of middle class sophistry? Such is the real test of the liberated man who seeks to liberate others. Thus, my dear Darrol, we explained your position and environment and discovered that you are at a crossroads: you either become a grave-digger and join the revolutionary procession or return to the shell, to a life of retreat, withdrawal, and lamentations on past blunders. What will you choose, Darrol? Will you forsake yourself and submerge your humanity in the procession of servitude, falsehood and abdication, or will you march fearless and naked before the sun proclaiming the coming of man? Will you listen to the voice of your conscience and follow your imagination, or will you submit to the babbling harlots of academe and the blandishments of liberal society? Will you, my dear Darrol, rise above "family and friends" and reach for your authentic self in the region of the stars, or will you confess that you are of the clay repentant substance of the earth that is ready to be remoulded for other uses? What will you do, as you move towards an Easter of life? Will the view from the mountain enable you to sell your soul, or will you in a mighty upsurge of life turn your back on slavery and look to the heavens for inspiration? These are some of the questions you must answer for yourself in your aloneness, in the solitudes of the coming weeks, months, years.

# PART 2

# Sparticist: Black and White

# Chapter 6

## Lutheran Fossil

*Great empires and little minds go ill together.*
—Edmund Burke

### Introduction to the Introduction

When I was fired from Waterloo Lutheran in late 1967, I thought that Lutheran was a peculiarly parochial outlet of civilization on the frontiers of Heidelberg. Therefore, I wistfully decided to write a satire on the whole affair. Satire, however, turned into bitter diatribe as the forces of obscurantism and religious bigotry took up the cudgel to smash a nascent challenge to its bureaucratic Christian rule of saints. Lutheran officialdom, it seemed to me, must have felt that I was a greater threat to Lutheranism than the Counter-Reformation. Thus, on behalf of God, truth, and justice, they proceeded to deceive, befuddle, harass, and cajole their critics. All was fair play in the effort to crush the satanic forces that sought to undermine the church triumphant. Nothing was to be spared: cowardly tactics, character assassination by the so-called deans and acting chairmen before the Committee of Chairmen, conspiracy with the executive Committee of the Faculty association and subsequent promotive rewards to each member, the generation and expansion of faculty hostility, the manipulation of student council to withdraw its support from the boycott of classes, the propaganda by the professors and their interviews with strategic students to urge them to cease and desist, and finally the purchase of the student-editor to deliver a coup de grace in the last edition of the paper in the most graceless and despicable fashion. All that occurred at Lutheran, and I thought that it was a uniquely Christian experiment of barbarity. But I was wrong. I have learned, after thorough research, that Lutheran is not unique. Lutheran is the concretization of the universal, the march of institutional and mental feudalism in North America. Every university is Lutheran; every professor is a self-immolating chatterbox; every administrator is a white-collar thief; every student is a worm. The fault lies not with those involved; it is the system that makes them non-people, clerks, amoralists, indeed, at times criminals. Most cannot understand their victimization, and their political sophistication reaches about the level of grade two. They are slaves who pray to their masters and accept their gifts with humility and absolute abandon.

There have been personnel changes at Lutheran since 1967; but these in no way alter the character, structure, or outlook of Lutheran. Indeed, the commercial propensity has been strengthened, the fundamentalist behavior enhanced, the counterrevolutionary content intensified. Moreover, a feeble-minded president has been replaced by an administrative comprador who surrounds himself by a group of oligarchies that sport corporate banditry, service-club philosophy, and illiterate humanism. The students remain as flunky as ever, and I remain a social misfit by the standards of bourgeois psychology, if not a complete paranoiac. Therefore, I see no reason why anything substantive should be deleted from my 1967 account of the Lutheran debacle. Indeed, I now think that I was, without knowing it, describing universal types in an advanced colonial society: people without humanity, integrity, self-respect. In Mao's name, I pray for the salvation of their souls and the salvaging of their shipwreck.


## Introduction

The aim of this collection of disjointed diatribes is to alienate the few remaining friends I have to give the "enemies of the people" the opportunity of suing me. Let me hasten to add that my huge assets have all been transferred to Swiss banks, and my prospective plaintiffs will not be able to collect any money to soothe their bruised psyches. I still have a few dollars in Canadian banks, and I would rather go to jail than surrender my hard-earned Lutheran public money to "coprophiliacs." Besides, I think they are cowardly enough not to face me on the campus, and they will not dare confront me in court where I will have a chance to cross-examine them. Insofar as I know, the Canadian court system has not been corrupted by Lutherans, American colons, and ex-feudal East European Nazis.

A good many names that appear in my "unscholarly" work are there not only for the purpose of identifying village "philosophers" and demonstrating their intellectual bankruptcy but also for the purpose of increasing the prospects of selling my "junk." Anyway, even adverse publicity has an uplifting effect on the forgotten, and since this is probably the only time in their lives that certain people will see their names in print, what better place and time than now? And since this "stuff" is intended for local consumption, why not celebrate the oracles of Waterloo and exhibit them as good, loving, decent, Christian people, who hate injustice and love truth, especially if the latter happens to be their kind of baby? At any rate, names will not be deleted now so that their people may develop illusions of grandeur and historic significance.

Hubris—the revolt against the gods—was initially conceived as a pamphlet to advance a theory of freedom, education, and revolution using my experience as a case study. But as the conflict with the Lutherans unfolded, it became imperative to mercilessly expose their absolutism, inhumanity, and bureaucracy. What impelled me to begin the publication of Sparticist was the elementary discovery of the Manichean self-image, which characterized the actions and thoughts of the Lutherans— the chasm between Christian principles and bureaucratic brutality. Moreover, what astounded me most was the fact that "scholars," who were allegedly committed to the "truth," lent a hand to the popularization and origination of falsehood. It was bad enough that professors had nothing to spout forth except the platitudes of the dominant order, but when they engaged in petty conspiracies of silence and character assassination, it became impossible for me not to face the issue head-on. Since I was not to be given a hearing and not to be treated as a human being, I had no choice but to submit my case to public scrutiny, particularly after the Wagner BA (Mr. Endress) disclosed it and gave generously of his time to the press. Thus, the disclosure of the case, the animosity of the clerks, and the "moral turpitude" manifested by all must not go unchallenged. It is for these and other reasons that I resolved to publish my notes.

I hope my friends—if I still have any—will not feel embarrassed by the adulatory remarks. You see, I am a "fair-minded" person, and I give credit where credit is due; and since I am on the side of history—or if you prefer the reverse—my accolades ought to prove a benediction in the coming Marxian kingdom. Meanwhile, Lutheran Babylon prevails, and I hope the central committee of the board of saints will not expel any of them before they are ready to depart in peace and without harassment.

As to my students-friends and the students in political science who fought for justice, morality, and personal dignity, I hope we have created enough problems to cause the remaining clerks some mental anguish; but I fear that middle-class babbitry in collaboration with the regime of repression will succeed in silencing any outward revolutionary manifestation. But the "metaphysical guilt" we injected into the stunted Lutheran conscience cannot be conjured away by the sprinkling of holy water and the burning of incense on Grebb's altar. The ontological experiment we underwent has left its imprints on the minds of the wayfarer and the intellectually alert, and that cannot be erased by fists issued by cobblers and grocers. We have opened axiological questions that can never be ignored again, and the heuristic effect of these and other attendant issues will long survive our passing.

Lastly, I thought it was obligation to put my case before the students since they proved to be the only susceptible people in this "Christian environment." A good many of them have shown more intestinal fortitude than I expected. I only hope this experiment was their launching on the path of manhood and life rather than slavery and death, which abound in North America. I hope the students who participated in the struggle and observed the pathological operations of bureaucracy and the immorality of its accomplices will never again be deceived by the false reasonableness of inauthentic people who, under the guise of persuasion, issue commands and demand nothing short of absolute obedience. To my students, I say: revolution is my vocation; and I will go and fight for liberty wherever the struggle is being waged, be it in Vietnam, in Palestine, in America, or in Waterloo. You have seen skirmishing against death. From now on, it will be warfare to end the history of death.

I dedicate these notes to the "friends of liberty" and to those who cherish the spirit of revolution and, above all, to June, Bertrand, and Bonnie Anne. I wish them love, life, and liberty.

## Open Letter to the Parliament of Ontario

On October 26, 1967, the board of governors at WLU issued a Statement of University Objectives, which is being embodied in the structure, operations, and activities of the university. Three items in the statement ought to be of interest to the legislators and taxpayers of Ontario, and it is in my capacity as a taxpayer that I wish to bring to the attention of the legislature the following:

As a church-related university, it [WLU] should serve to bring contemporary theology into an effective relationship with secular matters so as to stimulate and foster the personal development of students and increase their understanding of religion and its relation to life.

As a church-related university, it [WLU] should provide a Christian environment that is meaningful and forthright in its purpose and coordinates the efforts of religious bodies to serve the spiritual needs of students.

Faculty, administration, staff and students should be encouraged to give evidence of their commitment to the educational, cultural, and spiritual objectives of the university and be provided opportunity to contribute toward the implementation of these objectives for the growth and development of the university.

If I understand the above *Statements* correctly, the Board of Governors which purports to preside over a "private university" affirms the absolutely denominational character of the school—an affirmation which is not in consonance with the spirit of secular humanism which characterizes the Ontario system of education. Moreover, the Board, which is solely Lutheran, rejects the principle of counterpoise, the operational code and the quintessence of democratic society. Indeed, the Board unabashedly proclaims itself a theocracy and operates a "university" on totalitarian principles by appointing employees on confessional grounds, requiring them to profess a religion in harmony with "the spiritual objectives of the university" and by encouraging the staff to work actively towards the achievement of Lutheranism as defined by Lutheran corporate magnates and their spiritual apologists.

It appears to me that the province's university system is being subverted and undermined by the kind of concessions made by Mr. Davis (minister of university affairs) to the Lutherans in granting and implicitly guaranteeing them in perpetuity about $1.5 million annually. While as a citizen I do not question the right of any citizen or group of citizens to

form and operate any kind of corporation under law, I do contest the use
of public monies for private purposes, especially if the users abuse the
power granted them by the province and flagrantly trample underfoot
the democratic procedures of this country. And as if these despicable
actions were not enough, the Lutherans are planning to establish a school
of religion within Waterloo University College, and I suspect that it will
be financed by the province. If this were allowed to happen, the province
would be regressing to the age of religious accomplice. Thus, such excuses
as this is "compensatory" money to replace federal grants is completely
unacceptable; and one cannot acquiesce in this form of legal subterfuge,
particularly since the Catholic universities (Windsor, Laurentian, Ottawa,
etc.) have all been nationalized and appropriate arrangements made so
that standards of academic excellence are relatively uniform throughout
the province. But the exception to the rule has been WLU, where the
standards of admission and the quality of instruction are deplorably
low. Yet this institution is subsidized by public monies without being
accountable to anyone except its American operators in New York who
manage it as a part of the branch-plant economy to promote the religious
and moral economy of a certain brand of ultraconservative Lutheranism.

It is true, however, that the managers of WLU pay lip service to
"democratic procedure," "intellectual curiosity," and "professional
competence"; but upon close scrutiny, all these laudable attributes will
be found wanting. And I can assure you, fellow citizens, that I speak
with authority when I say WLU is run strictly like a private corporation,
which is saturated with business norms and values and operated on
the principles of Stalinist authoritarianism. Education, the nurturing
of the soul, and the cultivation of emotional and intellectual growth
in a democratic environment are alien to the spirit of hush puppiness,
which permeates "education" at WLU. Indeed, WLU is no more than a
public relations agency to buttress Lutheran religiosity in Ontario and
give honorific titles to Lutheran businessmen and justify their predatory
business behavior.

As to democratic procedures and freedoms, I should like to point out
to the legislators that the Canadian Association of University Teachers has
recently stigmatized Lutheran procedure as "unacceptably authoritarian"
and their "freedoms" as "decidedly unacceptable." Moreover, CAUT has
seriously questioned the value of WLU as a university and whether in
the light of its operations on the part of CAUT cannot be ignored, and I

trust that the legislature will review its $1.5 million commitment to the Lutherans and hopefully eliminate it.

It should also be pointed out that the CAUT judgment was the result of a complaint I lodged with reference to my unjustifiable dismissal from WLU, a dismissal that was carried out without a semblance of democratic procedure or respect for intellectual values. Unhappily, the dismissal has been buried by my profession and the conspiracy of silence on the part of the mass media. I can understand why. I am not a Jew, and I am not a liberal commodity that can excite editors and civil libertarians who profess a love for the implementation of justice and the restoration of denied rights. I am an Arab and a radical, and these qualities do not appeal to the "sensitive" consciences of the "intellectual mafia" who are numbed by Zionist mythology and liberal guilt complexes. The Arab people have no lobbies to counter Zionism and weaken its impact on Canadian policymakers. They do not own newspapers to popularize their just cause. They own no huge corporations that decide the fate of this country, and they have no legislators to defend the trammeled rights of George Haggar. In brief, the Arabs are poor, and poverty is a sin under monopoly capitalism, and being a small minority somehow makes the Arabs non-people and non-citizens. I wonder what the honorable legislators, or indeed Mr. Davis, might have done had I been other than Arab. And will Mr. Davis excuse his inaction by contending that WLU is a "private university"?

I suppose many more questions could be asked of Mr. Davis, but the crucial ones are on what grounds and for which purposes have the Lutherans been exempted from provincialization? Is it because they are controlled from abroad? Is it because they have invisible powerful political and corporate friends? Or is it because their kind of vocationalism provides lower echelon clerks to maintain and enhance the well-being of corporate managerialism?

Other important issues could be raised, and I would be very happy to appear before the Bar of the House or the Education Committee to state them.[1] I should be very grateful to hear from the Speaker of the House on this matter.

---

[1]  The prime minister of Ontario, Mr. Robarts; the minister of university affairs, Mr. Davis; and the leader of the official opposition, Mr. Nixon, did not have the integrity to acknowledge receipt of this.

## Prelude to the Fall

In the cosmos of heavens, heavens abound in a variety of manifestations. There are lesser heavens, higher heavens, and mediocre heavens for the training of prospective angels. The brighter ones go to the higher heavens to be trained in the manners of great angels and to be taught to emulate the forerunners in their respective fields. The less-gifted ones move in a different orbit of heavens. They go to northern or southern climes to receive training for functions in the lesser heavens. In the hierarchy of heavens, there is a coterie of mini-gods, which co-opts prospective angels and appoints them to the tribe of angels. This clique consists of waspish salesmen and an exclusivist tribe known as the persecuted. These two elements, by and large, dominate the heavens of the northern climes. Connection with them means closeness to the seats of the gods. Remoteness spells doom and exile. The tightness of this circle cannot be described in words because the population of the planets are very suspicious of authors who attempt to describe the state of heavenly bliss in less-than-blissful terms. However, we cannot feel hampered by the tyranny of opinion, and we must proceed with our task of analysis. This begins our story, the story of the anointed angel whose fall we hope to adumbrate.

Our angel has a long history of angelness dating back to his friar days. In other words, his vocation to the altars of the super-gods has a history of its own, which we only mention in passing to explain the virulence of his temperament and the certainty of his rectitude. The anointed one, having graduated from a higher heaven, was recruited by a lesser heaven. This he considered a partial fall since he had hoped that mediocre heavens would at least offer him a post. The reason for their silence was very simple. Lacking the manners and the social distinction of their class, he was deemed unfit for mediocrity. Therefore, higher and mediocre heavens had no place for this unwashed angel who merely possessed training and intelligence and had neither the graces nor the contacts necessary for the circulation in mediocre and higher heavens. Thus, by fate, our angel had only lesser heavens to seek and be sought by. Hence, his unhappy consignment to a heaven where neither intelligence nor scholarship mattered and where piety prevailed. The conditions of piety are simple and clear. One from above, pleases flunky prospective angels and learns to appreciate the environment of Christian love and beatitude of his superiors who in turn bless and honor their superiors. All levels of superiors are the civil servants of the board of gods, the fountainhead of goodness, wisdom, love, virtue, prudence, and all conceivable values. In this seat of power, the true gods dwell. The executors of their orders are to be henceforth known as the seraphim. In other lands, the seraphim are known as professors whose mission it is to disseminate the wisdom of the gods and make it possible for them to perpetuate their rule. Since the board of gods is preoccupied in dealing with other gods at the same level, it follows that the seraphim are the functionaries of our heaven. Now the seraphim are of two kinds: Napoleons and mini-Napoleons with one Napoleon at the apex and four at the base of the pyramid. From these four, orders go to all corners of our kingdom. However, there is one Napoleon whose relationship with the second category of seraphim is paramount. He is the liaison officer, and his word is regarded as sacred.

Our anointed one, the angelic upstart, began his career in the council of lesser seraphim. Two weeks after his appointment, he was accused of importing foreign doctrines to our heaven. Having been cajoled and threatened, persuaded and intimidated, he was finally told to desist forthwith from this alien enterprise. Our angel, being a recent acquisition, was forgiven for his youthful enthusiasm and admired for his resistance and fearlessness. In brief, he refused to kowtow to the apostle of a mini-Napoleon and was left unhampered. This triumph conduced in our angel a secret belief in his infallibility and in the capacity of the higher council of seraphim to extol his deeds. It also engendered in him a feeling of superiority, bordering on pride. In the ensuing dialogues, he manifested the virtue of his learned intelligence and exuded the warmth of a vibrant mind.[2]

Pride breeds insolence; insolence breeds vulgarity; vulgarity means banishment from heaven. That is the fate of the proud and the vain who cannot accommodate themselves to the will of heaven!

Our angel, being a man of depth and scrupulous virtue, began to write epistles in the lingo of heaven, and it was discovered that this historic achievement was a sign of the adaptability and capacity for adjustment of the anointed one. The doctors in the seraphim class were astounded by his newly acquired gloss. They saw in him a man of deep profundity whose final conversion to the truth was pleasing to the gods. Word spread in the kingdom that the potentially obdurate angel had seen the light,

---

[2]    Communication: Apparently, there are more Jewish voters and bagmen in Ontario than there are Araba. But that is waspish justice!

and the council of seraphim rejoiced in this great act of transformation. The anointed one was showered with praise, his name became legend in higher and lower councils, and the happy family of heaven received him with a filial embrace. The anointed one was himself surprised, for he had not changed theses or abandoned his ways. He had merely broadened his critique and deepened his knowledge of reality. Because of the familiarity of the conventional topics dealt with, the seraphim interpreted the change in topic and verbiage as a change of heart and mind. What a sad day when word *change* is felt to mean a replacement for integrity and a stylistic amendment is interpreted as a repudiation of the social question. Thus, the inexorable march of events, the inevitable confrontation of views, and the consequent shock felt by the seraphim when the anointed one regressed to his previous lingo.

The conflagration that culminated in the fallenness of our angel was brought about when the council of seraphim read in the chronicle of heaven a critique on the conditions of heavenly bliss. Our angel had written an epistle evaluating the quality of the lesser seraphim and had, by implication, criticized the higher seraphim and the board of gods. What vituperation, what vulgarity, what opprobrium this insignificant angel was to heap on the gods! Preaching rebellion, disobedience, and resistance in the midst of family harmony cannot be condoned. Fear and terror plagued the kingdom, and a special self-appointed army of the seraphim visited a member of the ruling triumvirate to insist that Judas be exiled. Being a lover of pacifism, peace, order, and harmony, the triumvir summoned a mini-Napoleon and ordered him to communicate to our angel the news of his impending exile. This mini-Napoleon, being a functionary, called in our angel and excoriated him. The latter was informed that he was not original but verbose, sloganeering, and a charlatan. Patiently, the anointed one explained his epistle. Perplexed and confused, the mini-Napoleon, in the ensuing dialogue, agreed upon the contents of the epistle but disapproved of the style and expressed his envy of the anointed one who wrote so fearlessly and indignantly without the gods' permission.

Instead of expressing heartfelt thanks for the disapprobation and promising to recant, the anointed one pledged to spread more terror in the kingdom by writing further epistles. Not to be silenced, he even introduced such irrelevant concepts of outer space as academic freedom and the intellectual as a revolutionary. The tribe of mini-Napoleons were greatly disturbed by such unprofessional behavior, by this violation of senatorial courtesy, and the debauchery of the anointed one in identifying himself with a lesser breed of specks in the universe who were competing to gain a place in an ordered heaven.

Our mini-Napoleon, outraged by the stubbornness of the anointed one, returned to the triumvir to inform him that the anointed one would not abjure his misdeeds. Thereupon, the two enumerated the sins of the anointed one, submitted them to the upper triumvir who sought their approval by the board of the gods. Weeks elapsed—time being of no essence in our heaven—and the anointed one was not informed of his prospective banishment. Finally, impatient, he knocked on the doors of the mighty to find out what was their will. He was given an assortment of lies explaining why he should look for another heaven as a place of abode. Weeks passed by and, the higher triumvir, feeling that the estranged angel might launch an attack on heaven, pre-empted the fallen and, to justify his action, offered fairy tales, which were widely believed throughout the kingdom. The disclosure of the banishment of our angel was explained by the council of seraphim in terms of ineptness and naiveté on the part of the higher triumvir. Neither the merits of the case nor the welfare of the angel involved raised serious questioning. The seraphim respected and loved authority, and the office of authority had spoken. Thus it was written, thus it was accepted, thus it was upheld. Such matters as possible innocence could not be entertained, and our angel was deemed guilty until proven innocent—in contravention of the most elementary laws of justice and heavenly decency. The doctors, on this occasion, had buried their learning and, with it, their morality and humanity. They, like other citizens in totalitarian heavens, had accepted the role of the sycophant, the careerist, the bureaucrat. Hence, conscience was a characteristic of juniors who had not yet learned the ropes and who, in due course, would acquire the wisdom of the gods and preach the value of obedience to them. In brief, to be a seraphim was to be wingless, to be caged, to be circumscribed, to be chained, and to feel free, happy, and unbound. That is the only infinite we assert: the infinite capacity of our sycophants to deceive themselves and others.

Since the assumption required sophistry and the latter needed apostles to propagate it, the tribe of seraphim was best fitted to practise such an ignoble art. Therefore, it unleashed with fury all its power to tame the natives, squash dissent, and trample upon the rights of the anointed one. Their feeling of certainty stemmed from an audience with a mini-Napoleon who had informed the council of mini-Napoleons how, in fact, he had on his own independent initiative sought the proscription of the fallen and how neither exogenous pressure nor endogenous chicanery had impelled him to perform this great deed. He asserted his complete autonomy, and the council of mini-Napoleons lacked the integrity to ask the reason for this unheroic deed. That is to say, they neglected to exercise the rudiments of reason or cite the attributes of legality and morality they so frequently prattled about in their creative verbal pyrotechnics. The children who pretended to embody reason had abdicated reason and consigned her to the realm of oblivion where she belonged. The lovers of truth and wisdom had replaced morality by manners, principle by expediency, integrity by prostitution. In brief, they had all become prostrate prostitutes, and those with nagging consciences had been suppressed unless they wished to suffer the fate of the anointed one. Thus, silence prevailed and the conspiracy of silence stultified, all means of expression while the splenetic indictments of the fallen angel continued unabated and denunciations multiplied without parallel in their frenzy. Meanwhile, gods and non-gods, saints and lesser saints, cherubim and seraphim, all went about their business as if not a ripple had troubled our ocean of peace; and the external world acted as if no such event had taken place. Our fallen angel wondered what would have happened if he had been a Jew or a Commie, what civil libertarians and the intellectual mafia would have done and what the editorial writers would have written had he been black, yellow, or brown. What a wonderful cosmos to be in where equality before the law predominates, where rich and poor sit at the same tables, where love and peace engross the entire multitude, where decency and integrity are the guiding principles!

Finally, heaven and hell, go thy way! We will neither bend nor destroy you. Neither shall we redeem you, nor will we be silent in our defiance. We cannot be cowed into submission. We shall be free, and we shall not fear you. Your banishment will not annihilate us. It has humanized us and given us the ether of liberation, and lest you feel, O heaven, that you have vanquished us, let us remind you of Gibran who asks, "Who shall command the skylark not to sing?"

# Not a Fable of Gods, Toads, and Reptiles

Once upon a time, on a distant, distant island, in the distant, distant past, a volcano erupted. The mammals of the kingdom assembled to study the causes of the upheaval. As usual, in a kingdom of such a size, some gallant citizens regarded it their responsibility to examine the causes of the disaster and rectify the error, if any. Other citizens, of course, preferred to remain aloof and detached from the turmoil, which they assumed to be caused by citizens from other islands. Nevertheless, the citizens assembled. Most notable among them were the tribes of Toads, Worms, Reptiles, and Grasshoppers. Initially, the tribes were receptive to the voices from heaven. The angels of heaven had informed the tribes of the causes of the evil. Seeing that the voice of heaven was sincere and authoritative, a Council of Toads was assembled. The Toads proclaimed unequivocally: "Be it declared and known to all our subjects that the voice of heaven has spoken. We hereby decree that all citizens henceforth must not indulge in sexual lust for the period of one year. If the voice of heaven is obeyed, heaven will indeed listen to our prayers and will hearken to the voice of continence." The Council of Toads was also authoritatively informed by a group of grasshoppers who had access to the voice of heaven. They had seen the entire divine plan for the kingdom of Freedom. Since they communed with the spirits, they were firmly convinced that the spirits' wrath could be averted only if continence became a perpetual project. Hearing the divine commands, the Council of Toads reflected deeply and thoughtfully, and they, jointly with the grasshoppers, declared a plan for perpetual war on lust. The entire tribe of Toads was stirred and agitated by the proclamation. Some citizens were frightened; others became very anxious; the enlightened among them, especially anti-Semitic Toads and sundry flunkies who had selected to come to a lesser heaven after having been rejected by other heavens, felt that this didn't sound like the voice of heaven. Their allegiance to the local deities was above the level of standard devotion, and their fanaticism for the pursuit of truth could not be surpassed by those of other heavens. Yet some felt that the time had come to conquer lust. Suddenly, when the proclamation became known worldwide, the true gods also discovered it. Hurriedly, they sent their messengers to all corners of the kingdom of Toads. Anxiety spread. Doubt and fear prevailed in the kingdom; and as the archangel VON VULGAR dispatched his forces and charged his chariot toward the parliament of Toads, everyone stood stunned, shocked, and surprised. They all lay prostrate, for they could recognize the halo of the archangel whom they had seen before. "Speak to us, true archangel," they all beseeched him earnestly. He, haltingly, spoke to them with decorum and true authority, saying, "I have come to discuss with you the recommendations of the Committee on Committees and the cause of malaise in the land of Hellas." They all huddled together and raised their heads to hear the words of truth and wisdom. The true archangel informed them that the author of their action was not the voice of heaven but that of a degraded heavenly object in exile. "Speak more," they all insisted, cringing before him. And he said, "That fallen heavenly object has disintegrated in space. But before his disintegration, the Holy Trinity had warned him against his sins, pleaded with him to return to the fold, and offered apology for his creation. Moreover, as pride took possession of his soul, he challenged the gods' authority. That is why we banished him from heaven. That is my message to you from the Lord, the creator, whose happiness and yours are forever intertwined." And the archangel ascended to heaven.

With these tidings from heaven, the Council of Toads resolved to resolve the unresolvable. They agreed that it would be impolitic to announce that, in fact, they had been deceived by the fallen object of heaven. In order to go through the democratic process, in which they all take pride because it is fair and impartial, they ought to hold another secret session to give a hearing to the fallen angel. For it was written in their constitution that justice was not for those who have but for those who have not. But the "have-nots," according to the law of the kingdom, were nonexistent. Therefore, the constitution in essence meant that the law was for those who have, especially the anointed, the redeemed, and those in the process of redemption.

The fallen heavenly object and his armed conspiracy discovered the plot and sent their messengers to the Council of Toads to determine whether or not the gods had actually discovered the plot and had exposed it to all the people of all the planets. The Toads keenly assured the disciples of evil that the Council of Toads would permit no interference in its affairs and that, as Autonomous Toads, they would examine the subterranean causes of the volcano's eruption. On a historic day, the Council of Toads dutifully assembled with three female toads among the multitudes and a broken-down ex-Toad who had been elevated to the kingdom of the gods. The latter was sitting in the chair. Beside him stood a baby reptile that had been trained in the art of sophistry, which is to say, upon request, he could declaim against anyone for a price. Abruptly, the fallen heavenly object descended on the scene with his halo somewhat shattered but nevertheless there. He gave an impression of self-assurance to the representative of the Toads who had come to determine whether or not he had been properly expelled from heaven and if heaven wasn't right after all. The fallen object earnestly answered questions and expounded on the beauty of evil, the greatness of evil, and the joy of exile. The Toads, excited by his remarks, listened carefully and attentively. Some wondered whether exile was the best place for him after all. Having delivered his encomium, the fallen object departed with the clear knowledge that a counter-heaven was the best place for him. The Council of Toads, with the guiding intelligence of our baby reptile and the ominous, threatening presence of a broken-down corpse, decided that they were, after all, in heaven and somehow been misled and driven a millimeter away from heaven. Swiftly, they all returned to heaven, pleading mercy and forgiveness and disowning their proclamation. The entire population of heaven hailed the wisdom of this responsible and respectable act and welcomed back into the fold the little lost Toads. They sprinkled them with holy water and purified them with incense and accepted them back into the kingdom.

When the Grasshoppers got hold of the news, their angry voices screamed betrayal. The procession must go on. Equality must be given to the fallen and to the local warlords. The show went on, and all types of Toads came to see the parade. Those leading the parade were the Grasshoppers, fallen angels, and interpreters of the will of the gods to all Toads everywhere. The fallen angels explained the causes of their fall, decrying the justice of heaven and appealing to the assembled Toads to reason with unreason and become untoady in a kingdom of Toadyism. Patiently, the Toads listened while Toads and counter-Toads spoke for and against heaven, the abode of the blessed, who had sent only cherubim to listen and report back to the gods, the reason being that heaven— disdainful of untidiness, unhappiness, and horror—did not wish to be troubled by the discordant voices of fallen men. For it had been decreed that if the fallen wished to return to the kingdom and get an audience with the gods, they would have to repent and drench themselves with the tears of happiness and joy. But like all fallen angels, they were obstinate, talking about such foolish things as dignity, integrity, and authenticity, with the passions of a distant land called Mother Earth. The gods were not to be troubled with the morality of other planets and the schemes of alien conspirators. They knew the law, they were the law, they had issued the law, which stated clearly, "In our happy and harmonious heaven, there shall be peace and we shall know war no more. Away, away with obstructionists, schemers, and thinking people. They are dangerous and interfere with the harmonious process of our family relations, a necessary condition in the programming of Toads and creating of robots that conform to the laws of Toadyism and know their function in the scheme of heaven and its allies. We cannot condone discord, for our task is to hush the conscience of Toads and still the barking puppies who prey upon the flock. Harmony for eternity, peace in perpetuity, Toadyism forevermore—let this be our motto."

The tribe of lesser saints in the kingdom of heaven was greatly disturbed by the movements and counter-movements of Toads; shocked by the insolence of the fallen object; and, to some extent, envious and even longing for the day of fallenness. However, the council of lesser saints, overwhelmed by messages from heaven, moved slowly and assuredly to arbitrate between toads and lesser saints. Having commended the Council of Toads for its inactivity, it advised the lesser saints to take precautions against the contagion of fallenness. Fear spread among the lesser saints. Courage found a few upholders, and conspiracy found themselves allies. Suddenly, reptiles, ancient and new, took it upon themselves, as learned professors in the art of Toadyism, to correct the impressions of Toads and spread doubt about this previous history of the fallen angels. The ancient reptiles highly esteemed by all authoritatively declared that the fallen angels had a history, beginning from time immemorial, of thinking of lust, contemplating it, and cleverly executing the plots of lust. As apostles of fatherly harmony and exponents of upper-class stolidity, they felt it incumbent upon themselves to disseminate the good news and slay the dragons. Those who paraded as ape trainers and excelled in being the traitors of heaven were utterly dismayed and horrified by the culpability of the fallen angel. They sought out the gods and insisted in the name of heaven that the fallen angel be forever forgotten since he had organized 1,001 plots to denigrate the goodness of heaven, the distribution of its largesse, and the operations of its proficient commands. Along with ancient and new reptiles, valiantly they stood at the side of heaven and proclaimed her righteousness, justifying the divine plan for apostles, saints, angels, and Toads. The ape trainers and their allies, the reptiles, moved with historical, mathematical, and geographic precision to successfully convert deviant Toads by the effeminate diction of their voices, the pleasant countenance of their smiles, and the magic of their wands. The feminine voices of the trainers and reptiles and the graceful contortions of their bodies and words seduced the Toads and tamed the oscillating and schizophrenic among them. As a result of this process, the Toads, shocked and surprised, further repented for having broken the counsel of the fallen. Word quickly reached every part of the kingdom that the fallen were indeed sources of evil and terror who deserved nothing but fallenness and the banishment of exile. Thereupon, all resolved that the fallen must be proscribed in order that happiness, peace, and family life would forever reign in heaven and in the kingdom of the Toads.

# SPARTICIST I

## Open Letter to Lutheran CAUT

*Well knows he who uses to consider, that our faith and
knowledge thrive by exercise, as well as our limbs and
complexion. Truth is compared in scripture to a streaming
fountain; if her waters flow not in a perpetual progression they
sicken into a muddy pool of conformity and tradition.*
—John Milton, *Areopagitica*

The local executive of CAUT has without the advice and consent of its membership issued a statement in which it proclaimed the University's right now to renew my contract and asserted that my academic freedom was not infringed upon. How the executive arrived at its judgment, I do not pretend to know; but I know for certain that I have never been interviewed by the executive as a collectivity and I have never submitted for its consideration any documentation of my charges against the regime which has been condemned by the national CAUT as "unacceptably authoritarian." How the executive without a hearing, without evidence and without cross-examination can conclude that my academic freedom was not violated leaves me baffled and stunned by is readiness to prejudice the case without giving the faculty a chance to hear both parties to the dispute and judge for themselves as to who is or is not at fault. The executive declares that "it has no evidence that academic freedom was involved in the denial of a new contract to Dr. Haggar." What evidence does the executive have to deny that freedom was not abridged? Are the five Wisemen (The Executive Committee of the Association) aware of the statements issued by Mr. Endress to me and to the press? Are they conscious of the elementary fact that the ruling regime stated clearly that I was a capable scholar and teacher? Or are we to dismiss all that as naiveté and ineptness on the part of Mr. Endress as the prudent men of the faculty lounge have whispered? A whitewash gentlemen of the executive and a leaf from the writings of Mr. Endress: "The question . . . [is] closed." The question is wide open and no unctuousness can conceal it.

In its assumed position the executive, it seems to me, are allowing person to replace principle and status to supplant the intellectual value of academic freedom. The gentlemen in question appear to confuse social organization and tenure with academic freedom and treat these concepts as if they were interchangeable. Such is not the case and any person with an M.A. or Ph.D. should know the difference, a distinction which seems to have escaped the National Association as well.

Since the faculty's integrity is at stake a few facts should be known to all:

1. Although initially the Dean offered two flimsy excuses for the non-renewal of my contract—unhappiness and non-recommendation by the acting chairman—since then the list of sins has extended to other areas and rumour-mongering has become the order of the day. If anyone has any charges to make let him or her surface and face me at a place and time of their choosing. It is no coincidence that open-ended statements in the classrooms are so abundant, and the silence of the grave prevails.

2. The Acting President has informed me in writing that no contract was being offered because he believes that I am not happy with the philosophy, structure, operation, and personnel of W.L.U. The gentleman in question at least possesses a simple honesty which states the case without equivocation—a rare commodity among sophisticated academics.

3. Neither the Acting President nor the Dean nor the Acting Chairman apprised me of their intentions not to renew my contract on the 15th of December as stipulated in my contract nor before or after, until I initiated an inquiry into the matter on the 19th of December. Indeed, I have never been in the office of either Acting President or Dean. All the rest is fairy-tale and selective perception.

4.  A significant number of colleagues have been told that the Acting Chairman informed me on two occasions (December 1 and 15) that my contract would not be renewed. That is an ABSOLUTE LIE.[3] On December 1, he called me to his office and accused me of verbosity, lack of originality, and sloganeering for writing the article on the clerks. Immediately I asked whether he was speaking as a colleague, chairman, or administration messenger. He assured me that he was speaking as a colleague. In the course of an hour he agreed with the contents of the article but violently disapproved of the "way" it was written. And in this process of recrimination he admired a letter in the issue of *The Cord* before him which attacked my position. I advised the Acting Chairman that I intended to reply and I did in the letter on Servility. However, as I was leaving his office, he said to me that he could no longer "shield" me—a comment that was to have meaning on the 19th of December. I have been authoritatively informed since then that he was instructed to tell me that no contract was forthcoming. That he never did.

5.  It is very obvious for anyone who has conscience, reason, and self-respect, and wishes to use them, that my academic freedom has been violated and my civil rights trampled upon. It is indeed regrettable that the executive's vision of reality is just as myopic as the tunnel vision of the administration and that both of them have assumed all the way that I am guilty until proven innocent. What a system of justice for a "community of scholars" in the paradise of Christian love!

"All that is necessary for the forces of evil to win the world is for enough good men to do nothing."

(Edmund Burke)

---

[3]  According to Frank Cornelius Peters, the then Mennonite Lutheran dean and now president, Mr. Aun told his superiors that he informed me on December 15, 1967, that I would not be rehired. In a January 4 letter to me, Mr. Endress, a Christian liar, stated: "I was in Dr. Peters' office at the time of the conversation and therefore I am aware of the flow of the conversation and your own confirmation at the end that Dr. Aun informed you that no contract would be offered." What is a lie or two for Christ, Luther, or Henry Endress for that matter?

# SPARTICIST II

## Note on Scholarship and Humanism

*No man is an iland, intire of itself; every man is a peece of the maine; if a Clod be washed away by the Sea, Europe is the lesse, as well as if a promontorie were, as well as if a Mannor of thy friends or thine owne were; any mans death diminishes me, because I am involved in Mankinde.*

—John Donne

A significant number of WLU "scholars" have been greatly disturbed by remarks I made pertaining to their scholarship. Since these people profess to be empirically oriented, may I recommend a rereading of "Faculty Notes," which are, in effect, the intellectual biographies of the faculty and are to be found in *Campus*, defunct *Scoop*, and *Memo from the President's Office*. Perhaps on the basis of empiricism, we might have a convergence point, and my allegations will prove to be either valid or false. If false, why not call them false; if true, will you continue to do what you have been doing? It is the style, the way, the emotions, the tirades, etc., that cloud the vision of Haggar, and therefore he is not scholarly.

It must be pointed out that those who are making these scurrilous attacks on my scholarship are the flunkiest dead-enders on the staff. They seem to think contract equals scholarship, and "bodies" of triflers in the classroom and agreement with autocracy are the essence of scholarship. Wrong again, clerks.

You ought to remember that on January 17, 1968, I stated publicly that the university should have three main concerns vis-à-vis its staff: (a) whether or not a professor is competent, (b) whether or not he is performing his assigned work, (c) whether or not he has working relations with his students and immediate colleagues. The acting president told the *Globe* (January 18/68) that I am "probably a very good teacher"; and in letters to me, he has spoken in glowing terms about my publications, public appearances, and work at the university. Are we to interpret these comments the way Mr. Hellyer did on February 16, 1968, when he stated that the Endress letter was "to soften the blow on Haggar," or are we to accept them? Moreover, the dean has assured me in front of two people that the question of competence was never raised and that he would give me "the best recommendation." And Mr. Aun has said something to the same effect.

I should point out to my readers that these "promises" are of no value to me, and I will neither request "recommendations" from these "honorable gentlemen," nor will I do them homage by using their names for reference. In my view, the only reference a man needs is his educated manhood. This is something no one can bestow or withhold. And if one's manhood runs counter to accepted "civilization," then up with a "civilization" that is anti-man.

It is obvious then that the Lutherans should know by now that Haggar will not bend or kneel to tyranny, arbitrariness, and caprice; and they should know that they will be no more than a footnote in the history of George Haggar. As to their owners and the worms who are defending them, I say: the "holy" trinity of Grebb, Endress, and Peters have no divine right to destroy people and feel justice was done because enough prostitutes admired their decisiveness. Do you not know, you people of little wisdom, that "law is for him that has against him that has not and for the strong against the weak"? Thus, the vital question here is to what extent will Christian depravity descend to encompass every conceivable sin that I might have perpetrated? And are there bounds to the psychic bestiality to which the doctors of philosophy can sink in the hope of redeeming a decadent bureaucracy without moral authority and without a single speck of humanism? That, fellow "academics," is the dilemma that must be confronted, and no self-deception such as "Haggar dug his own grave" will ever excuse your submission to Hitlerism and your kowtowing to tyranny.

As to your accusation of "vindictiveness," I say I am not a Christian; therefore, I can afford to be vindictive, and I need no biblical quotations to justify me.

As a humanist, every death diminishes me; and nothing diminishes me more than the smiling falsehoods of the objective, sane, and dedicated teachers of my profession.

You tell me that you feel offended by the labels pinned on you by Haggar. And I tell you that you have overfulfilled my expectations. You have transmuted my labels into living monuments and my observations into eternal laws. You hate abdicationism. Indeed, you are not only prepared to submit to Mr. Boss, but you are prepared to justify him, explain his human ways, and prostrate before his awesome majesty, however fraudulent he might be. Citizens of the Fourth Reich, you are the intellectual marines of the American empire, the verbal and human napalm of monopoly capitalism, the blessed pirates of Christianity, and the honored "professionals" of every dictatorship!

"Dogmatism!" cries out the enemy; but is there anything more repugnant to the intellect than the centrist dogmatism of the middle class and the apologias proffered on the altar of its daily debaucheries in the name of order, authority, and compromise? Yes to dogmatism if it supports that ruling elite, no to liberty if it means accountability for the middle class and the exercise of virtue! This is the essential message of reigning liberalism and its advocates. And since competence is in question, it must be regarded as a new promotion by the ruling oligarchy.

For my part, I think what should be said is that middle-class rationalizations do not constitute scholarship, and what passes for scholarship in Canadian universities is not necessarily scholarly. Manners, morals, and scholarship are involved at the local level; and perceptual defensiveness is the fault of my critics, who would do well to begin exploring the tenets of these disciplines.

# SPARTICIST II

## The Politics of Politics

It was widely disseminated that Mr. Aun initiated independently the move again the non-renewal of my contract. After the exposure of that fallacy, the friends of order and authoritarianism resorted to the selective resuscitations of past events, which allegedly demonstrated the human protection Mr. Aun accorded me to ward off the attacks of the previous regime. This desperate attempt at face saving and malignant rumoring cannot go unchallenged, and self-respecting people must begin to examine the entire evidence not in terms of personality but in terms of verifiability for the purpose of establishing the truth. For this and other reasons, I submit for investigation my whole experience with the department beginning with my appointment in the spring of 1965 to my last encounter with the CAUT executive on February 16, 1968.

Since a considerable segment of the faculty have interpreted my relative silence as a weakness of case and have hoped to see me fade away without troubling their sensitive consciences, perhaps I should briefly explain the strategy behind my quietism. It appeared to me that my accusers felt that upon release of the case, the old impetuous Haggar would run out to the press screaming "Fascist bastards" and in the process discredit himself and demonstrate how rightfully he deserved to be dismissed. Having decided on the basis of reputation rather than knowledge of Haggar, the regime must have felt that if a battle were to be waged, it would be between Haggar and the department or Haggar and the staff who support the ruling bureaucrats. Therefore, whatever Haggar did, he was doomed because the faculty were very much antagonized by the article on the clerks and by the general non-middle-class behavior of this proletarian boor. It does follow then that the regime felt secure in the knowledge that to get rid of Haggar was almost unanimously acceptable to the faculty, and therefore the time was propitious to move and sacrifice that disgraceful muckraker. If this were the general calculation of the regime, at least it was accurate in its estimation of the reaction of the faculty. But Haggar's reticence has bewildered many, and he did not behave in the expected manner. His stoicism, instead of being thought of as a plan, has been considered a feebleness of case. That is why the regime and faculty are in a state of consternation, and Mr. Endress has been placed in the untenable position of having disclosed the case and of having revealed "unnecessary" details, providing Haggar with a store of ammunition. In brief, my plan was not to give my critics more excuses than necessary to justify the truculence and invidiousness of their behind-closed-doors and classroom attacks.

Secondly, I have held the view that the regime committed a very serious blunder and a deep wrong against me. Therefore, I decided to give them elbow room to maneuver and retreat without losing too much face—this being the first law of political negotiation. However, the regime has no intention to budge one inch. Mr. Endress informed me in writing that the case is "closed" and has told others that the decision will not be reversed. Indeed, a gentleman of impeccable credentials who sought to begin the process of negotiation has been ruthlessly silenced. If the regime were interested in negotiation, their opportunity came when the National CAUT issued its report. The magnanimous thing to do was to issue a statement to the effect that an impartial body had investigated the case, and in the light of developments, we would offer Haggar a contract. So much for charity, enlightenment, and Christian magnanimity! I cannot help but think that Mr. Hellyer and his executive were not interested in exploring the possibility of reversing the decision but in upholding the autogracy in the hope that after the Haggar departure, the statement on academic freedom might be slightly amended and the men who helped bury the Haggar affair be rewarded. How many a CAUT president has received a promotion or a scholarship after his incumbency?

Thirdly, I have deliberately and consciously endeavored to keep Mr. Aun out of the picture on the grounds that he did what he did at the behest of the regime and not on his own initiative. I have known him for nearly three years and know something about his mental makeup. Besides, friendship and loyalty to him prevented me from involving him. But since he did nothing to clear his name and publicly stuck to the idea of "joint decision," I was perturbed but not angry enough to divulge his role. However, since he told the chairman that he acted autonomously and the latter have spread the word in their fiefs and are behaving like mini-Napoleons in his defense, I feel that such double talk and doublethink must be answered. And since the CAUT president was trying to dragoon the faculty association into upholding their executive, I feel no obligation to anyone except my students, my friends, my honor, and the truth, which has been so badly mutilated by its alleged advocates.

## 1965

Let us now return to the beginning of the beginning, not to the ransacking of history. I was appointed to Waterloo Lutheran in the spring of 1965. The interview was conducted by Mr. Aun and a host of others, including Mr. Overgaard and a former classmate, Mr. Miljan. Before coming for the interview, I was not aware of the existence of two schools here or of the fact that Mr. Miljan was an employee at WLU. I feared that if I did not disclose my commitments to the interviewers, Mr. Miljan would; and since we were strong political "enemies" at U of T, his disclosures would prejudice my prospective appointment. Happily, Mr. Miljan had forgotten the debating battles at U of T and the pamphlets I published as a parliamentary CCF-NDP leader there. Indeed, Miljan expressed deep interest in the emerging Socialism, which I advocated, and assured me that undergraduate differences would constitute no roadblock to my appointment. Therefore, there was no need to conceal the past, and the interviewers were told about my political career as a student and politician. More specifically, they were advised that I was a very fervent supporter of Afro-Asian Socialism and that the U of T group I led was disowned by the CCF for its left-wing radicalism. The interviewers, in other words, recommended my appointment in the full knowledge that I was a radical Socialist and not merely a middle-class NDP supporter who engages in dissent as a show of liberality. There were no false pretenses. Haggar was, still is, and will forever be for social revolution, for the overthrow of capitalism, for the eradication of injustice, and for the end of exploitation of man by man!

The first test of my Socialism came when the NDP campus club invited me to give a lecture on the subject. I did, and the *Cord* reported a garbled version of what I said on October 1, 1965. Mr. Overgaard's self-appointed informers told him that I predicted the demise of capitalism within five to ten years. After reading the *Cord* report, I felt obliged to correct the paper's misunderstanding (October 15, 1965) and wrote in explanation of my thesis that "coalition politics (brokerage) may have worked in the past, and might still work in the foreseeable future, but it will not work in about two decades hence, because the economic foundation of our society will have been radically altered as a result of the triple revolution—cybernation, weaponry, and human rights for the subjugated people." Moreover, I contended that the cybernation revolution is being deferred by monopoly capitalism for fear of violent social upheaval since its mainstay is the petty bourgeois elements, and these are the social forces that have to consigned to perpetual unemployment if the technological revolution were carried out precipitately. Therefore, because of the class between the bourgeois ethos and the technological substructure, bourgeois ideology has become a fetter on the evolution and growth of society, and the time will come when capitalism will be replaced by a more humane Socialist order.

Mr. Bartmann (a student then and presently a lecturer) took up the gauntlet and launched an attack on "Mr. Haggar's Marxist determinism" but kindly placed me in the galaxy of Socialist luminaries like Marx and Deutscher (November 5, 1965). Several other letters were written while Mr. Overgaard's fever rose rapidly. Feeling that he could no longer condone this "Socialist nonsense," he ordered Mr. Aun to tell me that if I wanted to return next year to stop writing immediately. Mr. Aun conveyed the message and assured me that he did *not* share the views of Mr. Overgaard. He was convinced that I was a "Social Democrat," and he respected my views, providing I did not blunder into Communism. This first academic experience shook me up because I had been conditioned by my liberal professors to believe that the universities were the citadels of truth and all ideologies were to confront one another in this marketplace of ideas. Believing profoundly in the collision of ideas, I recommended a debate on the matter, but the proposal fell on deaf ears. Thereupon, I angrily told Aun that if Overgaard opened his mouth again, I would have a contract-burning ceremony on *This Hour Has Seven Days*. Mr. Overgaard never raised the issue again. But a move was made in the department by the Dow Chemical "scholar" to have me expelled. Members of the department opposed the move, and the issue was dropped. Meanwhile, the *Cord* was ordered to stop publishing letters for or against me, and that was that.

In this whole incident, I did not need protection from the previous regime as Mr. Overgaard reported to the CAUT meeting on February 16, 1968. What I needed was protection from Mr. Overgaard, and when Overgaard discovered that his threats were of no value, he desisted.

Moreover, the confrontation with Overgaard did not affect or in any way delay the issuance of my contract. Therefore, those who informed Students Council (when it was convened to repudiate its call for the boycott and inquiry of January 17, 1968) that my contract had been withheld before and there was always a reservation about their issuance were telling the council blatant lies. In retrospect, Overgaard's intimidations did not hinder but facilitated my subsequent communications with the former president, who believed in the Arabic adage the enemy of my enemy is my friend.

## 1966

In the autumn of 1965, Mr. Hauge, with whom I shared an office, started his campaign to introduce the semester system into the department and "behavioralism." I was very sympathetic but did not care to champion the cause because I knew Mr. Aun was bitterly opposed, and I was much more interested in social issues than in the reform of WLU (which I thought was a fruitless undertaking). The controversy over the matter reached the boiling point when both the former dean and Mr. Aun recommended that Mr. Hauge be denied a contract for the academic year 1967–1968. Villaume overruled them and gave Mr. Hauge a contract. The revolution was on. Aun issued a harassing six-point directive, which was aimed at Hauge. In essence, Aun proclaimed his mini-Napoleonness and expected us to acknowledge it. We dismissed it as latent Estonian Stalinism.

The Hauge affair merely illustrated Aun's hankering after authority, which we did not recognize and therefore Aun did not render the deference he sought. My partial sympathy from his stemmed from direct knowledge of the conditions of exile and the psychological problems of alienation, which afflict a European who does not feel that "vulgar" North Americans appreciate him. My opposition to Aun was grounded on the conviction that he has a feudal frame of mind, an authoritarian personality, and an inflated vision of himself as a forgotten demigod. Moreover, his profound suspicion of innovation and his romantic hierarchism made it impossible for him to work within a framework of relative democracy. Thus the crux of the matter: traditionalism and absolutism versus radicalism and revolutionism. The conflict was inexorable.

Hauge had a keen mind, but his appointment to teach Canadian government reveals the lack of Lutheran commitment to university education. Hauge's basic interest was U.S. municipal government, and we offered no course in such a field. He taught Canadian government and did the best he could, but the students were very much aware of his very limited knowledge of his subject. They protested to the dean and Aun, and quite frequently, a large number of them came to attend my classes. Instead of heeding student demands, Aun, in the spring of 1966, with the dean's approval, gave Mr. Hauge sole responsibility for teaching the three sections in Canadian government. This was very shocking to me because I was teaching the honors class and I expected to be teaching it in 1966–67. Needless to say, this change of policy occurred without my consultation, and Mr. Aun informed me on the phone. A few days later, he tried to assuage me by saying we could better work together teaching Politics 20, the introductory course.

The second most important incident in 1966–67 was with regard to teaching Politics 20. Aun, for about eight years, has been using the Hodgett book for the course. He is by training and conviction committed to a traditionalist approach to teaching, which requires neither imagination nor serious preparation nor reflective work and research. The approach is simple: the teacher reads to the students the constitutions, the electoral laws of a given polity, and gives them a pseudo-historic account of the institutions under review. The students are impressed by the use of legal language, and some are overawed by the wide learning of their professor. They are predisposed to rote memory; thus, the approach is palatable and satisfying to such high-schoolish minds. This approach in my view is anti-education and anti-political analysis but useful for the legal study of politics. Thus, the fundamental problem that has to be faced in planning a course that embraces the entire field of political science. Aun asked me to plan the course, and I did, taking into consideration his views. After many sessions, a course outline was agreed upon, and we agreed that we would only have joint final examinations.

On November 4, 1966, Mr. Aun unilaterally and without prior notice to me announced to the students that they ought to buy a new textbook he had just ordered: Hodgett, a book we had rejected. The students had invested about $15 in books, and the change affected over four hundred of them. Besides, I was away attending a Windsor seminar and returned to face an agitated class. I told the students that I contemplated no change in the direction of the course and did not expect them to purchase Hodgett's book. Aun was very disturbed and became very angry because I challenged his authority publicly. Then a few weeks after the incident, Aun announced to the students that we were having a joint test, and all of them became terrorized because they did not know what to expect. For my part, I told my students not to worry, that the test would be prepared by me and not Aun. However, the battle was on when he decided that we were to have a joint examination after he had reversed the course in midstream. I submitted my exam for typing, and he withdrew it. Immediately, I informed the former president, who ordered him to return it. I told my students if one word of my final exam was changed, I would resign on the spot. Aun was told to stop his badgering or else. He did.

## 1967

The third incident spans the entire 1966–67 academic year, and this relates to Mr. Aun's position and mine in the department. Villaume blocked Aun's appointment as chairman because he held that Aun was "incompetent." Aun was made acting chairman, and the faculty was led to believe that he did not want to be chairman. At any rate, in the autumn of 1966, I asked Aun to petition the dean on my behalf for a nine-hour load for 1967–68. After one month, he did not move a finger to advance this request. Thereupon, I went directly to the dean, who seemed very sympathetic and told me that my request would be complied with. However, when I took sick in January of 1967, Mr. Aun visited me at the hospital and told me that I had misinterpreted the dean in reporting to Aun that the dean was agreeable. I told Aun I thought the misdeed was despicable and that if both thought they could take advantage of my illness they ought to consider me as having resigned. Aun said not to worry and that he was for me.

It should be pointed out at this juncture that neither man had known that Villaume considered me his "brain truster" and publicly regarded me as the university's symbol of diversity. By going through the motion, I was merely playing to procedure. They knew and I knew Villaume was the boss. What they did not know was that their opinion of me, favorable or adverse, was of no consequence to Villaume. Aun decided to promote my cause because he felt that I deserved the consideration, but in retrospect, it seems that he needed my neutrality or support vis-à-vis Hauge, who was out to remove him. The request was granted by Villaume and without reservations and not because Aun said so.

The central problem facing the department in 1967 was the replacement of Aun and the recruitment of two eminent scholars so that the department could find a place on the map of this country. Two very good prospects were available, but when one of them learned about the impending struggle in the department, the entire plan fell through, and we had to rely on making junior appointments. This brings us back to the problem of whether or not a department with serious scholars can be run autocratically and whether it is possible ever to build a department with Aun presiding. The answer is a resounding no. The reasons are simple: authoritarianism, academic ossification, and complete inability to grasp the significance of the revolution in political science.

The fourth incident took place in the fall of 1967. Aun and Overgaard were instrumental in proposing the Bonning Centennial lecture. Aun never mentioned the proposal to me. But Villaume did. After an hour's discussion with Villaume, he agreed to extend the proposal into a series and asked me to draft an outline specifying topics and indicating which names were to be considered for each. An accord was rapidly reached, and I went through the motion of informing Aun and asking him to put forward the "proposal." And he immediately did. Aun wanted the series to be conducted by the department. So did I. But Villaume had no confidence in Aun, and he unilaterally placed the series under the auspices of the Cultural Affairs Committee. Aun was slighted and rightly felt offended, especially when he was not asked to introduce any of the invited guests. The university decided to publish the lectures. After Villaume's departure, the PR people turned over the manuscripts to Aun, who did nothing on the question of the editing and preparation of an introduction. However, in the autumn of 1967, he asked me to read the lectures and offer a critique, which I did. It seemed to me that Aun appeared to be asking me to do the work and let it appear under his name; therefore I proposed that I be given some research assistance and I would do it on the understanding that I would have a smaller load next year. Nothing came out of the suggestion, and my suspicion was confirmed when in a heated discussion over the matter in the presence of Mr. Nyiri, the latter proposed "joint editorship" and Mr. Aun responded with stunned silence. A few days afterward, he spread the word that he could not give Haggar what he wanted for next year—i.e., associate status. My reaction to this well-planted rumor was a sardonic smile.

The fifth incident of my "happy" experience with the Lutherans was over the Middle East and my role as Arab spokesman. When in the spring of 1967 the turbulent Mideast monopolized the headlines, I defended the Arab revolution and contended that an assault was being planned against it by Washington, Ottawa, and Tel Aviv. My attacks on the insidious plans of Zionism did not please Mr. Grebb, chairman of the board of governors. Villaume seemed to have liked what I was saying and doing and regarded it as good publicity for the university. To assuage Grebb, he cancelled (the exact word was *postponed*) on very short notice an invitation to Mr. Healy (a former professor of business who was offered Mr. Overgaard's post, and currently academic vice president) and invited me to address the Rotary Club of Kitchener so that Mr. Grebb and his "friends" would hear the "raving Arab." Unhappily, Mr. Grebb failed to attend the meeting, and he was never to be educated on the Palestine question and the rights of the Arab people. Grebb's displeasure with my continued defense of the Arabs was so widely known that the PR men discussed it in the Torque Room in the presence of several people. It was at that time that my well-publicized comment on Mr. Grebb was made: it will be the case of the professor versus the cobbler.

The footnote to this incident was written by Mr. Endress when he asked me to speak to the faculty dinner in the autumn of 1967. Endress told the *Globe* (January 18, 1968) that he had asked me to speak on the Arab family, or something like that, and he implied that he had to stop the storming multitude from destroying me for giving a speech on the Arab-Israeli conflict, in which I launched an attack on Zionism. Mr. Endress also told the *Globe* we had to defer to the Jewish "professors," etc. Insofar as I am concerned, I would have given Mr. Endress a lecture on quantum mechanics or the theory of relativity before I would agree to speak on "Arab family life." What Mr. Endress apparently wanted of me was to say something innocuous or perhaps laudatory of American imperialism. His right-wing republicanism and the Goldwaterism of the American colons on this campus must have been offended when I traced the conflict to American machinations on the wheat question and to the impact of American Zionism on the formulation and execution of foreign policy in the Fourth Reich. As to the "Jewish professors":[4] who is Jewish on this campus besides Ms. Berman unless Mr. Endress has become Jewish recently in the hope of financing an "independent" Lutheran University? And this question brings to mind the confessional character of recruitment, which has been hidden under the rubric of a university and defended as a right to discriminate against non-professing believers, which is a violation of the fair employment practices law of Ontario—a policy that may be of interest to the ministries of university affairs and labor.

Therefore, a basic question must be posed: is institutional bigotry to remain in this province and is public money to be allowed to go to a coterie of American colons to use it for private advantage? This question, I trust, will be answered by the legislature.

The final incident is, of course, the current one, which was unleashed by the article on the clerks and the subsequent efforts of the autocracy to override the laws of morality, human decency, and elementary justice. The tragedy of it all is that my profession has proved itself unworthy of the trust conferred upon it by society as the custodian of truth. Its members have demonstrated that they are without morality, honor, or principles.

Thus, I must tell my profession: I am not a Christian; therefore, I cannot be a hypocrite. I am not a wasp; therefore I cannot be a brutish Caliban. I am not of middle-class origin; therefore, I cannot be a living lie!

> *The tree of liberty must be refreshed from time to time with the blood of patriots and tyrants. It is its natural manure.*
> —Thomas Jefferson

---

4    I understand that Lutheran has made some conservative Jewish appointments recently.

# SPARTICIST III

## Open letter to Professor Milner

Professor Milner is a U of T professor of law. In 1967–68, he was chairman of the CAUT Committee on Academic Freedom and Tenure.

Your letter of February 22, 1968 reached me on March 6, 1968 with a postmark of March 4. Part of its contents were revealed to me by an administration emissary on February 27, 1968. He told me that he was "authorized" to inform me that the real ground for the non-renewal of my contract was "personal incompatibility"—an expression never uttered before by the administration or its apologists. Moreover, he assured me that Mr. Aun would give me "good recommendations" if I remained silent. Since he did not divulge the source which coined the term "incompatibility," I assumed that the regime was merely expanding my list of sins to deceive the faculty further. As it turned out, the term was taken from your letter and your remarks on the Lutheran school were buried. Put briefly, they used your letter selectively to justify their barbarism and they feel vindicated by the findings of the "impartial investigators." The kind of manipulation that has been going on leads me to believe that Mr. Hellyer has been acting as the Dean's agent and it is very probable that the copy of the letter you sent him is in Mr. Peters' office. For this reason I must send you an open letter.

1. As private citizens, you and I agree entirely that WLU. is not worthy of the title "university." Indeed, it is no more than a glorified vocational business college.
2. As a civil Libertarian and former "university" teacher, I think that no corporation—be it a business enterprise or a university—has the right to appoint or deny appointment to people on grounds

of confessionalism or any other discriminatory practices. It was this matter to which I was alluding when I referred to Labour laws, fair employment practices or bills of rights in my letter to Professor Smith.[5] In arguing in this vein, I was not challenging the rights of any citizen or group of citizens to freely associate. I was merely asserting that every corporation is under law and the laws of the country and province override the laws of Lutheran bigotry or any other sectarian provincialism.

3.    It saddens me to read, "the real ground (for the non-renewal of my contract) was personal incompatibility." It seems to me that you are ignoring the two letters the university sent me and the comments Mr. Endress made to the press which very clearly stated that the reasons were my "unhappiness" and disagreement with the university's alleged "philosophy." You seem to be doing what Mr. Hellyer did on February 16, 1968 at a faculty meeting when he described the letters and comments as an effort to "soften the blow on Haggar." I can forgive Mr. Hellyer for being a careerist. I cannot excuse a lawyer for his preparedness to dismiss tangible evidence so glibly.

While I do not profess any love for Mr. Aun, I must tell you that he had nothing to do with my dismissal (or shall we play the lawyer's game and call it non-renewal?) but merely acted as an amoral functionary. It may be of interest to you to know that he confessed at a Faculty Association meeting (March 4) that "Toronto calls" (meaning Jewish) and local pressure (business hucksters) had a good deal to do with the so-called "joint decision." Moreover, I am now in a position to tell you that 21 concerned people met on January 18, 1968 to explore the prospects of an accord with the university with a view to reinstatement. Mr. Hellyer and his executive issued a statement on January 22, 1968 declaring that they felt "strongly that further action should be withheld" and commending Student Council for reversing its decision in support of the Student Inquiry into my case. This same executive on February 16, 1968 issued a statement which was

---

5    Professor Percy Smith was the CAUT secretary in 1967-68. He and Milner came to Lutheran to investigate my complaint. They were brainwashed by the executive of the Faculty Association at Lutheran. They did not even make an effort to arrange for a peaceful settlement between me and Lutheran.

sheer balderdash and defended the autocracy at a meeting held on the same day (my answer to the executive's statement and the prevarications they, the Administration and their supporters are expressing is referred to elsewhere). I expect shortly to issue a detailed account of what transpired at the meetings of February 16 and March 4, at which time the Lutheran oligarchy was upheld by its clerks. It might also be of interest to you to know that those puppets attacked Professor Smith's "unprofessional procedure" in a letter to the faculty dated February 16, 1968.

4. The so-called executive of the Association was perturbed when I contacted Professor Smith directly. Initially, I sought an investigation through its "good officers." However, when I discovered that so-called "senior scholars," the business school, and other interested parties had exerted pressure on the regime to dismiss me and when I learned that the executive was unsympathetic towards me on personal grounds, I lodged my complaint with the National Office. Its hostilities since have amply justified my decision.

5. On January 23, Professor Siirale and Pastor Urdhal arranged an off-the-record luncheon with Dean Peters and myself. Since Hellyer and Co. reported this meeting to the faculty on February 16, I feel it is no breach of faith to tell you what happened. At the meeting, Peters specifically stated that the article I wrote on the clerks (November 24, 1967) was the decisive issue. He interpreted it literally and regarded my criticisms of the profession as "unethical." He also acknowledged "internal pressures" and introduced the idea of my lack of communication with the university when I was abroad last summer. On this item I pointed out to him that Mr. Aun and I had breakfasted together on June 10, 1967 and I never implied that I was not planning to return to WLU. I wrote him two letters and three post cards during the summer. I also sent the university a telegram on August 6 informing them that I had had an operation and that I would be hospitalized for about three weeks. As it turned out, I was in the hospital for five weeks and arrived on campus on September 20, 1967—two days after classes began.

6. On the question of Vietnam, the Mideast and the pressures of insurance companies and Zionists in the K-W area, I believe I

told you on January 26, 1968 that my evidence on these matters was verbal and therefore less tangible than the evidence I had on the question of the violation of academic freedom i.e. the Endress letters and comments to the press. However, I am appalled by the fact that you accepted the "evidence" of the regime as factual by virtue of its defensive denials. Endress and his advisers are Americans who are very agile on questions of truth and falsehood—a path well-blazed by their presidents. Or did you simply believe them because they are in authority and I am not? It seems to me that in your view the onus is on me and I am guilty until proven innocent. I tell you now and I have told everyone within my reach that a hearing should be granted me at which time my evidence and theirs would be cross-examined. Then I believe the truth will prevail. However, they have been able to conceal themselves behind the "sanctity" of their offices and with the connivance of the Association and the Faculty who have merely reaffirmed part of your decision without giving me a hearing and allowing me to confront my accusers. Is this what you call justice, Mr. Lawyer, and Mr. Professor of academic freedom, or have you merely adopted the position of Mr. Charlie? But I suppose according to your reasoning I must succumb to authority and accept my Waterloo. That I will not do and I will fight on. Moreover, I regret that you and Professor Smith seemed to have accepted the idea which Hellyer and Co. and Endress and sycophants reported to you i.e. that I did not give a damn about a contract and did not want one. I certainly did not want a contract which requires me to abjure my humanity and lead a life of submission and defeat. Such conditions can only be condoned by the dead who await the grave diggers to do away with their stench.

In retrospect, all I can say on this matter is that I was a fool to have remained in the intellectual desert for more than a year. But it was a brief essay in freedom under despotism.

7.  You to seem to have been overwhelmed by Mr. Endress' "good faith." I am surprised that P.R. smiles and fraudulent Lutheran humility have overcome your sense of right and justice. But I pity you and hope someday to teach you and my profession something about legalism, legality, morality, clerks, academics

and intellectuals, and about social organization and intellectual attributes. Meanwhile you will be interested to know that at the insistence of my "liberal friends" I answered ads in my field at 13 universities. All answers to my letters of inquiry are negative.[6] Let me therefore thank you for believing that I have "a good deal to contribute to Canadian University life." You see, Professor Milner, Liberalism has reached the end of its tether and my critique of the universities was not only valid for the Lutherans but for all.

The universities have spoken and autocracy has prevailed. Little wonder we have no intellectuals, no philosophers, no men of towering intellect and no thinkers or critics in this country. And the supplicant order which CAUT represents is making no contribution to freedom in equating it with tenure and upholding the rights of salesmen to act arbitrarily and live deceptively as honoured "intellectual leaders" in academic circles.

---

6    In 1969, I answered eleven. Most universities did not stoop to reply.

# SPARTICIST IV

## Intellectual Masturbation: Faculty Style

One of the fundamental problems facing undergraduates is that of distinguishing between frauds and learned professors in order to select the right courses and the knowledgeable teachers. However, a more serious problem arises from the fact that, by definition (insofar as the student is concerned), an MA or PhD holder is someone who knows something; and since "university" teachers come from the upper social classes, their deficiencies are compensated for by manners, graces, and palpable reasonableness. Thus, the central problem of knowledge and ignorance is concealed. Since virtue and knowledge are separate compartments, it follows that a little knowledge combined with a diploma and the right approach is more than sufficient in pleasing middle-class students, who come to be entertained and to receive a BA at the same time. Not being committed to learning—learning will not buy positions for junior executives—they are generally overwhelmed by the voluble irrelevance of the PhD or MA in front of them. In other words, the student confuses PhDs with knowledge, manners with morals, commas with learning, nastiness with analysis, words with concepts, journalism with scholarship, anxiety with happiness, appearance with reality, utility with morality, contingency with existence, and—this is undoubtedly the most serious error—"class" with humanism.

Although I do not expect to expunge this impermeable wall in the comments I am about to make, I do hope to demonstrate to those students willing to reflect that rationality and emotionality are also the psychosomatic afflictions from which their "professors" suffer with joy and complete smugness. By reproducing the "minutes" during which the army of the clerks debated my fate, I wish also to underscore the rudimentary truth that all things about which professors prattle, such as democracy, liberty, due process, etc., mean nothing when they are directly involved. Professors endlessly discuss the merits and demerits of this or that undertaking, the fairness of this or that action, but they are neither able nor willing to consider their own deeds, petty jealousies and meager achievements. Tribes of professors spend their lifetimes dialogizing about nothing, reading their favorite cartoons, celebrating their inactivity, and proclaiming the eternalness and righteousness of their mythological disciplines. What is incomprehensible and inconceivable to them is the possibility that professors, in brief, are unaware of the pervasive condition of academic idiocy and abdication. Being multi-segmented beings, they are completely incapable of grasping reality as a whole; and since they do not even know what man is, his function, mission, value, and humaneness, it follows that their actions are just as absurd as the work of the mob or the jacquerie. If you have not given up and damned me, here are the minutes of the meetings. This information is not "privileged," and you are just as entitled as Mr. Grebb to know what happened. After all, "niggers" are people in my book.

The scene is 208, the date February 16, 1968. The professors assemble at very short notice late Friday afternoon to hear a report from their "executive," who has just issued a statement endorsing the Lutheran humanists in their well-considered decision to expel a Semite of the wrong kind. The professors silently and dutifully file in, reading their favorite *Sparticist I*. Their local Fuehrer Mr. Hellyer reads the overpublicized CAUT national statement on Haggar and proceeds to perform the last rites on a dead ghost, which still haunts the Lutheran land of happiness. Not wishing to disturb the ceremony, nobody dares criticize his faithful and loyal executive for issuing a statement that nails Haggar to the Lutheran cross. Two scribes, Bonner and Overgaard, second the motion, which states that academic freedom has not been violated, and question the wisdom of exhuming a dissolved corpse. Then a conscientious "Christian" named Bryant wonders aloud whether or not the evidence has even been seriously examined by the central committee of the Lutheran party. The Fuehrer silences him by arguing that Endress was "hasty" in writing those letters to Haggar and that he did so merely to soften the blow on Haggar. Thereupon, a "psychologist of abnormal learning," Mary Kay Lane-Brown, desires to know what constitutes evidence and proves violation of academic freedom. She implies Haggar may be incompetent, which is the only ground for dismissal. Sweet, the hobbledehoy of the scholars demands that Sparticist be suppressed, and the Fuehrer intervenes to tell Lane-Brown that, in due course, academic freedom will be dealt with, but we should not spotlight it now for obvious reasons.

Two friends of liberty—Calder and Kitchen, who will be disposed of for their humanity—accuse CAUT of sidestepping the issue. Calder reports that, in talks he and Siirela have held with Aun, the latter has advocated the reinstatement of Haggar and regrets that the incident has taken place. Moreover, Calder introduces a motion of reinstatement. Overgaard, fearing that a conspiracy is in the making, proclaims that the chairmen, not the administration, was responsible for the dismissal of Haggar, and he points out that Aun has protected Haggar from the previous regime. Then, the dissimulated prince of paralogical verbal warfare Subins declares that he is envious of geniuses such as Haggar, announces that the latter should banished, and asserts that CAUT has no right to recommend Haggar's reinstatement. Dawson, a clerk recently promoted to the status of full professor for no scholarly achievements, supports the Subins-Overgaard line.

Langen, the philosopher, refutes the allegations of Calder by declaring that Aun has no interest in reinstating Haggar although his mind may not be closed on the matter (assuming that An has a mind and a conscience, a rather false premise for a philosopher, but Langen must be forgiven for, after all, he is a Lutheran and an atavistic theologian). Andersen, suffering from emotional ambiguity, thinks the whole situation is mixed up and misinterpreted. He expresses the profound opinion that Haggar may have incorrectly interpreted the situation, and since he cannot be certain of Haggar's interpretation, he is opposed to the motion for reinstatement. Fearing that a kind of subterranean sympathy is manifesting itself as the scholars read *Sparticist I*, the Fuehrer points out that "if we make a decision to reinstate Haggar now, we may face the same problem next year and also that of tenure." In his effort to bulldoze the faculty to go along with their executive, the Fuehrer is backed by Whitney, PhD, eviscerated geographer of the world, articulate spokesman for authoritarianism, who not only condemns Haggar but demands the withdrawal of the motion in his support as the Fuehrer incessantly badgers Calder for the lack of clarity of the motion.

To solve this problem, smiling Jesus, Mr. Dolbeer, recommends that the motion be referred to a Committee on Committees to study it. Dawson, the man of puerile humor—which so impresses the old community of scholars—seconds the motion of withdrawal. Secord—the mathematician from Windsor, knowledgeable on questions of axioms—declares he is confused. Anderson and Mother Hen (Ms. Roy), the unheroic hero worshiper, express similar misgivings. Ms. Lambert, forever lovely, asks the Fuehrer to invite the administration and Haggar to present their cases before the faculty. The Fuehrer says no and strongly implies that this would be giving Haggar equality if he were to face the dean or some administrative spokesman.

Langen suggests that all documents be submitted for examination. (Langen was a member of the executive committee that decided that Haggar's academic freedom was not violated.) MacLean, the classical scholar and trifler, concurs with this oblique suggestion. Roy, who at this time allows her humanity to overcome her head, points out that Haggar's career has been ruined and asks for a secret vote. Thereupon, the question of voting is raised, and the meeting adjourns for lack of a quorum.

The time is 7:30 p.m., the scene 2E6, the date March 4, 1968. The faculty's annual meeting opens. The Haggar item is last on the agenda. Shelton, with historical grasp and English insight, raises the question of precedence of motion. He is voted down. The meeting proceeds as scheduled by the executive, which is concerned with constitutional sophistry and the election of incoming officers. Over two hours elapse. Then, Calder reads his motion of reinstatement. Peter Downing, speaking for Waterloo Trust morality and their affiliates on the campus, asks if it is responsible on the part of an academic to use such terms as *cobbler*, etc., but gets no response for his effort. Calder explains why Haggar should be reinstated and Subins provides the comic relief by asking, "Is knowledge democratic? Is truth democratic?" In this atmosphere of receptivity, Siirala, humane and moral, explains that academic freedom was seriously violated and underscores the fact that the spiritual conditions of freedom are lacking at WLU. He demonstrates that Haggar is a good scholar, a very impressive teacher, a promising theoretician and reminds the Lutherans that, if they have any intellectual prestige, it is attributable to Haggar. He, of course, demands Haggar's reinstatement and advises the faculty that Haggar's dismissal is an act of excommunication. Paape, buffoon and sycophant, is greatly antagonized by the term *excommunication* and questions the wisdom of using such language. Whitney assails the motion and says there is no evidence of violation of academic freedom (no one asks him what the evidence is for his position or questions the empiricism of this man of high intellect).

Kitchen takes the floor. In speaking for the motion, he says that the university's methods are faulty; and although admittedly he doesn't know much about academic freedom, he does know why the faculty are unhappy about Haggar and oppose him. Haggar is a challenge to their beliefs and values, and he is frightening to most of them because he states his opinions publicly. Sweet (forever sweet) acknowledges the point made by Kitchen but declares that Haggar's problem is that he states his opinions publicly and that is improper. (Haggar is too vocal, and he is not a hippie. That is why Mr. Sweet is opposed.) Aun, a collaborationist of long standing, declares his opposition to the motion on the grounds that Haggar's freedom was not violated. He contends that Haggar's manners and behavior are not appropriate. Besides, calls from Toronto questioned whether or not a professor should be allowed to make statements on political matters. Moreover, he says that Haggar did not sign his contracts on time and that he didn't know where Haggar was last summer. However, he grudgingly admits that Haggar is a very good teacher despite his bad behavior. (Mr. Aun and his supporters had called several students to their offices to tell them that Haggar was not a scholar and that his moral principles were lower than the students thought. Mr. Friddle had the audacity to state in his class that "we could ruin Haggar if we wanted to and that the university had information that could wreck him for life if divulged." I confronted Mr. Friddle and challenged him to produce such information or shut up. He did shut up, but the whispering behind closed doors continued.)

Principal Carrigan, realizing the clear and present danger inherent in the actions of the university, castigates Aun for his defective reasoning and the absurdity of his analysis. He states that he is very disturbed by such arbitrary action and points out that, by comparison, Haggar's criticism of the faculty is mild to that expressed in the faculty lounge by a good many people. The only difference is that Haggar says what he believes irrespective of place. Overgaard, the ex-director of the School of Business Administration, forgets for a moment his past and present activities and declares that he has never criticized the faculty or administration. (The tragedy is that no one stood up to tell Mr. Overgaard that his memory was extremely defective or asked him why he was the ex-director.)

Thereupon, a new line of attack is adopted by the friends of autocracy (the Downing line, which was intended to argue that Haggar was guilty of non-professional ethics having failed), and Mr. Albright, the agile business negotiator, begins stressing the authority of chairmen and the right of chairmen to dismiss people even on grounds of disliking their looks. The only misgiving he has is that Haggar may not have been adequately warned. Aun springs to his feet, declaring that Haggar was warned by implication. Sweet returns to his old thesis that Haggar talks too much in public. Overgaard takes up the question again, emphasizing that authority is in the hands of the department heads who make the decisions. Mother Hen (Ms. Roy) forgets her remarks of February 16 and says that the chairmen must be upheld.

Then the "sincere" Mr. Anderson expresses the profound judgment that Haggar may be incapable of conceiving the fact that he is undesirable, and the stolid Mr. Paape declares in his inimitable mental sclerosis that the motion should be voted down since "we cannot assume responsibility for Haggar's inability to obtain a position elsewhere, and whatever happens to Haggar is of no concern to us." Langen, attacking the supporters of the motion, accuses them of selecting reasons arbitrarily and declares that the association has no right to tell the university whom to employ.

The motion is voted down 47–24, with 4 abstentions.

Carrigan moves that "the faculty deems unacceptable as grounds for non-renewal of contract the following:

1.  claims of being unhappy with the university and its aims,
2.  criticism of the administration, and
3.  criticism of the faculty."

Vanderlip—a former high school teacher of classics, whose authoritarianism is exemplary of most of the lower echelon scribes— contends the motion appears to be too negative; and Fred Little, a proprietary claimant to WLU and a presidential hopeful who was instrumental in the expulsion of Villaume, moves for the tabling of the resolution. He is seconded by the BD non-sociological friend George Durst. The motion is buried.

Paape, an American colon and a non-historian who chairs the History Department, moves the following: "The Faculty Association requests prompt re-examination of the policy and procedures pertaining to appointments and tenure by the Board of Governors and the Committee on Contracts."

The manicured Mr. Priddle, the darling of perception and middle-class humaneness, seconds this heroic, revolutionary motion. Little or no discussion ensues, and the motion is passed almost unanimously.

Oh yes, we almost forgot. Mrs. Cheyne, aloof scholar and East European political émigré, wonders why, at the outset of the meeting, the Haggar case is placed on the agenda since he is not a member of the association and he did not pay his $28 for CAUT membership. (I left CAUT because it has been used by the "old guard" as a privileged sanctuary from which to attack the administration and advance the cause of Little, Overgaard, and company. In 1966, a number of radicals, who have already left, and I were involved in a systematic study of the university, the status of the teachers here, and the salary scales. In two emergency meetings, our plan was upheld 44–0 with myself in the chair and in charge of the studies undertaken. When the die-hards discovered that control might be slipping out of their hands, Mr. Dawson, who was president of CAUT, asked me on their behalf to step down on the professional ground that I was a "junior" and my leadership of the faculty might be offensive to Villaume and alienating to the "senior" professors. I informed my colleagues on the committees, and we determined to work for the implementation of the proposals. Of these the most dangerous from the point of view of the "scholars" was, of course, our effort to unionize CAUT and affiliate with The Canadian Labour Congress. The thought of an intellectual proletariat was repugnant to the professors. Therefore, I was purged as chairman, and Mr. Thiery presided over the Beacom Motel emergency meeting where every proposal we offered was voted down 57–7. The friends of "liberty" recovered their complete hegemony over faculty matters, and I am the last of the radical crew to depart.)

The jury has spoken without examining the evidence. No further comment. The deed is an eternal testament to the shamelessness of the clerks!

# Chapter 7

# The Suno Upheaval: The Birth Pangs of Black Freedom

*Stop telling weak-minded people how underprivileged they are. When you tell people day after day that they're being persecuted, that they're being denied, that they don't really need to work, you're asking for trouble. . . . We need good Americans, we need good citizens, we need good, strong Christian leadership.*
—Fred L. Tannehill, *New Orleans States-Item*

## Introduction

A black man—a liberated man—does not hate white people per se. Indeed, the more black a man is, the less likely he is to be a racist. He hates injustice, inhumanity, insincerity. These manifestations happen to be perpetrated by white people who control the loci of power in neo-colonialist, imperialist America. The black affirmation, which is the supreme goal of the black man, is the aim of the black revolution—a revolution to transform America, its people, and all mankind. Such is the mission of the black man and the burden he must cherish and endure. Because of this enormous historic task, all of us must subscribe to the goals of the black revolution and do our utmost to help black people actualize their freedom and ours.

As a witness to the SUNO upheaval, I wish I could have done more. But I trust that others in the years ahead will do their share as I am certain that they will—the taste of freedom has enhanced our desire for greater freedom. Then as I depart, I will not say good-bye to my black friends. I will say my thoughts will always be with you, and I shall watch and record your progress so that future generations will celebrate your deeds and look upon you as models. We shall meet in the kingdom of freedom!

To Sandra Marcelin and all black people.

## LETTER TO A SOUL BROTHER

When I accepted a teaching position at Southern University in New Orleans, you suggested that I keep my eyes open constantly and record the events I witnessed here. I thought the proposal was excellent and decided to maintain persistent vigilance as I assumed my teaching responsibilities. Since my impressions are still vivid, I thought it might be useful to record them as a reminder to myself and in the hope that they might provide some insight to others into the character, operation, and atmosphere of a "Negro college." Also, you will recall, you advised me not to be too assertive and to "keep my cool" until I established rapport with the students and faculty. You will be happy to know that I remained relatively silent for about a month and refrained from making public declarations concerning the intellectual environment at Southern. In other words, I alienated no one consciously and created neither great enemies nor friends. I simply listened carefully and tried to understand the inner statics and dynamics of Southern, before beginning my critique of the institution and offering plans for its demise and reconstruction. Now that sufficient time has elapsed, I am in a position to proffer an evaluation in the context of the experiences I underwent. My impressions are the following:

1.  SUNO is not a college but a rehabilitation centre to fulfill some of the illusions of black whites and place them in subordinate positions in a depersonalized, bureaucratized world. It is much more accurate to characterize it as an open prison that provides neither food nor shelter to its inmates. It provides an intellectually crippling diet that imprisons the black soul, and dehumanizes teacher and student alike in this oriental ritual dance of gods and atomized rascals. SUNO is an intellectual experience and a laboratory to the outsider. It is the continuation of the ghetto by American means, not the catalyst that aids in self-discovery

and in the articulation of one's hopes and aspirations. SUNO is *de facto* intellectual death for both oppressed and oppressor. For only a few, it serves as a useful means of ascent in the structure of institutional racism and its exploitative relations. SUNO, as a university, is a fraud, a pernicious fraud perpetrated by white society to justify its racist ideology and contain the black people. Therefore, every serious person must mercilessly expose this symbol of fraudulence, deception, treachery.

2. SUNO and one hundred ten other SUNOs in America can only be justified as rehabilitation centres. The only justification for SUNO's existence is that it provides about one hundred fifty jobs for otherwise unemployable "niggers" who participate in the deliberate destruction of their fellows. The only relationship between these people and the centre is that of the cash nexus since the environment is structured in such a way as to make it impossible to build a community, even for those who seek to do so. It is a prison visited daily by specialized wardens who poison the minds and paralyze the bodies of their students—a function performed with dignified submission and meticulous authoritarianism. Therefore, the more deleterious does it become in its impact and effect.

3. SUNO is a miniature bureaucratic empire where authority is vested in one man. He, alone, has usurped the functions of teaching, educating, and managing the centre for the convenience and well-being of the "companions of the table." Thus, the *raison d'etre* of a university has been subverted to serve the pure poses of the miseducated Negro class rather than to uplift the black community and revolutionize it. SUNO is an instrument of social control, a socializing agency and an ideological outlet for the diffusion of white slavery. Its overseers see it as an institution to make "niggers" safe for exploitation. They, therefore, faithfully apply white norms, values, beliefs, and mores with the added touch of the converted—the marginal neophytes of the inquisition.

4. There is only one prescription for SUNO and its counterparts the world over: they must be abolished along with the socio-economic structures that undergird them, and be replaced by a new order of freedom.

Now that I have given my impressions, let me retrace my steps to the point at which my story begins.

I arrived in New Orleans at the end of August, having been delayed briefly at the border for not possessing the exact bureaucratic form required by the border police at Detroit, Michigan. The latter relished the idea of telling the professor off and returning him to Canada. Their strict adherence to America's laws and their refusal to admit an alien into the "land of the free" (although he possessed a Canadian passport which entitled him to enter the USA at will) seemed to intensify their feeling of patriotism. With triumphant pleasure, they extorted my signature and rapidly flashed my name to other points of entry, making certain that the Arab culprit would not escape America's justice. Since the incident occurred over a weekend, I was unable to contact the higher bureaucrats in Washington, Detroit, or New Orleans to solve my predicament. Therefore, I was forced to wait until Monday morning, at which time I appeared before a kindly, worldly bureaucrat at the U.S. consulate in Windsor. He explained to me the anxious rivalry that exists between the representatives of the justice department (the border guards) and those of the state department (the PR people of the CIA, like himself) in carrying out U.S. laws. At any rate, the issue was clarified, and I was finally allowed to crash my way to freedom.

Having lived and studied in America for three years at Fordham and Columbia in New York, I thought I had acquired a certain amount of knowledge about the great republic. However, my sojourn at Southern was such an educative experience that it proved infinitely superior to the intellectual experience of Columbia. When I arrived in New Orleans, I discovered that Southern was engaged in a morbid monologue with itself for the purpose of fulfilling the periodic accreditation requirements of American "higher education." Instead of being a moment of soul-searching, analysis and self-criticism, the occasion known as "self study" was a parade of endemic, irrelevant reports that had apparently engaged the attention of Southern scholars for a year and were destined to plague the chairman for yet another. What was unique about this affair was the Dean's performance: he stood before a faculty of trembling eunuchs and told them point black that none of them was indispensable, that anyone who disagreed with the way he was handling matters could resign on the spot. In brief, the Dean acted and talked as if the school were his private patrimony and the faculty his indentured laborers who, in exchange for menial intellectual functions to be performed under his military command and prescribed conditions, had forsaken their freedom and moral obligations. Neither he nor his audience seemed to have heard of intellectual integrity, academic freedom, university autonomy, scholarly pursuits. As I learned, this regular ritual which he performed on the eve of each semester to castigate the assembled multitudes for their infantile behaviour and shame them for their evil misdeeds. Moreover, in fulfilling the functions of vassal, vicar, and overseer, he was constantly flanked by a coterie of obedient assistants who moved according to his rhythm as he beckoned them to corroborate the veracity of his just wrath and lordly anger.

At the outset, I was shocked to hear the Dean deliver such a tirade and suspected that some crimes of high misdemeanor or malfeasance had been committed. This was not the case. Therefore, I was appalled and stunned to note that every professor remained silent, uttering not a single word of protest. I enquired again to verify whether the man on the podium was actually the dean and was assured that it was he. Leaping forward to pose some questions, I suddenly remembered my moratorium pledge of silence for one month which deterred me from pursuing the matter any further. Brother, the dean's speech was an unforgettable experience which, I believed, could occur only once in a million years or possibly in a nightmare. I could not have written a better speech to caricature a tyrannical dean. At any rate, I son discovered that nightmares are universal rules at SUNO, and that their perpetrators and victims justify them as part of a rational and irrevocable order. Moreover, some of my seasoned and experienced informants thought that what I was witnessing was applicable to all Negro colleges (112) and probably to most white colleges in the South. As the days rolled by and the "university community" commenced the academic year, I began to understand the meaning of unfreedom and the effects of the suffocating environment at SUNO. The university lacked even the physical facilities of communal interaction, and the faculty was an accidental collocation of intellectual robots, acting as temporary foster parents, from whose mouths spouted forth an endless stream of middle class froth. However, needless to say, all possessed the pleasant countenance of slaves and terrorized employees, trembling before Mr. Boss. As for the students, I am still not certain that there is such a commodity at SUNO. Granted, twenty or thirty people appeared in several of my countless classes. Therefore, I decided to educate "them niggers," addressing them in the idiom of the polished Ivy Leaguer revolutionary who was untarnished by the compromises of white liberalism. Since they listed respectfully and nodded, I assumed that they had understood my words. Suddenly, I discovered that they had neither understood my lectures nor were they remotely interested in books. Discarding my white blinkers and fictitious terms, I tried to talk *to* rather than *at* them. The result was overwhelming: an ocean of humanity poured forth which, I suspect, white society will be unable to understand. Surprising as it may seem, the years of slavery have not damaged the black as much as they have dehumanized the white. And, in the midst of all this, I found a flicker of hope which will not begin to glow in the whites until they recover their humanity! Thus, in a short time, I discovered the two sides of the black students: the side that submits to injustice, insult, and injury and the human side which has not been crushed by the barbarity of the oppressor. It is the latter which gives us hope for the future. It is the former which we must strive to abolish. Therefore, I abandoned note-taking and critical detachment in favor or involvement in this pathological milieu and sought to grasp its inner and outer dynamics. It seems as if the gods conspired to provide me with an occasion to penetrate the seemingly impermeable outer shield of Southern as a visiting team from Southern, Baton Rouge, descended in our midst. The "scholars" from abroad were perturbed by the prospective refusal of accreditation to Southern after a pre-accreditation committee had dubbed their painstakingly-prepared report a "whitewash." Therefore, they had come "to ascertain the facts and the views of the faculty" and began their task by assembling the administration and chairmen. Their next step was to arrange a separate meeting with the faculty, in the hope that they might elicit more straightforward responses. The visitors were provocative—in the bourgeois sense of the word—posing what appeared to be relevant and formidable questions but expecting no answers or only self-fulfilling short replies. However, within two hours, the conditioned and structured responses exploded into a babel of tongues and a sea of righteous indignation. And this is what ensued.

A few inaudible and peripheral remarks were whispered. White teachers prodded their black-skinned colleagues to take the lead but the "niggers" remained unmoved. Their anxious or indifferent grimaces seemed to indicate that, in their opinion, silence was the golden mean at this time; jobs were more important than truth; careerism more sacred than martyrdom; platitudes safer than critiques. Dismayed and angered by this cowardice, a few whites launched a massive and extensive critique of every facet of the university. The administration was assailed as a one-man dictatorship. The faculty was scolded for its intellectual abdication and lack of esprit-de-corps. The entire environment was characterized as being permeated by a spirit of servitude and submission. Every facility, service, and outlet was labeled inadequate, its personnel incompetent, its management arbitrary.

During his group therapy session, the "colored" professors were inwardly delighted but outwardly reserved and disturbed, as befits slaves unaccustomed to the expression and exercise of freedom. A few, however, ventured to march to the microphone and proclaim their "thing" amidst cheerful approval and loud applause. Most simply took cover as a handful of slave-minded clerks launched a counter-offensive in which they adopted the despicable stance of all counter-revolutionaries: they equated the dean *with,* rather than distinguished him *from,* the college; they confused an empirical and contingent account with the principles of education; they failed to differentiate between a position and an offense. In other words, they contended that an attack on the dean was an attack on Southern, the black community and its right to state education. The "revolutionaries" brushed aside these arguments and their implied threats and countered rhetorically, point by point.

The visitors were visibly shaken and disconcerted by this welling ocean of pent-up discontent and hostility. They appeared somewhat relieved when a self-seeking white worm privately assured them that those who had spoken were recent acquisitions and, for this reason, were neither an integral part of SUNO nor representative of the faculty. Thereafter, all departed feeling buoyant and triumphant.

To me, the whole affair appeared as a great therapy session in which I was a participant-observer. Other participants felt that their sins and troubles had been washed away by living a spontaneous moment without a wall of inhibitions. For participant and observer, however, one positive development came out of the exhibition—a movement to organize a faculty association for the purpose of promoting faculty solidarity, fostering academic and intellectual freedom, and providing a counterpose to administrative tyranny.

Beginning as an instinctive moment of the oppressed, the Faculty Association began to lose some of the "senior scholars" as its ideas, function, organization, and leadership crystallized. Initial animosity was expressed by minor administrative barons on behalf of the overseer, and the "senior professionals" took their cues and gradually abandoned the hopeless and transient attempt. Indeed, in their generalized critique of the association, the "professionals" emulated the arrogant techniques of their master by adopting his contemptuous approach toward the faculty, emphasizing its powerlessness, impotence, and expendability. Intimidation and dire threats reached a smashing climax as blanket-labeling (malingerers and quarterbacks were the favorite terms), indiscriminate, implicating innuendoes, as well as invocative incantations concerning "education" at Negro colleges, followed in a parade of hopeless despair, academic silence and surrender.

Meanwhile, student agitation surfaced and eleven students were arrested and charged with "criminal trespass." Amazingly, however, not a single voice of protest was heard in the faculty ranks though white cops invaded the campus at the behest of a "nigger" dean and nabbed the students. Because of the apparent indifference to, acquiescence in and nodding approval on the part of the "university community" of their heinous crime, the dean must have felt greatly reinforced and justified in his misdeed. Strengthened by the lack of counter-measures on his plantation, he swiftly moved to expunge the "outside agitators of SDS and SNCC and eliminate their agents on the campus. To smash the conspiracy, the dean's counter-insurgents undertook the task of ferreting out the guerrillas and seizing and pacifying the Afro-American Society and the Political Science Club. Sponsors of these organizations had traditionally been used as absolute village mayors to perform functions deemed appropriate by the overseer and his patrons. They were selected for their authoritarian character and willingness to exercise arbitrary power over their "fellow-niggers." The only frustrating difference in this encounter, however, was that these natives were shedding the habit of servitude and asserting blackness as an inchoate substitute. The doctrine constituted a cultural rather than social upheaval and manifested itself in the African hairdo and other assorted concoctions that had nothing to do with Africa. Nevertheless, the doctrine embodies the revolutionary principle of self-determination and the poetic notion of racial superiority which, if recognized, would undermine the whole foundation of "niggerness" and its deformed and monstrous institutions. Thereupon, an avalanche of bureaucratic procedure was unleashed and overwhelmed the pseudo-liberated who had thought the revolution was simply an Afro hairdo rather than the seizure of power and the attainment of black and universal freedom. Instead of resisting and politicizing the student body, the Afros dispersed, and most reverted to "niggerness," The black remnant, however, decided to organize the *Bad Niggers for Regression* which turned out a prophetic appellation for a group of students who sought to discover the black soul, to tap its resources and to enshrine it in black life, action, work, love, and art. In their pursuit of soulness, the "Niggers" were immeasurably aided and abetted by bureaucratic obscurantism and high-handedness and by futile tradition-bound pacification measures. administrative blandishments and seductive persuasions proved totally fruitless, as the students became agitated and radicalized by a series of heroic steps on the part of the "Niggers" and by the repressive counter-measure undertaken by the "honky overseers" and ordered by the racist, white power structure. The genesis of the open struggle may be traced back to late January of '69. But fermentation, sporadic individual outbursts and the spread of a militant cultural nationalism were already discernible in the autumn of '68. At this stage, however, the movement seemed to have no momentum of its own, and it appeared as a continuation of previously registered discontent which, at its peak, was a localized boycott against high schoolish regulations rather than a systematic effort aimed at the transformation of the university into a black institution responding to the needs of suppressed ghettoized life. Thus, in late January, many students were perturbed and angered by the arrest and mistreatment of their colleagues, but few, if any, defended them publicly or expected to participate with them in historic actions on April 2 and 9 when all stood up and pledged allegiance to the Flag of Black Liberation. For nearly two weeks thereafter, the students carried out the most effective boycott in the history of American education (90–95% of the students participated in the strike). A fantastic reservoir of human passion and commitment suddenly burst asunder the mental and emotional shackles that crippled the subjects of neo-colonialist America. All that is black and beautiful crystallized and struck a mortal blow at the symbol of racist exploitation and the ramparts of its violence-ridden, socio-economic edifice. A new nation was born in the entrails of the imperial system—a nation that will penetrate the pores of the American behemoth, snatch its heart, break its backbone and paralyze its nervous system. It all came like a thief in the night and most observers have not been able to catch their breath or overtake the "Black Liberation Express."

A nascent evolutionary movement is forming: surprise, mobility, and action are the order of the day. All the tactics of guerilla warfare are being mastered. A revolutionary core is about to be born from the intellectual and emotional chaos that prevails. The ideological guidelines are slowly assuming operational codes. The Movement can no longer be snuffed out by fiat, no matter what "discretionary powers" the racist legislature confers on little administrative tyrants and no matter what penalties are imposed. These measures are likely to frighten away the "liberals" who fear "disruption" and oppose "violence." Their demise will contribute to further polarization on campus and in society. As to the prospect of moving from the stage of agitation and periodic confrontation to the stage of ideology and seizure, it will be determined by endogenous and exogenous factors such as the Vietnam War, the pervasiveness of ascendant McCarthyism and repression, the quality of the leadership on the campus, the kind of alliances that are formed on campus and in the community, and finally, the intelligence or stupidity of the administration.

In March, no one could have predicted the April uprising. However, a few incidents occurred that laid the foundation for it. The administration has always been nervous about and fearful of "white radicals" on the campus. In his semi-annual scolding of the faculty (February 13), the Dean revealed his edginess. He accused the author of being "the quarterback of the Revolution" and said "one of Dr. Haggar's little students was carrying messages and orders from SNCC on how to disrupt registration." As befits slaves, the faculty heartily laughed approval or Mr. pseudo-boss and applauded his firmness—a cue-emitting incident that portended ill for the future. In other words, the Dean and his cohorts subscribed at the outset to the Devil Theory of history and continuously assumed that the "honky Arab" was the sole cause of the "trouble." This criminal and erroneous theory culminated in my dismissal ad subsequent reinstatement on April 12, 1969. On April 8 and 9, it manifested itself by my public character assassination by a multitude of nigger henchmen. Lastly, it resulted in my peremptory and final dismissal on May 6. This conspiracy theory absolved the administration of its nepotism, immorality, abuse of power, lethargy, incompetence and arbitrariness; it excused the immense majority of the faculty for their lack of professional ethos, non-intellectual commitment to scholarship and moral cretinism concerning the defense and advancement of the black revolution. Above all, the Devil Theory illustrated how devilish a "white mercenary"—allegedly sent by foreign powers to overthrow the American government—can become by identifying himself as a black man or a third worlder, by infiltrating "naïve" black student organizations and "using" them to "glorify himself" and advance the "Arab cause." This escapist theory postulates eternal and total incapacity for self-determination, self-respect, self-regeneration on the part of the blacks and presupposes the absolute damnation and subjugation of the oppressed tenth of America. In brief, (according to the theory), the blacks are incapable of thinking for themselves or acting on their own independent initiative, History, I trust, will have no mercy for the blind, no pity for the main streamers and Negro apologists, and it will offer no charity in a Nordic heaven for the integrationists and their ilk.

Though spasmodic in February student agitation became coherent and intense in March. It reached its apogee on campus during Honors Day (February 17) when about 300 students walked out of a meeting that was supposed to have been addressed by the president who failed to show up. The students held a rally of their own outside the cafeteria and denounced administrative malpractices. The Dean, who, in behalf of the presidents, spoke to the remnant left behind, declared that he respected "peaceful dissent." But the verbal concession had a hollow ring, for the Dean had done his utmost to ban critical student publications on campus.

In March, the "Bad Niggers" lulled everyone to sleep by concentrating on open wiener roasts and supercilious and impotent marches on the state office building in New Orleans in protest of the $50 hike in tuition fees. The administration seemed extremely pleased with itself, particularly on March 13, after the president met with five hand-picked faculty members and the "student leaders." To avert further student dissent, the president played on the mystique of the skin and deflected the students by telling them that white teachers come to SUNO to experiment, to study, and to exploit the blacks. The news reached me within a half hour after the meeting. I was saddened but, for the time being, remained silent. Then on March 18, at a campus book party for James Forman, I was attacked by a loudmouth do-gooder (Millie) as an "exploiter of the black people." The incident astounded me, but won me a few friends who assured me that they have the highest respect for my scholarship and integrity. However, I was truly appalled that a so-called colleague had the temerity to attack me so savagely and viciously in public when I had not uttered a single word during the meeting. Thereupon, I resolved to make the issue public without naming the source of this malicious rumor-mongering about white instructors. The following letter was written and appeared in the March issue of the *SUNO Observer:*

"While it is not my aim at this point to offer a thorough-going critique of SUNO, I discern a sinister phenomenon on the campus that I think ought to be faced head-on and exposed—the anti-whiteness of several faculty members and a significant number of students.

"Evidently some people are of the opinion that a black faculty is an insurance and guarantee that black-skinned students will be taught 'Black consciousness' and blacks unlike whites know and can "tell it like it is." I have news for these inverted racists. Black teachers, like their white counterparts are habituated and socialized in the doctrines and values of middle class society and most blacks—for psychological and economic reasons—are much more conformist and submissive than whites.

"Moreover, to cultivate black consciousness, it is assumed that a black faculty is all that is needed. If this were the case, Negro colleges should have been hotbeds of revolutionary activities and they are not. Indeed, they still seem to be bent on being socializing agencies for white society rather than becoming the 'revolutionary vanguard.' Why this vicious circle of servitudes continues is not hard to discover: black-skinned teachers and other middle class mimics, instead of adopting liberationist and communalist values and working for the amelioration of Negro life, first abandon their people physically, then spiritually as they become incorporated into the structure of institutional racism.

"What is happening at the moment is that the 'integrationist' values of the black bourgeois are being challenged and those elements are being bypassed, ignored, and eclipsed by the 'militants.' Why is this coming to pass? Objectively speaking, because 'integration' is not a viable proposition between unequal parties in the political economy of capitalism. And since 'whites' are in general opposed to true integration, the black Anglo-Saxons are becoming the victims of their illusions and the traitors of the black masses. Therefore, the 'integrationist' option of niggerness which is propounded by the NAACP cosmopolitans and its followers is irrelevant, and they feel psychologically threatened by the rise of an alternative leadership and program.

"Thus we reach the crux of the argument: integration or liberation. Liberation means rejection of racist values, beliefs, institutions; a commitment to blackness. Here black consciousness enters the picture in its cultural and socio-economic impact. The Afro hairdo as a cultural expression is a symbol of resistance, but if the cultural does not merge with the social it becomes a symbol of silent despair. Therefore, black consciousness is not only pride of heritage, but also a program for abolishing the dominion of freedom. And this can only be achieved by identifying with the oppressed everywhere and by rejecting the current nigger leadership that pacifies and deceives the blacks while ascending to white society at the expense of the black multitudes.

"Lastly, it behooves the racist escapists on this campus to examine their positions and learn that the enemy may be within and not in the increasing proportion of white teachers at Southern which I suspect will be beneficial rather than inimical to the evolution of black consciousness. George Haggar"

Although no concrete feedback on the letter was received, its contents reverberated throughout the institution; it provoked some, annoyed others and antagonized the reactionary nationalists of the bushy hairdo tribe. Meanwhile, the pig brutalization of the black community and its students accelerated as a city-wide Black Student Union emerged which aimed at linking together newly-founded youthful black organizations and workers. Furthermore, a black "city council" representing the dynamic sectors of the black community, was being established as an all-encompassing organization. Their only achievements thus far have been the formulation of demands relating to redistricting, the attempt to obtain equal treatment at racist city hall, and the Martin Luther King first anniversary assassination march.

In March, apparently quietism prevailed on the campus. Abruptly, on April 2, to the astonishment of all (including myself), the Black Liberation Flag replaced America's symbol of tyranny in front of the administration building. Although on April 1, Lynn French, co-chairman of the Afro-American Society had delivered a scathing attack on the administration and issued ten non-negotiable demands. No one suspected that a new nation was on the verge of birth. On April 2, black students proclaimed their independence and in face seceded from the American

Union—they sowed the seed that will doubtless germinate and bring forth the blossoming of a beautiful black spring!

This historic and heroic deed shook the white power structure to its foundation but it gladdened the hearts of black men. Outmaneuvered and outnumbered for the moment, the pigs and the administration tried to persuade the students to take down the "black rag" by reminding them of their obligations as American citizens and of the fact that lowering the flag was an act of desecration. The Negro dean pitifully cried, "I served under the American flag in Italy in 1942; it is my flag." I was exhilarated to witness this historic birth of freedom, the unleashing of the black conscience. As chairman of the Faculty Association, I called a meeting to endorse student demands. Fortunately, the reactionaries and pseudo-blacks failed to carry the day and the Association passed a nine-point resolution to support student demands—from autonomous black studies to swimming pools. In the afternoon, I appeared with Lynn French at a press conference and assailed racism, capitalism, and imperialism; exposed neo-colonialism and contended that the black revolution was an essential part of the world revolution of the oppressed. Naturally, the media picked up the latter part of the speech and ignored the faculty resolution. The administration and its allies were outraged; the entire racist structure mobilized its forces to quell our efforts. The nigger infidels of SUNO organized a lynching party that pilloried me in absentia on April 8, and accused me of crimes ranging from being a foreign agent to being guilty of moral turpitude. A former CIA agent, and a Berkeley man at that, reported that Haggar "duped us." Another, with the active and anxious collaboration of both the nigger president of Southern University and the SUNO dean, demanded my deportation— an order for which was issued on May 26, at the behest of the Justice Department in which McCarthyism reigns in Washington, racism in Baton Rouge, and police power in New Orleans. Still another described me as a foreign agitator and a trouble-maker dispatched by the Arab states to foment campus turmoil in America and avenge Arab defeat at the hands of American Zionism. Gerald Ford (R. Michigan) House leader, made the same charges with reference to Arab students in America a few days later.

On the eve of April 9, the entire pig power of New Orleans was mobilized to smash the revolution. Infuriated racists and Negro "moderates" formed a solid phalanx of opposition to the students. All the forces of repression united behind the American banner. Those alleged lovers of "law and order" could not condone the "desecration" of "Old Glory." Every petty tyrant was ready to demolish SUNO's citadel of freedom and all had the absolute collaboration of the Negroes in attempting to suffocate the foetus of black hope. The media of communications which prides itself on being an "arm of the police," performed with meticulous care by turning cameras off, or the other way whenever the police charged the students. Indeed, in the following few weeks, the media did its utmost to discredit the movement, to help defeat it, and to ensure the arrest and imprisonment of about 35 students, the dismissal of the author, and the expulsion of at least 10 other students. But the students were not to be dissuaded or intimidated by the barbarity and the cacophony of those prattling despots, and on April 9, at about 8:30 a.m., in the presence of over 100 pigs, they majestically and fearlessly moved forward, lowered the American flag and raised the Black Liberation Flag. For a few moments, the reign of freedom prevailed. Alas, they revolution had no army—only revolutionary cadres. With naked and consummate brutality official violence was immediately invoked, and each of the six students involved was pounced upon by at least half a dozen cops. Within an hour, 27 students were arrested as hundreds tried in vain to break the police siege of SUNO. The administration true to the nigger tradition of submission, openly sought to divide student ranks and organized terror squads that engaged several faculty members in bitter and insulting debate and that invaded my office to "lynch the white man" who "masterminded" the uprising. However, most students came to my defense, and no physical injury was inflicted. This racist approach in the counter-revolutionary offensive failed dismally—the administration's ploy of scapegoating me in the hope of dividing the students and projecting its autocracy and barbarity on a foreign citizen. At any rate, racism did not stop with my expulsion. Indeed, the president, dean, and senior faculty who equated white with radical, issued commends that no white man may be appointed in the Southern University system. *Racism in reverse is not a characteristic of black people, but of niggers who serve white racist America and worship its idols.* Furthermore, this racism contributed to the progressive decline of the administration's moral authority as the students learned to distinguish between ordered liberty and ordered tyranny and sought to expunge the latter and supplant it by an order of black freedom!

On April 8, without consultation, the dean appointed a rubber-stamp committee of predominantly fawning faculty and students. The Afro-American Society was invited to its meeting; but when its representatives discovered that the aim of the committee was diversion rather than negotiation, they withdrew and exposed the nature of the committee. Such concocting of committees was to persist for the balance of the season. Its impact on the students was nil, but its effect on the semi-idiots of the Louisiana power structure and the mass media was phenomenal. Those racists actually believed that "reasonable" student demands were being implemented when neither the administration nor the State Board of Education accepted a *SINGLE* student demand in principle (the so-called "crayfish pond" was not a student demand). Moreover, the partial "restructuring" of the administration merely elevated an existing office (the head of student personnel was named dean of students) without change of personnel and assigned the minor task of draft counselor to an Establishment negro lawyer who is a friend of the military, not of the black people. Thus it is patently clear that the administration and its white sponsors are not acting and have not acted in good faith. Indeed, fraudulence and deception are the hallmark of this coterie of bureaucrats. To illustrate, let us return to the faculty committee of sixteen ciphers that was created on April 12. On that historic day, the administration huddled with the chairmen and decided on a strategy of deception implicating Haggar and company in the upheaval and holding them accountable for it. At the outset, the president played the role of the gray-haired black father whose love is education, self-sacrifice, and reasonableness was boundless. He did not identify himself with the preceding administration, though he was its scion and its most dedicated tool and this tactic won him the naïve sector of the faculty. As strategy unfolded, I exploded it and took the offensive while two or three colleagues pressed the president about "total amnesty" for the students. (None of us at the time suspected that Ron Evans and I, with four other students, were being expelled that very afternoon.) In the midst of this cross-fire, the president order the faculty to "elect" a committee of 16 on the basis of school divisions rather than at large. The faculty acquiesced without protest with the full knowledge that the committee would be stacked. As it turned out, the committee gave verbal endorsement to marginal student demands and glossed over the essential demand of converting the university into a black institution. Moreover, the committee arrogated to itself—probably at the behest of the administration—the right to break the student boycott. But it committed on fundamental error; it pleaded with the students to exercise their convictions, intelligences and consciences and they did so by rejecting the committee's please and dubbing its members "oreos."

Thus we see the miserable failure of the faculty committees that the president and his overseer dean improvised as a buffer zone between them and the students. Consequently, most of the faculty became discredited agents of the administration and, to avenge themselves, carried out retaliatory measures against the students in the classrooms. Such are the deeds of scoundrels who parade themselves as blacks and act as niggers.

Meanwhile (on April 12), the administration committed its biggest blunder. It suspended several students and sent special delivery letters of dismissal to Roland Evans and to the author. The administration almost succeeded in executing its plot and carrying out its strategy. Happily, however, Valerie Ferdinand, the articulate minister of information of the Afro-American Society, was allowed to appear on a television program which broadcasts student activities. On that program, a SUNO student senate meeting was in progress and Mr. Ferdinand disclosed the student suspensions. Those present were stunned and the senate, in a moment of spontaneity, endorsed the student strike—an endorsement that was withdrawn a few days afterwards under extreme pressure from "moderate" faculty and the administration. I was informed of my own dismissal at about 5:30 p.m., April 12. Aware of the chicanery of the power structure, the collaboration of the local mass media, and the absence of a liberal opposition in the south, I gave an interview to a UPI correspondent who immediately put the news on the national wires. As a result, the local media was forced to carry the item once or twice on the air and for the next few days remained completely silent. With this pre-emptive disclosure, the administration was forced to retreat and rescind the dismissals after trying a final legal trick that "listed" rather than "lifted" the expulsions. My response to these machinations was an open letter to the dean:

Dear Dr. Pseudo-Boss:

Please be advised that I have no intention of requesting a hearing before my so-called "peers" with reference to the "termination" of my services at SUNO. Those "peers" held a meeting on April 8—I suspect at the instigation of your office, since both your subordinates, Keller and Furr were present and said absolutely nothing to deflate the hysteria that prevailed. Although a number of colleagues at the kangaroo court endeavored to defend me, they were silenced and ignored and scurrilous attacks were delivered against my person with what appears to be the approval and connivance of your most trusted confidants. Furthermore, since your office has been a house of slander, fraud, and deception, I take it that it would be gullible on my part to seek justice or redress of grievances from you or your Fascist-niggers, house-niggers, black bourgeois masochists, or the white liberals who, when all is said and done will come down on the side of "law and order."

Moreover, I want you to know that I find it repugnant and contemptible to see you and the other house-niggers who surround you drape yourselves with the American flag—the symbol not of justice, freedom, and liberation for the Black people, but the symbol of their oppression, the symbol of world exploitation, the napalming of the Viet-Namese and Arab people, the vampiring of the Afro-Asian and Latin people. Also I want you to know that I stand for the eradication of racism, capitalism, and imperialism and no McCarthyite tactics emanating from your office or the white supremacists at City Hall or Baton Rouge will deter me from pursuing the goal of smashing the enemy of human progress—American imperialism.

Lastly, let me repeat to you in writing my reply to Mr. Furr—your henchman—who stated at the faculty meeting of April 12, that "a faculty member designed the Black Liberation Flag and advised the students on how to use it;" I said that I was not responsible for the slavery of the Black people, for four hundred years, the rape of their women, the pulverization of their manhood; I was not responsible for the arbitrariness, incompetence and dictatorship of the administration; I was not responsible for the inadequate facilities of SUNO, its swamps, its decadence; above all, I was not responsible for the poverty and shoddiness of your curriculum and the low-caliber of your faculty. But most important, you and the "companions of the table" who hoodwinked you, should remember what I said that the Black Liberation Flag was not designed by me, but by Marcus Garvey in the 1920's and that you should be ashamed to call yourselves black men or professors and not know such an elementary fact.

Yours for the deniggerization of the world!

George Haggar

It should be made absolutely clear that the president circumvented answering the question of student amnesty a number of times during the faculty meeting of April 12. Furthermore, there was no intimation that either faculty members or students were being dismissed. Thus the administration perpetrated an open fraud and a deception on the faculty and the latter have not yet and will never make a move to censure those clowns. Such is the state of honor, self-respect, and "black pride" of the SUNO faculty, a faculty that refused to sign a petition (only four of eighty blacks signed) whose contents were incontrovertible:

"A number of colleagues have been using subtle and overt intimidation to break the student boycott. Some have indeed openly promised A's to students who return to classes, while others have given double assignments and tests on very short notices. Such Uncle Tomism is most reprehensible.

"While we do not contest the rights of students and teachers to be in classes, we unreservedly condemn the callous attitudes of some teachers and their servility to the bureaucratic system that oppresses us all. Therefore, we call upon all teachers to honor the boycott and declare their solidarity with the students. We believe that the administration and its allies have used every trick in the book to deceive, hoodwink and coerce the faculty and students to submit to its arbitrariness and dictatorship.

"We urge all teachers and students to continue to press for their demands and work together toward a true university to serve the needs of the black students and black community."

The failure of the faculty to pacify the students and break the strike did not end the administration's scheming. It organized a committee of so-called Concerned Students to work alongside the faculty—the author was the group's major target. Those "niggers" inundated in the campus with hate literature against the "Arab Honky" and a pseudo-colored woman wrote a piece of mental diarrhea exposing the "white alien" who controlled the black revolution. In a few days, however, the Concerned Students announced publicly that they were working under a "lie" and the administration and faculty committee could not obtain and "plenipotentiary power" they needed to negotiate with the strikers. The administration lost its "liberal" friends, but it never lost hope. First, the highest authority in the system—the president—tried twice to bribe

Mr. Evans (advisor of the Afro-American Society) and asked him to call the strike off. Then shapely Negro women knocked on my door but to no avail—the two goddesses, money and sex, could not wield the magic wand. But perseverance paid off for the administration. On April 18, without consultation with other participants in the strike, the student senate official withdrew its endorsement as Negroes mobilized their forces to visit the mayor and other local potentates who expressed verbal sympathy to the cause without committing their treasures. These side shows and activities deceived many students and about 20% trickled back to classes which, theoretically, had never stopped. Then a new "Concerned Student-Faculty Committee" was organized as the media spread a rumor concerning the prospective merger of SUNO with LSUNO as a junior division. Every conceivable effort was made to smash the strike; the media reported on the hour that all was normal at SUNO; the administration used pigs to guard non-strikers; the governor declared he could not come to the campus under "duress" and made threatening noises. On April 21, however, he not only came under "duress," but by force—he was taken as "war prisoner." It took over 500 students to perform the coup and seize the governor at Church Hall. Lynn French, Charles Williams and the author confronted the governor and told him he had to come to the campus or else. He came. The author, who had the confidence of the students, had the fortune of riding with the governor to the campus. After a quick briefing, the governor asked me whether I thought "Negroes were intelligent enough to be in college" or had "enough motivation" to become "better people." This line of questioning stunned me as did his continuing remarks to the effect that niggers are incapable of doing anything more than minor mechanical and heavy physical labor. I wondered what he would tell the students and whether the administration and the Negro establishment shared his views. His brief campus speech divulged the supremacist's strategy and the tactics of managing a racist society. As to the obsequiousness of the black bourgeois, hardly anything need be said.

Upon our arrival on campus, the dean and his followers came to welcome "their" governor and tried to take over the meeting and deprive the students of their historic deed—blacks had seized a white southern governor and forced him to come to their school despite his refusal to come! The author was astonished by the audacity of the dean. Seeing that the students were about to acquiesce to this insolence, he shoved the dean aside and told the students not to be fooled by a rapacious enemy whose aim was the fragmentation and dissipation of the Movement. Thereupon, the meeting was turned over to Valerie Ferdinand who introduced the governor and had a brief dialogue with him on the meaning of the flag: black, he said, symbolizes the unity of the black people; red represents their blood, toil and sweat in a land of slavery; green expresses their hopes and aspirations for a land of their own. The governor was unmoved and asked that the black flag be removed. It was, but to the discredit of Ferdinand. The racist politician praised "old glory" to the heavens; few students applauded, but Israel Augustine, the stooge of the white power structure did most heartily (he was given a judgeship in mid-June in recognition of his role as anaesthetist of the black people) when the governor pointed out that "black Americans" were dying under the flag in Vietnam. The governor promised immediate action on the "crayfish pond" and met with the students briefly after they agreed to return to classes. In this atmosphere of false harmony, the governor announced that a number of student demands were "legitimate" and would be acted upon. The strike was over without any firm pledges; the Negroes demonstrated their "responsibility and dignity," the white power structure was delighted that it could dupe "them niggers" again with promises that would not be fulfilled. Thus started the political chicanery phase that enabled the administration and its allies to accede to token demands and appoint sycophants of their own choosing to carry out the "administrative restructuring of the university"—an action that was meant to demonstrate that progress was being made and that students had already made their points and gained their demands. In terms of public folklore, the students, therefore, would now learn to be patient and give the administration an opportunity to implement the "new program." Furthermore, Damocles' sword of merger with LSUNO remained constant, while large segments of the student body thought the revolution was consummated. However, in the midst of this confusion, the Negro integrationists proposed a peaceful march on Baton Rouge on May 2. Unfortunately for those Uncle Toms, however, the Afro-American Society decided to participate and quickly took over the sponsorship of the march as the pacifists and legalists gracefully beat a hasty retreat. The idea that originated with civil rights advocates and the dozen racist, legislator pacifiers that came to campus was converted into a human rights march that witnessed the symbolic conquest of Louisiana by the black people and the hoisting of their Flag from the 34ᵗʰ floor of the State Capitol building in Baton Rouge. This moral victory bolstered the Movement and impelled it to organize a "takeover" of the administration on May 5 and to install its own administrators. The "takeover" shook Louisiana and the south. The governor instantly dispatched 1300 guardsmen to recapture the "administration." On the 6ᵗʰ, the author was honored by a new "suspension" and ordered to "vacate the office and campus." *In consonance with the best traditions of Southern liberty, no specific charges were made, no hearing was to be granted, no trial was to be held.* On the 7ᵗʰ, the author returned to the campus as did 280 guardsmen and 100 policemen who failed to capture him. The chief of police was infuriated and, accompanied by the general in charge of the guards and the dean, he went on the air to threaten and intimidate the author in the style of the 1930's. on the 8ᵗʰ, however, the author submitted to arrest without resistance to 53 policemen and four reconnaissance helicopters and he was charged with "criminal trespass." Meanwhile, the students marked their "finest hour" by defending a "white man" whom the administration used as a scapegoat in the hope of dividing them and trying to defeat the revolution. The administration revived a committee of its own making and decided to give the students "due process" after it denied it to the author. This legalist phase was brief: the committee put six students on "strict probation"—an action that was not appreciated by a revenge-seeking society nor admired by the media for its scholastic "moderation." A few days later, eight "suspensions" were issued by the dean, who had abolished his own disciplinary committee, and, overnight, numerous "expulsions" by special delivery letters were delivered. It appears that about 15 students were affected by administrative machinations and on May 31, five liberal-conservative faculty members were dismissed without reason—only the false explanation that they do not hold Ph.D.'s. This came from a university where less than one-fifth of the faculty hold Ph.D.'s. Racism—not Ph.D.'s—caused their dismissal.

SUNO is now in the terror stage of counter-revolution and counter-insurgency. The administration has been armed by the military and moral support of its racist sponsors. It will doubtlessly endeavor to eradicate revolutionism and uproot every prospective revolutionary. It will henceforth move with absolute alacrity to coping with "disruptive students." It will continue "to suspend" critics, "to expel" peaceful demonstrators. However, these policies will intensify the struggle and transfer its locus to the community where the "honkies" will need the army, not the guards, to pulverize the revolution. In other words, the prospects on campus appear a bit bleak at the moment but on the whole, the Negro establishment and racist America are irrevocably doomed and the revolution is engulfing the entire nation. Our hope is based on the development of black ideology and the black "implosion" which are becoming embedded in the consciousness of black people. And very significantly, this hope is anchored in the firm belief that the emerging leadership is radical, not reformist, however confused it may be at this juncture. The new prototype is the local charismatic leader, deeply steeped in the regional traditions, who understands local problems and conditions and knows people by their first names. His intelligence and leadership will be tested by whether or not he adopts a strategy "of flexible response" rather than romantic adventurism or retreatism guised as verbal violence. In other words, because the leader is elected by the people and springs from their midst, he will not be able to bargain at their expense in order to co-opt himself and his immediate advisors. If he does, this time the assassin will be black not white.

While the Movement evolved from the stage of cultural nationalism (characterized by the Afro hairdo and a variety of ostentatious affectations about blackness) to the convergence of progressive nationalism with communalist humanitarianism and the assumption of an anti-capitalist socio-economic stance, several SUNO students assumed prominence. Among these students, mention must be made of Lynn French, the ideologue and strategist of the Movement; Charles Williams, chief security officer and brilliant agitator; and Valerie Ferdinand, minister of information and most articulate and magnetic proponent of the black university. These developing revolutionaries were augmented by the organizational ability of the *Bad Niggers* who prefer anonymity to visibility but who work relentlessly for the triumph of the revolution. The new breed is completely dedicated and beholden only to its people, to its destiny, to the making of a new black man, a new society, a new tomorrow.

Such is the state of SUNO; its appalling conditions and half-consequential but indicative activities brutally, nakedly, and crudely reflect the state of college life in American universities in general and Negro college life in particular. Moreover, the contemporary ferment is the first uncertain and hesitant step toward the emergence of liberationist consciousness on campus. The immediate recourse of black administrators to police violence to nip the revolution in the bud unmasks the irrelevance of deferential liberalism and undermines all evolutionary movements of reform in this milieu of the over-bureaucratized, intellectual plantation. The exercise and use of naked power may purchase time for the overseer, but since they are incapable of conceiving, initiating or carrying out badly-needed reforms, they are likely to dam the revolutionary forces until they make the revolution inevitable. As for the students, the experience of being sent to jail by a black dean may not have been necessary, even though it was illuminating and instructive. It will leave an indelible imprint on their minds as they realize that "fellow-niggers" are part of the enemy's structure of authority and agents in his apparatus of oppression. In short, *the experience of oppression should shatter their well-nourished illusion that black skin is a measure of goodness, rectitude, love, and liberation.* It should convince everyone who has not turned a deaf ear to reality that the Negroes don't "tell it like it is," nor do they have the stomach to do so. If they did, black schools would be oases of freedom rather than mirages on the intellectual map. Thus, the color of one's skin is no sign of one's liberation, nor is it a sufficient bond for a brotherhood of the oppressed. The struggle, moreover, should clarify for those concerned that the achievement of black freedom is a universal and human struggle, not a kind of localized display of bravado to capture a headline in a racist newspaper or obtain an interview on a privately-censored radio or television station. Once this reality is grasped and the oppressive stratification of Negro society is appreciated, and once black people discover how their potential power is manipulated for the benefits of white society, going to jail or having a record will become a badge of honor rather than a symbol of agitated despair and frustrated hopes. Participation in the revolution will become the order of the day as fear, submission, alienation, and withdrawal are stored in the museum of plantation economy, morality, and police power.

Thus, the impact of the abuse of power on oppressor and oppressed may be a clarification of the order of battle and a definition of the boundaries of expectations. The oppressor is more likely to rely on force, having demonstrated his capacity to use it, as he confers token liberalism on the oppressed. If the latter mistake this strategy for "liberalism" and relax their efforts, nothing will have changed. If, on the other hand, the oppressed opt for hipsterish white liberalism, they will be suppressed as a disgrace to the race. Only by planning well and converting the current ripple of Bayou St. SUNO into a tidal wave will they, in a moment of historic redemption, wash away the muck of the ages, the sediments of history, the conditions of enslaved "niggerness" and establish a localized kingdom of blackness and liberty. But before that is realized, the entre power of institutional racism will be brought to bear upon and crush their experiment in human freedom. Hence, we are left with persistent and undramatic struggle for the protection of group solidarity. In due course, the mounting of massive group violence on a universal scale will be necessary to found a new society, to create a new man. Meanwhile, we are all "niggers" on the verge of entering the age of blackness—the revolution of the Third Alternative against the metropolitan civilization of Waspish hegemony.

In the final analysis, the struggle at Southern is a microscopic and mortal combat against the universal virus of tyranny, servitude, suppression, and authoritarianism the world over. Therefore, the link between the specifically local and the general, the particular and the universal, is not only logical and necessary, but also inevitable and compellingly urgent. Hence, it is imperative for us to know our present situation and the direction in which we are heading. We should know that we are "niggers" in a society which has reached a state of advanced decay and depravity and in whose womb we discern the outline of a new order. We, therefore, must strive to overcome not only "white racism"; its institutional apparatus and moralistic rationalizations, but also "niggers" whose circumscribed and subordinate roles determine our immediate fate and destiny. Moreover, we must identify "niggers"—white and black-skinned—and concentrate our efforts on whittling down their authority and, if possible, seize their powers by all available means. In this "nigger" stage, pride of race, heritage and aims must be stressed and a leadership of black revolutionaries created. Self-identification, self-reliance, and self-determination must become the hallmarks of the movement, and all revolutionaries, brothers—brothers in blood, in soul, in total union. Yes, soul brother, you are a brother, you are a brother, but only if you possess a gun, know how to use it and plan to aim it at our mutual enemy! Then, as I depart, I shall not say good-bye for I shall return with the northern wind when you set America in flames—not to lead but to partake in this creative enterprise!

Blacks of all countries, unite!

You have nothing to lose but your
Rat-infested ghettoes!

## THE DAYS OF MAY

To the ancient Egyptians (Africans), the month of May was the
month of festivals to honor the abundance of nature and celebrate the
coming of spring. The mighty Nile inundated the "Valley of Kings"
and wrought in its wake the seeds of life (silt) from the mountains and
plains of East and Central Africa. Behold the Nile, the physical cement
of the African people, the channel of communications among them, the
spiritual bridge between them and the Mediterranean, the expression
of eternal togetherness, the testament to an overpowering African
civilization, the symbol of fertility, the gift of the gods to a rhythmic
people, the declaration of indestructible unity between man, nature, and
their craftsmanship!

In the nineteenth century, without recognition of the origin of May
Day, the European working class adopted it as a symbol of working-
class solidarity to demonstrate against oppression, injustice, and ruling-
class barbarity. The universalization of May Day, though adopted on
the initiative of American workers to celebrate the achievements of
labor and record its heroic strides, never became a national holiday
in America. Racist America thought she had no workers and that she
was merely composed of free republican proprietors with slaves as
chattels—a fact that troubled a few consciences but caused no public
compunction, indignation, or outrage. For these reasons, it behooves
the descendants of the African people to revive the May Day tradition as
integral to their cultural renaissance and as a symbolic gesture, not only
to honor their origin and identify with the oppressed of mankind but
also to do homage to the memory of the 1969 generation for its symbolic
conquest and founding of a New African nation in the state of Louisiana.
This generation seceded from the American Union on April 2, 1969, at
Southern University in New Orleans by replacing the American rag with
the flag of Black Liberation and proclaimed Louisiana a new African
state on May 2, 1969, and hoisted the black flag from the state capitol in
Baton Rouge, thus creating a formal cradle for an African civilization.
The issue now is how to concretize the vision; how to endow it with a
working reality; how to give it substantial territory; and how to organize

an army to extend, to defend, and to carry out the mission and the will of the new nation. To this task, all the oppressed must address themselves. My function, however, is the clarification of issues and the elucidation of relevant facts.

At the outset, let it be recorded that the midwife of the new nation was SUNO's Afro-American society: a group of young men and women who are trying to emancipate themselves from the mental shackles of slavery and the socioeconomic conditions of American neo-colonialism. As a developing generation of black men and women, they still stuffer occasional relapses of niggerness. But by and large, they have overcome that stage, though not the sentiments of bourgeois regression, which had been instilled in them and which they had internalized through the years of concerted brainwashing, which passed for Negro education—that is, "keeping them niggers in their place." Here, then, is the crux of the matter: how does a nigger become a black man, or alternatively, how does a chattel cease being a commodity and become a free man? The answer to this rudimentary question is simple yet very crucial. A man is not a man unless he seizes his own life and fashions it according to his tastes and desires. A man cannot have self-respect unless he can identify with a group—a group that has a heritage or that aims through collective labor to shape its own destiny through struggle. Pride can be acquired by individual or by group achievement. The group's mission can be formulated by its intellectual workers and carried out by the entire people. As it is, the black-skinned people are a people-in-being, a statistical group without a collective will, mission, or destiny. They are peripheral ciphers and subordinate beasts of burden in the making of the American empire (whatever the illusory self-image of the Negro establishment might be). The nigger is nigger, is nigger, is nigger! In this age of international American counter-insurgency and massive national repression, it is imperative to underscore and celebrate the two momentous movements of 1969: anti-ROTC demonstrations and black studies demands.

The reserve officer training corps is not merely an academic question to be discussed with detachment or Olympian disdain. ROTC symbolizes the subjugation and shotgun marriage of the university to the industrial-military complex. It symbolizes the penetration of American militarism into every aspect of life. This includes the thorough saturation of the university's curricula with amoral, positivistic scholasticism and the abdication of its instructional role as a humanizing and liberating agency. Thus, the militarization of liberal education cannot be defended as a freedom-of-choice question without implicitly acquiescing to the militarization and thereby fortifying an immoral stance. The professors should have spearheaded the assault on the industrial-military complex; most did not. It was left to the uncorrupted young to assume an adult role and face the oppressiveness of the "mainstreamers" and their professional and amateurish baiters. Students are the only vital force remaining in the deadly cesspool of American society. They are the spirit of a new age, the dawn of a brighter tomorrow, the messengers of a new order! By assuming this historic stance of questioning the validity of militarism, the civilian military metaphysicians, and the commercial hucksters of the American empire, the students are affirming the validity of the democratic ethos and the possibilities of the democratic man. Who indeed are "the neo-Fascists": the students standing for the democratization of life and its expansion or the administrators whose policies have dwarfed and depersonalized man, whose recourse to violence and police powers have eroded the democratic process? Who indeed are surrendering to totalitarianism: the students who are organizing the poor, the oppressed, the downtrodden or the administrators who are sitting on the boards of international corporations and putting their talents in the service of militarism and who justify wars of aggression as legitimate? Who indeed aim solely at the destruction of the society: students who seek the restructuring and development of their society or the administrators who live, preach, and eat the status quo—a crew that capitulates not to student demands but to the powers that be, to the dollar, to the personal and not to the communal good? Who indeed are the sentimentalists and romanticists: the students who endeavor to cultivate rationality and revive the human spirit by adhering to a strict universal ethical code or the administrators who act as thoughtless, chauvinistic worshipers of craven images and dead golden pasts? Who indeed are leading us to the "abyss of chaos": the student humanist revolutionaries who are trying to build a community of brotherhood or Dick Nixon and the hysterics that surround him who advocate repressive, bureaucratic policies? Who indeed care about education: the students who want education for life and living or the parents who sold out to the middle-class intolerance and want an education for status and hierarchy? Who indeed desires to assume responsibility within the structure of the university: the students who ask for it or the overseers, the professors, editors, and parents who deny them the right to participate in decisions affecting their lives? Who indeed is seeking disorder: the students who clamor for a responsive and relevant order or the citizens at large, who advocate total and unquestioning submission to an irrational and illegitimate disorder? Who indeed has refused to reform, improve, and meet reasonable grievances: the students who have petitioned, marched, and sat in for over a decade and who have pleaded for change or the presidents and deans who were decorating each other and granting honorary degrees to their patrons? Yes, indeed, yes, indeed, and a million yes, indeeds on a civilization that could only offer Dick Nixon, Hubert Humphrey, and George Wallace for the presidency of the Fourth Reich. That banal coterie of charlatans is symptomatic of a banal society of fattened sheep!

As to the second and more important aspect of the revolution—blackness—we must confess that black-skinned people are its most virulent enemies. We need not single out names. We speak of the black client-bourgeois, a nameless, faceless, worthless group of ciphers distinguished for its servility and outlandish mimicry of its master: the racist white power structure. Those invertebrates are the apostles of the commercial-industrial American bourgeois to the black community and its representatives in the Afro-Asian and Latin worlds. As a castrated pack of political opportunities, it has lost its moral authority with the black people. Only a residue of its former grandeur remains. Those people and their white sponsors do not understand that the issue of 1969 is no longer integration versus segregation but liberation versus annihilation. A substantial number of black people still believe in the America of middle-class egotism, of the Protestant work ethic, of the escape of their blackness. However, a significant minority has come to believe in blackness, which involves not civil but human rights, not integration on terms dictated by racism but liberation as the springboard of black freedom. It is this group, conscious of its blackness, that seeks to chart a new course for the black people of America. And this is the group whose destruction white America hopes to achieve under the guise of "law and order." However, this will not come to pass because the new generation is not fighting an isolated skirmish in Louisiana against enormous military odds but is part and parcel of the worldwide revolution of the oppressed, particularly those of the third world. For these reasons, we are not astonished to see the powers that be treat the new movement as if it were no more than spring enthusiasm, the assertion of masculinity, or the work of "outside agitators" and local radicals. The new movement is revolutionary; it cannot be accommodated because it is not seeking mainstream reform or co-optation. It is searching for dignity for black people; it is a movement to emancipate them and reclaim their heritage. Though many make it appear to be, it is not a black cultural hippiedom but a communalist upheaval that will culminate in the establishment of a Socialist confederacy. At the moment, it is a nation-in-becoming!

The disordered society of Dick Nixon and his attorney general will doubtless seek to destroy the new radicals whom they identify as the new barbarians, thereby conceding the prospective demise of the New Rome. Nixon and his clique have honored the movement by their appellation. But, alas, for their New Rome. Our legions are already in the empire, and the empire continues to disperse its legions to oversee the world. Furthermore, while they retain overwhelming physical power, the local overseers lack the moral prowess to exercise it or to go anywhere without immediately resorting to physical violence. If anything demonstrates the absolute decadence of America's ruling class, it is the resort to violence to deal with intellectual and social issues in the university. Violence and legalistic crutches, not moral authority or intellectual integrity, are the only instruments invoked by presidents and deans as professors silently acquiesce in the rape of the universities and the destruction of scholarship. With the blessings of Father Hesburgh and the semantic obscenities of General S. I. Hayakawa, Dick Nixon is burying America.

If our analysis were correct, the SUNO revolt assumes a cosmic dimension and SUNO becomes a laboratory for the study of black revolution. Here is a university nonentity created by a racist society to keep "education" segregated and produce menial workers and subservient Negro laborers for American neo-colonialism. At the outset, a handful of people liberated themselves, and in their struggle to convert a Negro university into a black one, over two hundred Negroes became black people. Agreement with the tactics or strategies is immaterial. The fact of the matter is that a magnetic and mobilizing leadership emerged and was *not* ignominiously defeated by the white power structure and its "honky overseers." The movement was *not* crushed, and that in itself is an accomplishment in the South. The spirit and the memory survive as the young revolutionaries go back to New Orleans' ghettoes, carrying the message of defiance and spreading the virus of black unity. However, we must not overlook the lessons of SUNO. For the first time in their lives, the black students said no. They challenged authority, although it appeared in black skin; and while doing so, they also discovered that skin is no standard for rectitude. Those expelled or imprisoned were expelled and imprisoned on the immediate order of a colored dean and his assistants who acted on behalf of racism and with the complete approval or silence of almost the entire colored faculty. The faculty, had it been Negro, would have at least insisted on internal self-government and due process. But the faculty consists of nigger ciphers of Uncle Bens and Aunt Jemimas, of intellectual harlots and moral morons, of stinking corpses without gravediggers to bury them, and of slaves who live for bread and mystery, not for freedom, not for love!

In saying no, the students also said yes. They said yes to blackness, yes to peoplehood, yes to emancipation. Herein lies the revolutionary message that struck dread, fear, and nightmares in the bosom of racist society and sent its soldiery to nip the revolution in the bud. The blacks negated and affirmed; therefore, they became men. They mobilized and worked collectively; therefore, they created a group identity and smashed the fossils of the old society. They tore the ideological masks off America; therefore, they ceased being Americans and became Afros. They said yes to nationhood, and they will say no to America's encroachments as they do their own thing; therefore, they joined the van of human progress, and they will sever the umbilical cord of servitude. As a result of their liberation, they have a right to reclaim May Day as a birthright and as a banner for the struggles ahead in building a New African nation in the heartland of America.

## NOTE ON U.S. JUSTICE

I was driven out of Canada (1968) by a combination of waspish depravity and Jewish conspiracy. These two groups, with the active connivance of my profession, denied my right to a livelihood in Canada's so-called universities. Consequently, I was forced to go to America where that unholy alliance was supplanted in 1969 by a combination of Southern racists—black and white—and the federal government of the USA. What transpired in America was elaborated upon elsewhere. Here, I am concerned with the obscenity of American "justice," on whose encounter I arrived at the following conclusion: the higher the authority, the bigger lie, the more immune that authority is to censure, sanction, and public condemnation. Authority in America need not fear a criticism, a vigilant press, or an alert intelligentsia. Authority is authority is authority; and all are to submit to militarism, regimentation, and disorder with abjectness and humor.

In order to perpetuate its role and maintain its imperialist hegemony in the black community, the white power structure uses the system of indirect government to keep the blacks tamed and within bounds. In brief, black-skinned people are employed by those colonialists to run and manage black institutions within the framework of separate but unequal.

Those black Anglo-Saxons do the bidding of their masters, select and designate prospective Negro middlemen, and execute the policies of institutional racism. As a group, the Anglo-Saxons relish exploiting their people for the benefit of others and pride themselves on being the servants of their people and citizens of the United States. They are Americans who consciously cherish and honor America's destruction of their race and her exploitation of the world. They enjoy dying in Louisiana or on the battlefields of Vietnam for old glory. Their words and deeds, however paralyzing and depersonalizing their efforts might be on the black people, are considered law—law that is a naked, instant, and overwhelming force to be invoked for the slightest of personal misdemeanors or for the most pacific collective action. It is the "law" of the "national guards," the bayonets, the shotguns, the helicopters, the chiefs of police, the generals, the governors, and the state boards of education. It is the man's law, a law applied without equivocation or hesitation. It discriminates not and reasons not; it is invoked, and it expects instant compliance; it moves swiftly and crushes every act of rebellion on the part of the blacks.

The man's law will be enforced no matter what the price is. Therefore, in America, law is the gun; the bigger the gun the greater the power, the more admired its wielder for his firmness and dedication to "law and order." The wielder of the gun is whitey; its object is the nigger. "Law and order" are the laws of America, and every American is a worshiper of these idols no matter what political stripe he or she sports.

Every American is a criminal from the president to the petty politician, from the army's chief of staff to the sheriff, from the biggest professor at Columbia to the most learned ignoramus in Mississippi, from Walter Cronkite to the most illiterate reporter, from the supreme court justices to the jurymen of the Sirhan trial, from the cardinal in Boston to the nun in New Orleans; from Billy Graham crusading in Madison Square Gardens to the littlest Baptist in Georgia. In America, crime walks with pride. She is adored and called police protection; she is worshiped and called the flag; she is obeyed and called justice; she is blessed and called humanity; she is honored and called constitutional government. In this realm of slavery, love is debauchery, life is servitude, man is cannibal. America is *not* beautiful; America is barbaric!

"You have no rights against our country," said the government lawyer as he began his arguments contending that I should be deported from the USA. Asked the Judge when the formal hearing commenced, "To what country would you like to be deported, Mr. Haggar?" Those present at the Federal Department of Injustice and Immigration sat silently. The reporters of the free press were there, but as usual, they reported the official side of the story only. The judge did not have to manage the news; the newsmen did so without compunction.

On May 23, 1969, I filed a reinstatement suit at federal district court in New Orleans. It was alleged that Southern University had violated my constitutional rights of free expression and due process (the First and Fourteenth Amendments) by dismissing me without charges, hearing, and trial. On May 26, 1969, the Federal Department of Injustice ordered my "voluntary" deportation and stipulated that I depart from the United States by June 4 or face forced deportation. The federal government in criminal conspiracy with its racists planned to retaliate, and the drama unfolded thus: On June 2, the Young Men's Business Club of New Orleans proudly announced that they had persuaded the federal government to deport Haggar. On May 16, the *Times-Picayune* reported that they and the white Citizens Council of Louisiana had requested the government to deport me—an announcement that forced the Department of Injustice to issue a clarifying statement (June 4) to the effect that Haggar was requested to leave the United States because his "purpose here has been served." Furthermore, it stated that "residency here was no longer justified since he is no longer employed by the university." In other words, the dismissal from Southern was the basis for the order. The Federal Department of Injustice neither denied nor confirmed that it was succumbing to obvious racist pressure.

My lawyer, Mr. George Strickler, a naive legalist, asked immigration to extend its deadline for my "voluntary" departure so that I could pursue my civil litigation against the university. As a gesture of liberality, its deadline was extended to June 12 whereas the hearing on my civil suit was scheduled for June 25. Since I did not trust Mr. Strickler because of his Americanism, I initiated private discussions with immigration in the presence of Hugh Murray Jr. It was clearly stated that immigration acted on the basis of a notification by the university on the part of "appropriate authorities" that my contract had been terminated and not at the request of racist groups. Immigration said they could not guarantee my unhampered re-entry if I departed voluntarily, and they promised not to arrest me if I did not depart. Immigration, however, did not plan to be outwitted tactically. Therefore, when they learned that I had indeed sued the university and intended to pursue my suit, they changed their grounds for my deportation, hoping in the process to undermine my case and ignoring the rudimentary fact that they had issued my exchange visa. They alleged (June 16) that my entry into the United States was illegal, and I, therefore, must depart or be deported. Meanwhile, on June 12, immigration issued a statement that indicated that I would be given a "hearing" on June 23 and that while they did not plan to call witnesses, I had a right to subpoena any witnesses I so desired. On June 16, fearing the prospect of an injunction enjoining dismissal on constitutional grounds, immigration informed me that I had entered the United States under an expired program of exchange. This action was tantamount to saying that they had discovered a technical error that they committed and for which I had to pay the price. At this juncture, I hoped to expose immigration and accuse them of collusion, but Mr. Strickler who had faith in American justice admonished me not to do so. As a true faithful, he studiously proceeded to file a motion to subpoena witnesses and request public disclosure of documents (June 17). Immigration almost instantly overruled him (by letter). The same man, Troy Adams, who had made the public statements on my unwarranted continued residence in the United States and my right to call witness denied Strickler's motion (June 19). Strickler, playing the lawyers' game, reapplied publicly to the immigration judge on June 23. The judge, Mr. Schrull, also denied the motion without a serious explanation. Mr. Strickler remained silent but appeared visibly perturbed. The assembled newsmen and a few spectators remained totally silent too. I thought the hearing was a fraud and said so publicly, but what was reported made the government's case impeccable. In sum, the American government deliberately deceived the public, and the press not only acquiesced but also reported only the government's side. That same government classified me as a white man in the records of that fraudulent republic whose justice proclaims itself color-blind. What was shocking was that I was insulted and adjudged on the orders of racists and was to be deported under the pretext of law—a law manipulated to serve and sustain and immoral social order and an effete elite. That was the obscenity of American justice, and I had to wait only two more days to witness not only a greater obscenity but also a greater crime and a more sordid system of justice.

On June 25, I appeared before the federal district court of Judge Lansing L. Mitchell, a Southern gentleman who made a mockery of justice. One could not tell whether Mitchell was the defense attorney or the judge. On several occasions during the trial, he praised Dean Bashful, the accused, as an honorable man who had served his people well and castigated me for calling the janitor, a janitor instead of a superintendent. He refused to understand the meaning of the constitutional issue at stake. The only thing he could understand was that I had "no legal contract"; therefore, I could not be reinstated. Besides, the judge authoritatively proclaimed, "There is no evidence to indicate that Dean Bashful, or anyone, ordered Dr. Haggar to refrain from making any statements sympathetic to student demands." Thus spake the judge who heard the dean testify in his court that I was expelled for allegedly having used my classrooms as a "political forum to project ideas connected with the demonstrations" and for having "delivered inflammatory speeches to the students." As to "due process," for which violation even the placid American Association of University Professors ordered the university to reinstate me immediately on May 15, the judge asserted that I denied myself a hearing by returning to the campus on May 8. "Dean Bashful had every intention of giving Dr. Haggar a hearing," the judge sonorously declared overlooking the published letter (*Times-Picayune*, May 8, pp. 1, 3) in which a request for a hearing was made. Moreover, the judge was advised that Mr. Strickler, the lawyer, called Bashful not once but five times on May 8 between 9 a.m. and 11 a.m. to arrange for a hearing, and each time Bashful's secretary told him that Bashful was "on a long-distance call" and his assistants were "out of town." As it turned out, Mr. Bashful was not "on a long-distance call" but was conferring with the National Guard general and the chief of police on how to find a pretext to arrest and dismiss me without provoking a violent confrontation with the students. The judge and his racist cohorts made up their minds not on June 25 but on May 8 when they resolved to crush the black students at Southern and got me expelled on the orders of a racist scoundrel, Governor McKeithen.

In the course of the trial, I tried to convert the court to a political forum. My lawyer opposed the idea, and the judge tried to silence me. Nevertheless, I managed to say enough to cast doubt on the validity of the hearing the supercilious legality of the judge and the lawyers.

After I pointed out that Southern was on the censured list of institutions by the AAUP for its arbitrariness and unresponsiveness to professional requirements, I declared that it was a Negro, not a black institution. Then I argued that the dean was a vicious and vengeful man, a colonial servant who along with his ilk aimed solely at the maintenance of his power and the continued division and suppression of his people. The judge was totally unmoved; his mind was already made up—he was an unreasoning product of a racist political culture. What else could one say other than "It has been said, Your Honor, that the law is ass, but I must add that it is doubly asinine when presided over by a mule!"

Case dismissed. Long live American justice!

# PART 3

# Academic Odyssey

# Chapter 8

## The Treason of the Clerks[7]

Intellectuals in North America seek status, not veritas. To them, propriety supersedes truth; manners, morals; rank, probity. In brief, the loyalties of these clerks are to mammon, not to man. As citizens of the Fourth Reich, they punctiliously worship the anointed idols of monopoly capitalism and proselytize its venal gods of tin, baubles, and symbols. In this ambiance of philistinism, human growth is stunted, life is mechanical, truth is legalistic formalism. No community exists, except the latent pseudo-expressed feeling of universal repression. It is, therefore, palpable that such devitalizing conditions can only produce robots with varying degrees of talents and susceptibilities suited to fulfill functions created by the pervasive division of labor and its invisible managers. Thus, North American capitalism is no fructiferous ground of intellect and intellectuals, and those who attain liberation are exceptional and few. Furthermore, in its most enlightened phase, capitalism condones and at times promotes bourgeois radicalism as a sign of liberality—a doctrine for which it has an enormous absorptive capacity. But this kind of verbal, surface, tactical, protective radicalism must not be confused with penetrative radicalism—a radicalism that begins with root causes and ends with their eradication. Hence, we discern the fundamental differences between the gadfly clerks of capitalist journalism (the reader can peruse for himself the adopted "radicals" of the *Toronto Daily Star* and the occasional liberal pranks of the *Globe* and *Telegram* and other establishment dailies and periodicals) and the revolutionary intellectuals and their commitment to mankind.

---

[7]    Julien Benda, *The Betrayal of The Intellectuals* (Boston: Beacon Press, 1959).

What should be stressed is that most people consider university teachers and students intellectuals. We do not.

Indeed, we consider them clerks and apprentices in the academic workshop of capitalism. However, unlike the student, the professor remains the eternal sophomore, the perpetual adolescent, the ubiquitous moral moron. This contagious malaise affects the student transitionally but the teacher permanently as he sets out to teach the "givens" without giving, the decreed without commanding, the commonplace without apprehending. In sum, he is both a transmission belt and a sanitary engineer of the intellect, who thinks he gives structure and coherence to the inert thoughts and chaotic sections of young mind. He does not realize or is capable of conceiving of himself as a truant officer or an errand boy in a system of academic mendacity. His failure to grasp the meaning of his position places him among the oppressed who cannot comprehend their conditions objectively and consider themselves "happy and contented" though somewhat "frustrated and alienated." Because of this clerkness, its transactional nature, didactic busybodiness, and stultifying routine, we classify the teacher as clerk in the commercial sense. In fact, we classify most people in all other departments of life as clerks. But our concern is with the teacher because of his strategic position and the damages he inflicts on others. Our rationale is that such clerkness neither creates nor stimulates. It merely processes and moulds; it crushes initiative and imagination; it obeys and carries out order bureaucratically. It is a civil service in an empire of ants composed of civil servants sustained with such illusions of grandeur as academic freedom and tenure, liberal fair play, and scientific objectivity.

If clerkness were the dominant feature of North American life in general and the "teaching profession" in particular, would it not follow that all teachers are clerks? Most are certainly not. As a matter of fact, three categories may be delineated: clerks (whom we have already sketched), scholars, intellectuals.

The most important characteristics of the scholar are competence and intelligence. By competence, we mean that the scholar has acquired the requisite training by specializing in a certain area of study; that he is capable of communicating his subject matter to others; that he is ready and able to impart his knowledge to students; and, finally, that he generally subscribes to the canons of scholarship, objectivity in the use of the scientific method, skepticism with reference to received dogma, and the appearance of modest humility when introducing innovation. By intelligence, we mean that in addition to possessing a scientific bent of mind and a semi-superior intelligence, the scholar amasses information, forms hypotheses, and enunciates doctrines whose implications may not necessarily reinforce the status quo. But by and large, most scholars, social and natural scientists included, espouse the ethical precepts and political dictas of the social system under which they live, and the pure scientific scholar is a rarity. Therefore, in his social and moral perspective, the scholar embodies the clerk; he surpasses him scientifically, not morally. However, because the scholar owns a more discriminating and superior intelligence, his marketability makes him less amenable to strict dogmatism and absolute servility and confers on him a feeling of independence and autonomy—a license to be a moral libertine if he elects to do so. Moreover, since scholars experiment, investigate, and write in a scholarly style, they could, if unified, pose a potential threat to their would-be masters. The probability of a united scientific class is a prospect of the future. At the moment, they lack the members and the will to act except individualistically and amorally. Their group consciousness is basically "professional" and marginally social.

Furthermore, it should be noted that we did not subsume disinterestedness or detachment as an attribute of scholarship though bourgeois intellectuals do so. The reason is rudimentary: there is no such creature. Whoever we are, whatever station we occupy in life, each one of us has been "socialized" into something, which specifically means that each person begins with a framework of moral presuppositions, desiderata, hopes, and aspirations, however vague. Scholarship, therefore, does not encompass the pretended disinterestedness of the academic or operates in a moral vacuum. In other words, it begins with a non-scientific premise and mobilizes scientific forces to give it a scientific gloss especially in the so-called social sciences. Scholarship is part and parcel of the ideological weaponry of every society, and wherever it is found, its practitioners give implicit or explicit assent to the environment under which they live and carry out assigned tasks prescribed by the political and moral mentors of that particular order. The scientific method may be neutral; science is not!

If the distinctive characteristics of the clerk are propagation or transmission and execution of orders, and those of the scholar, competence and intelligence, those of the intellectual are responsibility and leadership in addition to the qualities of clerk and scholar. By responsibility, we mean responsiveness to the working class, its needs and demands—a moral and historic obligation to be assumed by revolutionaries, no matter what the origin of their social class may be. By leadership, we mean actions conceived and undertaken in the name of the working people, the immense majority of mankind, and on their behalf. Furthermore, leadership and responsibility mean accountability to the workers, manual and intellectual; service to their cause; articulation of their interests. And all these needs, demands, and interests can be summed up in one synthetic conclusion: the abolition of capitalism as a social system and the construction of a socialist society!

Therefore, the intellectual is first and foremost a liberated man, not a PhD wielder. He has shed the garb of family and friend and assumed the mantle of the revolutionary—the unbound man of free humanity. He has smashed the shackles—intellectual, moral, and psychic—that entrap others and reduce them to the level of automatons. Has grasped "reality," seized it, and formed ideas about its demise and reconstruction. He does not fear public disapprobation, moral opprobrium, social ostracism. He says, "I am a man because I elected to be one, and I am prepared with other men to abolish the conditions that make manness impossible." In other words, the revolutionary affirms: I will; therefore, I am. However, he wills as an individual in a historical context under historical conditions independent of his "will." His will is, therefore, historically conditioned; and it is a good will only if it understands the evolution of society, its direction, and the meaning of its current stage. The good will is, therefore, a revolutionary will, and a revolutionary will wills the emancipation of mankind from the clutches of American imperialism and its client states the world over. Objectively speaking, the bourgeois university of North America is not and cannot be a place for the revolutionary, and the so-called university "revolutionaries" are no more than house niggers or house gurus of capitalism. Should, however, a revolutionary, by chance, be in the university, he should do his utmost to overthrow the crippling intellectual conditions that prevail there and devote himself to the unmasking of its treason. The intellectual then, as we see him, is not the remote, aloof, speculative, idle mind of universal university rhetoric, public stereotypy, and Julien Benda, whence we derive our title, but the engage par excellence, the man who embodies the march of the revolutionary in history, and the heir presumptive to an order of human freedom built on the ashes of imperialism.

The revolutionary is a historically bound man commissioned to create a human society in time: the terrestrial city. The traditional clerk was a heaven-bound man, a prophet preaching repentance, obedience, spiritual and moral redemption. He sought the celestial city. The modern clerk is a stomach-bound *number* in the pig city, a parasite-fleecing society in the garb of formal affinities with the medieval clerk. The differences among them are very great. Here are some of the salient features of the latter. The medieval clerk spoke, wrote, and acted in a transcendental manner. He regarded the world as ephemeral, "a place of exile," to use the Christian idiom. His concerns were otherworldly except in their implications for the upholding of absolute morality and the mortification of the flesh. The true clerk was a stoic, an ascetic person, a holy man, not a detached cynic seeking self-gratification and a privatized peace of mind. He was a Roman emperor without imperial possessions, a pontiff of the spirit, an apostle of the celestial city. Julien Benda designated as clerks:

"All those whose activity essentially is not the pursuit of practical aims, all those who seek their joy in the practice of an art or a science or metaphysical speculation, in short in the possession of non-material advantages, and hence in a certain manner say: 'My kingdom is not of this world.' Indeed, throughout history, for more than two thousand years until modern times, I see an uninterrupted series of philosophers, men of religion, men of literature, artists, men of learning (one might say almost all during this period), whose influence, whose life, were in direct opposition to the realism of the multitudes. To come down specifically to the political passions—the 'clerks' were in opposition to them in two ways. They were either entirely indifferent to these passions, and, like Leonardo da Vinci, Malbranche, Goethe, set an example of attachment to the purely disinterested activity of the mind and created a belief in the supreme value of this form of existence; or, gazing as moralists upon the conflict of human egotisms, like Erasmus, Kant, Renan, they preached, in the name of humanity or justice, the adoption of an abstract principle superior to and directly opposed to these passions. Although these 'clerks; founded the modern State to the extent that it dominates individual egotisms, their activity undoubtedly was chiefly theoretical, and they were unable to prevent the laymen from filling all history with the noise of their hatreds and their slaughters; but the 'clerks' did prevent the laymen from setting up their actions as a religion, they did prevent them from thinking themselves great men as they carried out these activities. It may be said that, thanks to the 'clerks,' humanity did evil for two thousand years, but honoured good. This contradiction was an honour to the human species, and formed the rift whereby civilization slipped into the world.

"Now, at the end of the nineteenth century a fundamental change occurred: The 'clerks' began to play a game of political passions. The men who had acted as a check on the realism of the people began to act as its stimulators" (pp. 30–31).

The clerk committed treason by adopting "political passions," by sharing "in the chorus of hatreds among races and political factions" (p. 31); by descending to the market place "determined to have the soul of a citizen and to make vigorous use of it" (p. 32); by flattering the vanity and "profound cupidity of his compatriots" (p. 51); by denigrating foreigners and asserting the moral superiority of his own people" (p. 54); by serving his nation with the pen and becoming part of the "spiritual militia of the material" (p. 51); by proclaiming attachment to the particular, egotistic and concrete and contempt for the universal, cosmopolitan, international (pp. 60–66); by divinizing politics (p. 86); by deifying national custom, history, and past (p. 92); by affirming the false doctrine of the romanticism of pessimism (p. 97); by extolling the cult of the warlike, apologizing for aggressive wars and venerating the man of arms "the archetype of moral beauty" (p. 101); by cultivating an affectationist bourgeois soul whose motto is "Display your zeal for the eternal, the God of battles" (p. 126); and, finally, by professing a plebeian morality as opposed to traditional morality.

Benda summarized it thus:

"It is impossible to exaggerate the importance of a movement whereby those who for twenty centuries taught Man that the criterion of the morality of an act is its disinterestedness, that good is a decree of his reason insofar as it is universal, that his will is only moral if its seeks its law outside its objects, should begin to teach him that the moral act is the act whereby he secures his existence against an environment which disputes it, that his will is moral insofar as it is a will 'to power,' that this part of his soul which determines what is good is its 'will to live' wherein it is most 'hostile to all reason,' that the morality of an act is measured by its adaptation to its end, and that the only morality is the morality of circumstances. The educators of the human mind now take sides with Callicles against Socrates, a revolution which I dare to say seems to me more important than all political upheavals" (p. 94).

Need we add more charges to the indictment of the modern clerk and his treason! Need we reiterate, "It is springtime for the revolution!"

# Chapter 9

## Student Protest

Students the world over have discovered in the past decade (beginning with the Turkish and Korean students who were instrumental in the overthrow of their autocratic governments) that if they cannot take over a given country, they can shake it to its roots, cause immeasurable disruption (the French and Italian students in the spring of 1968) and social dislocation, and give rise to repressive social trends (Germany and the USA). In the so-called "free world," most students had assumed that in a "free society," they had a right to petition, protest, agitate. In the past two or three years, they learned that the assumption was a rhetorical tool and a legal deception that served the ruling cliques and demonstrated their alleged open-mindedness.

In the so-called iron curtain countries and military dictatorships, no such illusions ruled. Therefore, students in East Europe, the United Arab Republic, Mexico, Argentina, Brazil, and elsewhere had to face their rulers head-on, get crushed, but win some "concessions" such as freedom of expression and less rigorous curricula. In the relatively pseudo-free societies, like Britain, Canada, and Japan, student agitators—lacking burning issues such as war, race, and complete autocracy—thrust themselves on the scene as a university-oriented movements whose aim was the "democratization of the university." It is true, however, that in the recent past, student movements in the West have been trying to ally themselves with the working class but thus far, without visible success.

Most students come from the privileged classes and carry in their bones the ideological reflexes of those classes. What is important, however, is that *some* of the students are defecting to the working class and betraying their objective class interests. This is the revolutionary impact

144

of the student rebellions from Berkeley (1964) to Berlin, Colombia, Mexico, Paris, and Rome (1968) to Southern, Cornell, Harvard, The City College of New York and Berkeley (1969). Other minor incidents in the United States, Europe, and Asia took place but had little or no repercussions. As to Canada, in the past two years, a few localized, personalized, isolated incidents occurred at Lutheran, Simon Fraser, New Brunswick, Sir George Williams, McGill, etc.; but none assumed cosmic dimensions. It is against this background that *Student Protest: The Student Radical in Search of Issues*[8] must be understood and evaluated.

Although the genesis and evolution of student radicalism and involvement are not sketched, and no systematic empirical study of a single upheaval is reported, *Student Protest* is a relevant book not because of the information it conveys (there is a little of that on the Canadian scene) but because of the principles and issues it raises.

The organization of *Student Protest* reflects the state of mind of the authors and, to a large extent, the student movements: it is without structure, and the articles assembled together seem like an amorphous hodgepodge with only "liberal" interconnecting threads. To give it some ordered coherence, let us commence our review with Halleck's article "Why Students Protest: A Psychiatrist's View," then proceed to look at the Canadian-Quebec scene and the principles of organization and ideology propounded by pacifist, liberal-minded, and Catholic ideologists. There is also an essay by Hardial Bains of the Internationalists, which is in a class by itself.

Halleck endeavors to explain why students rebel. He points out that critics of student protest use psychological interpretations in their evaluations of radicalism to impugn the motives and personalities of students. This technique casts doubt on the "mental stability" of the activists and "thereby insidiously questions the validity of the changes they seek" (p. 163). The aim is to depict the demonstrators as sick, mixed up, and immature so that they can be ignored and ridiculed. However, it cannot be denied that "there appears to be an inverse relationship between feelings of despair and activism" (p. 164). In other words, the glare of publicity and the sudden prominence activism gives to a few impels many to flock to the movement to seek recognition, excitement, and simple release from inhibitions. In his anatomy of stress, personal and general, Halleck delineates three forms of oppression that propel student activism: direct, indirect, and misperceived. He says that Western society

---

8    Gerald F. McCuigan et al., *Student Protest* (Toronto: Methuen Publications, 1968).

suffers from "interpersonal oppression" (p. 165), which takes on such patterns of behavior as arbitrary control, deprivation, and abuse; and the practitioners of these arts appear to be neglectful, selfish, and malevolent to those feeling the persecution. At any right, vague and nebulous forces as well as identifiable persons comingle and produce an atmosphere of general oppression. Thus, we can enumerate such issues as neglect by the professors, the demand for good academic performance, the feelings of guilt because of one's privileged status, and, in additional to these, the draft in the United States. Moreover, such momentous issues of our age, like nuclear annihilation, technological change, and wars add to "chronic uncertainty" among students. And in the absence of a tradition of service, sense of responsibility, and social purpose, students either become bored and despondent or join with others to alter the oppressive environment. Also, there are those who misperceive oppression and externalize their guilt by indiscriminately attacking "symbols of authority" (p. 170).

If the cause of revolt is oppression, personal and social, why do we have so few or almost no revolts in Canada? Is it because the university administrators are enlightened, or is it because there is only a counterrevolutionary tradition in this country? Or is it because of the fact that the students come from the upper classes and do not want to jeopardize their future careers? Neither Mr. Harding nor Mr. La Touche makes an effort to pose or answer these questions. Harding gives us an autobiographical report on student power in Canada that tells us more about James Harding than about radicalism. But Harding may be right. James Harding may be all there is to radicalism in Canada. If so, radicalism is no more than a group of individuals with a few followers here and there, and it is only capable of undertaking on occasional bravado stance as would appear after studying closely student power here. In this context, we must record with sadness the pathological rise and disintegration of student power. It is possible that the residual remnant might develop radical and orientation with the right circumstances and leadership.

Canadian students were forever in want of great issues. In the early sixties, they discovered the bomb; then, they discovered the Indians and community organizing. In the midsixties, some discovered Quebec; and belatedly, some discovered Canada. The fear of atomic holocaust forced the liberal minded to agitate against the bomb when the Americans decided to use La Macaza and North Bay as bases. They were resoundingly defeated, and the bomb were placed on Canadian soil. The "idealists" among them were persuaded to emulate the "radicals" of the American ally by going, as its radicals did, to the "people" to organize the poor and oppressed. They did so, and most of them became junior social workers by joining the Company of Young Canadians or opted out completely. A few went to the NDP, and a handful joined the Communist Party or became Internationalists. The upshot of all this is that in a few short years, the Canadian movement did not develop beyond a religious and aesthetic protest and disintegrated instead of going from the religious to the moral, to the political and, finally, to the military state of revolution. Let us face the facts: student power, surface university reforms, and adoption of a few students and professors by the news media are not tantamount to a revolution. Indeed, this is the traditional policy of liberal co-optation. The Student Union for Peace Action (formed in 1964 and dissolved in September of 1967) and CYC or whatever anarchic embodiments they may assume will remain liberal reform measures, not structural change; and above all, let us not confuse nationalistic groups and individuals with proletarian internationalism!

Moreover, the Canadian setting consists also of the French fact not clearly understood even by Frenchmen like Daniel La Touche. He tells us how student "syndicalism" emerged in Quebec and contrasts it with the student movements in Canada by way of four hypotheses: Quebec as one integrative link, radicalism as an instrument of integrating students into the surrounding society, student radicalism as the dominant ideology among students, and the ideology as a channel of social promotion. Although La Touche concedes that his "syndicalism" is a French transplant, he does not seem to understand that it has nothing to do with historic syndicalism except in name and that its aim is not social transformation but social collaboration. That is, the kind of syndicalism that La Touche espoused is Catholic solidarism predicated on the idea of social peace and organismic evolution rather than social class and revolutionary upheaval. What his syndicalism amounts to is Catholic collectivism a la Pope Leo XIII—a syndicalism that gave a liberal gloss to Italian Fascism, and in its current exposition gives Catholicism a veneer of liberality.

Syndicalism as a revolutionary theory postulates production as the basis of society and the producers (workers) as the rightful owners of that society, not the capitalists and their para-military and military agents. Moreover, syndicalism insists that only through working-class unity in industrial rather than in craft unions can capitalism be overthrown by the "general strike" of the oppressed; production, not consumption, is the basic tenet; class conflict, not social cohesion, is the cornerstone of syndicalist thought; struggle and combativeness, not religious pacifism, are the integrating force. That, in brief, is syndicalism and not its bastardization by La Touche and company.

As to the substance of La Touche's ideology, he states it thus: "The ideology is based on one definition and one axiom from which everything else is drawn. The student is by definition a young intellectual worker. And the axiom is that there is no such thing as a student problem. There are only student aspects of socio-national problems" (p. 121).

La Touche cites the charter of the University of Montreal to illustrate the meaning of the ideology. He says that the student is a "young citizen" and "an apprentice in a profession with which he will in the future serve society" (p. 122). Secondly, since the student has rights, he also has obligations; and among these, he has to "be honest and subordinate his own interests to those of society" (p. 123); thirdly, "just as the student has rights and obligations, so does the association of which he is a member" (p. 124).

Charter of Grenoble, student syndicalism, or whatever honorific title we confer on Mr. La Touche's syndicalism, it remains a tradition-bound, medieval Catholicism with intermediate organizations and groups that will not tamper with the foundation of society. Lastly, its authoritarian and latent institutional Fascism must not be obscured by the term *radicalism* unless we succumb to the "libertarian" vulgarities of George Woodcock and company[9] and identify contemporary radicalism as left-wing Fascism. Thus, we discern that the Canadian scene as portrayed by Harding and La Touche does not offer a substantial realm of revolutionary activity. On the contrary, we see nothing but stagnation, fragmentation, and decay. However, the potential is there, and those with clear revolutionary ideas that equip them with transformational strategies have a whole world to mobilize with little or no intellectual competitors except the bourgeois radicals and their ilk.

The paucity of revolutionary activities and the poverty of intellectual reflections on the left seem to stimulate the academic theorizing of the liberal center. Here we have to good Basilian fathers with what could be called a conscience: G. F. McGuigan, the editor of *Student Protest*, and Neil Kelly. As Catholics, they conceive of problems in moral, not

9    *Saturday Night*, July 1969, p. 19–22.

economic, terms. McGuigan, in particular, ascribes student protest to "the depression of human values" and contends that "uneasiness among most students remains nameless" (p. 18). He maintains that its most obvious signs are "a lack of hope and a confusion about goals and the purpose of life which in many cases borders on moral despair" (p. 19). He asserts that the students are theologically minded and that their discontent is not merely aimed at "rearranging society," "redistributing wealth," or reforming the "present system of government" but at "bringing under scrutiny the very role in society of rationality itself and the intellectual legitimacy of its paradigms (sets) of control and organization" (p. 21).

McGuigan tells us that to understand "radical" students, we must learn to appreciate that "action and thought are only true when united," and we must be willing "to participate in the more demanding notion of revolution as participation in order to understand, because understanding is 'doing,' and 'doing' is being" (p. 23). Out of these revolutionary processes, issues crystallize. One type can be solved within "a given set of values," another may be the occasion when "wo sets of value come into conflict, i.e., civil rights"; but the more important dimension of an issue is its "symbolic or sacramental character," which makes it "the occasion for a rejuvenation of human awareness" (p. 28). In this sense, truth to the new left is not propositional but existential, and their confrontations with the universities illustrate the point. Take, for instance, the much-vaunted liberal idea of academic freedom, which recognizes "free choice" but denies the correlation between thought and moral action, a denial that makes its pluralism an intellectual game without moral content. Here "the liberal educator does put limitations on academic freedom by categorically denying the validity of a particular intellectual approach which combines the intellectual and moral problem in effective action or by gratuitously assuming certain other moral values" (p. 30). Therefore, confrontation between the radical and the university becomes inevitable because the university refuses to relate intellectual opinion to moral commitment. Indeed, the university always "backs away from any other commitment except the establishment commitment" (p. 31), and confrontation shows who controls what for whose benefits. Confrontation simply unmasks the fraudulence of the university and exposes its treachery. It illustrates to us that liberalism is totalitarian because it offers "no true alternatives," and that is "the ability to decide against the liberal set of values" (p. 36).

Up to this point, McGuigan has a full grasp of radicalism if we accept his moral frame of reference. From hereon, he wants to expose the dangers of "the open-ended systems theory of the ongoing revolution" and to prescribe a solution that is so reminiscent of the beatic vision of communitarian Christianity. McGuigan is concerned with student arrogance, despair, intolerance, and impersonalism. He castigates the radicals for "the inhumanity of treating people according to a theory system" and points out that they do indeed "categorize" people as establishment, stereotype relations between people, and are "suspicious as to whether one is for them or against them," an approach that sins against their "own first principle and shows how they and the establishment are obsessed by the same theory of change in which the antagonisms of either side are necessary to one another in order to justify their violent actions and make the theory world" (p. 40). McGuigan is saying that left and right condition each other and live in a kind of hostile environment of coexistence. Now he concedes that the right has been demythologized but not the left. To do that, he foresees "one final radicalism—that which eschews and finally rejects the dichotomous views of reality as composed by the nature of opposites" (p. 47). McGuigan fears the prospect of the left becoming established and oppressive too. He, therefore, advocates stepping out of the "dichotomy and no longer playing the role of gods" (p. 48), which can only be done by "the common recognition of problems and mutual ignorance" (p. 49). It is at this point that Neil Kelly, the other Basilian, enters the picture, championing "personal institutionalizing." There is nothing new in Kelly's indictment of the church. What is interesting in his analysis is the correlation of "one's own experience with the experience of another" (p. 249). He wants structure and difference. To Kelly, personal life is "intentional living," the discovery of the value of "personal moral action," which is characterized by "personal freedom, personal decision, personal judgement as to means for the direction of purposes of action" (p. 252). By personalizing action and recognizing differences in others and relating to them, we replace establishment institutionalism by personal institutionalism and thereby enshrine sameness and variety.

From the Catholic prescription, we proceed to the secular "liberal" prescription. Here we have David Zirnhelt, Paul Goodman, Noam Chomsky, George Benello, and Dennis Lee. If these authors dislike being lumped together, let us remind them that they share a common abhorrence of revolutionary action. They are Girondists; they have one foot in the institutions of society and one foot outside it; they are essentially moralistic and pacifistic, and to them "resistance" is either agitating from within or withdrawal to parallel institutions or counter-communities plus occasional participation in marches to protest government policies and injustices.

Goodman and Chomsky are well advertised and celebrated by the liberal establishment as its gadflies. We can neither add to nor detract from their celebrity. Besides, what they say in *Student Protest* is marginal. Mr. Zirnhelt is still on the love-reason kick, and we intend to leave him there. As to Dennis Lee, his essay on Rochdale, better known as Roachdale, has been published in many places, and I deal with it in my review of the *University Game*. Briefly, it is another autobiographical account of a sensitive liberal person who found standard university education unbearable and opted out for "unstructured" education and living. It is an attempt at personal salvation rather than social redemption, but it is a start. Benello's article "Wasteland Culture" is a critique of managerialism and Marxism and a synthesis of organizational theory that posits the "therapeutic community" as an agency for social transformation and says absolutely nothing on how we can overcome the capitalist Leviathan.

Benello deplores the "power-centered personality" Western society produces and tells us about the fragmentation and deprivation that prevail in the technological order. He insists that modern bureaucracy is "dysfunctional" (p. 203), credits the New Left with the reintroduction of "utopian vision," and calls for a new kind of organization. His sources are the New Left theory of "participatory democracy" and counter-communities and the "vanguard management theory" of organic adaptiveness rather than bureaucratic structure. Benello's contribution consists of his cortical model of organization, the neuron structure of the brain. He states his case thus:

"Only in the lower reflex pathways is there a linear, specialized, chain-of-command form of organization. Here networks are specialized to control a particular function: reflex action in the limb, digestion, heart, and so on. But in the cortex, the neurone networks function in a manner similar to task forces. Any frequently repeated stimulation leads to the development of a 'cell assembly'—a structure consisting of many cells in the cortex and diencephalon which can act briefly as a closed system, relate to other closed systems, and also to motor channels" (pp. 207–208).

Benello's contention is that the dominant forms of organization "parallel the control organization of the lower brain" instead of following the "cortical model." To embody this model in institutions, we must use the mechanism of the "therapeutic community" not in Freudian fashion to deliver ourselves for "unexpressed aggression or sexuality, but rather to benefit from mutual openness, honesty, and an ethic of mutual aid." This community is based on the "primacy of the person," and we are expected to live in it, not merely talk about it (p. 211). He illustrates the principle of "intensive organization into cells" by citing communistic Christianity, the Birch Society, and Soka Gakkai in Japan. Benello is not advocating Fascism; he simply wants to point out that present society is manipulative and shows us how we can emancipate ourselves by face-to-face organization. He wants us to think "ecologically" and create "intentional communities or cooperative paradigms," which taken together are "mutually interdependent and thus form an ecosystem" (p. 218). From this angle of vision, Benello decrees that we need not get into power, but we need to know "how to transform and humanize it" (p. 218). And that is the crucial issue. How can we humanize something we do not control—that very something that brutalizes us? We can wax romantic about the "densely and intensively" organized society where the basic activities of life "interrelate," where we enjoy integrative democracy, where we can lead meaningful lives; but how do such activities affect the oppressed totality of mankind? How do we overcome the garrison state and its innumerable soldiery?

These are the fundamental questions Benello cannot answer. It is sad that we sinned and fell; it is sad that we are not as rational, computerized, and automated as Mr. Benello would like mankind to be; it is sad that utopian "projectors" learn so little from history!

Lastly, we come to Bains's "Necessity for Change," which is the only contribution to *Student Protest* that steps out of the liberal framework. Bains tells us that the "historical crib" into which we are born is not only stultifying but is also the source of our "anti-consciousness." The "historical crib" answers our emotional and social needs by giving us reassuring, simplistic answers and by assigning us roles to perform in a stratified society. The issue is how to smash this "historical crib," liberate ourselves, and construct a new society. Bains asserts that the "will to be" (p. 139) is always straining to be free: "When we say rebel, we mean transcend through consciousness the historical situation, and make it alive" (p. 140). But rebellion is rebellion for "something," and that something is "service to others," and it does not come because we understand or we are aware. It comes only when we are conscious, and consciousness is a state of being in a state of change, a state of having a "confrontational ethos" (pp. 145–146). This ethos is something acquired by struggle by which we spurn our Fascist being of the egocentric I and reject the consumerism of capitalism and vulgar Marxism: the index of our liberation is our "revolutionary zeal" and the energy we invest in the creation of liberated person, the Socialist man, the man who will combat the "ill effects of the environment" of which he must be conscious (p. 157). In the final analysis, "only the complete elimination of the basis of this exploitation and this dehumanization will liberate us" (p. 160).

In his introduction to *Student Protest*, George Payerle finds all his fellow authors quite congenial to his way of thinking and finds much that is worthwhile in Bains's article. However, Payerle dislikes Bains's insistence on his approach as being "the only correct way of seeing society" (p. 5) and considers it to be in "complete opposition" to the above thesis. Poor Mr. Payerle! His individual personal self-realization and continuing change rhetoric remain trapped in liberal utopianism and moralism. What is wrong with Bains is not that his way is false or correct but that he considers himself one of the few or about the only one in North America who understands Marxism-Leninism. Moreover, he falls into the bourgeois sociological trap of equating the Soviet Union with the capitalist view of material abundance; and indeed, Mr. Payerle fails to discern that pitfall. What Bains has in common with the authors of *Student Protest* is not a common perspective but a feeling that he is "saved" and others are damned. His inclusion in this collection may be a form of Catholic bait that anticipates conversion. Meanwhile, a Babel of babbling liberal tongues will prevail.

Contrary to their profession of humanism and criticism of official liberalism, the authors are a new liberal establishment that has not been canonized. Each, with the exception of Bains, is not only liberal but also an ultra-liberal outsider who is looking forward to his day of elevation. Bains is a Maoist fanatic without the suppleness of Maoism and its devotion to revolutionary activity. For this reason, Bains may also become one of the God-that-failed types and a rabid conservative! No slander intended, only struggle!

# Chapter 10

———◆◆◆———

# The University: Liberty or Servility?

The North American university was the by-product of three interacting forces: the sacerdotal, the regal, and the feudal industrial. Indeed, the religious origins and purposes of the medieval and early American universities cannot be doubted. The stated purpose was clearly the training of clerics to serve the tribal gods of that epoch. Likewise, the purpose of the regal or state university was the concoction of secular theologies to justify the expansion of absolute power in Europe or the dispossession of the Indian inhabitants of North America, and, in both instances, the university-trained people provided the necessary cadres for the maintenance of the prevailing social order. Moreover, with the coming of industrialism, the "captains of industry" with the active collaboration of the "captains of erudition" seized the university and turned it into a service station, a medicine shop, a public relations agency. In brief, the university, whatever its provenance and concretely specified purposes had been, has always been an instrument of social control, a provider of trained clerks for the powers that be, a special hunting grounds for the scions of the ruling class and its would-be emulators.

What is remarkable about *A Place of Liberty*[10] is that its authors begin with a correct view of reality, abandon it, then propose a panacea to and all their academic ills: self-government in the university. Here in summary fashion are the core ideas that represent the collective wisdom of the liberal ideologies of CAUT (Canadian Association of University Teachers).

---

[10]   George Whalley, ed. *A Place of Liberty* (Toronto: Clarke, Irwin and Co., 1964).

154

The late professor Stewart Reid, in a historic account of the "origins and portents" of the university, criticizes the absentee landlordism and omnipresence of the board and states that

"The American university has never been a self-governing community of scholars. Instead, it has usually been treated as if it were a somewhat peculiar type of business enterprise. Supreme authority is vested by charter or by Act of the legislature in a Board of Governors or Board of Trustees. This Board is the custodian of all the property of the university and is empowered to use or dispose of it as it sees fit. It has the authority to appoint or dismiss all employees from the President to the cleaning women. It erects buildings, buys equipment, and decides when and how "the plant" shall be operated. Legally, if not in practice, it determines the curriculum and sets requirements for admission and for degrees, since the academic Senate is always a subordinate agency. In short, the Board is the university. In many cases it is responsible to no one but itself and in some it is in fact self-perpetuating. Usually it does not directly or completely represent the public, the state government, or even any clearly identifiable public interest, and it avowedly does not represent either the teachers or the students of the institution. In its outward appearance and legal structure, then, the typical American university is, in Dr. Capen's words, "a Simon Pure example of authoritarian government," which illustrates the "curious paradox [that] the nation which has developed political and social democracy more completely than any other, has devised and perpetuated a plan of university control which, technically and legally, does not show even a chemical trace of democracy" (pp. 12–13).

Professor Reid's critique is either implicitly or explicitly shared by every one of his fellow contributors. Professor Rowat puts the case most succinctly in his article "The Business Analogy," in which he takes the "decision making" theoreticians of management consultancies to task. He rejects their "happy family" model of emphasis upon "agreement, unity, uniformity" efficiency, and business mindedness, and asserts that

"[T]his system has resulted in a formal hierarchy of control in the internal administration of our universities which is essentially authoritarian. Presidents, deans, directors, heads of departments and professors are all appointed and directed from the top down in a system of superior-subordinate relationships in which the President has potentially arbitrary control over the pay and promotion of any faculty member. The effect is to inhibit individual initiative and independence of mind. Thus the present system unwittingly militates against the free search for truth and the free expression of thought" (pp. 74–75).

If the university were an autocracy, a despotism, and a business enterprise, what should its purposes be? How should it function? What kind of government should it have? And what should be the role of the teachers? These are the crucial questions the professors attempt to raise and answer. Here are some excerpts. First, Professor Reid:

"We are constantly being told nowadays that the function of the university community in Canada is to preserve, to criticize, to augment, and to transmit all the knowledge and all the creative capacity that is available and possible for us. The scholars who are charged with that staggering responsibility can hardly be treated any longer as irresponsible servants, formally and specifically forbidden a voice in managing their own affairs, and subject always to the wiser influence and superior authority of their businessmen masters" (p. 25).

Professor Frank Scott contends that power must be conferred on those whose allegiance and duty is "the pursuit of truth for its own sake"—that is, the professor whose functions are research, scholarship, and teaching. Only they, and not the businessmen, can understand the "special nature of the university" and advance it as a center of learning. Businessmen, by temperament alone, care for the conventional, useful, practical, and have a "congenital horror of controversy" (p. 33). According to Scott, these ideas are contrary to the idea of the university, because it must pursue the truth

"in its various disciplines to the farthest reaches of human thought, and reveal its findings to society through writing and teaching. The free university is indeed one of the greatest inventions of men, and without it no society can flourish. It is far too delicate, complex, and precious an instrument to entrust to any but those trained to its use by long practice" (p. 34).

In other words, the university is not a "plant," and what distinguishes it from all other institutions as Professor Percy Smith sees it is its "intellectual commitment." He defines the latter as a "responsibility for the extension of knowledge through discovery and assessment, and for the awakening of young minds to intellectual excitement and challenge" (p. 43). The supreme function of the university is not the preparation of youth for life but the presentation of "a way of life, the way of the questing mind, and inviting and encouraging every student to participate in it" (p. 45). Smith embraces "intellectual wakefulness," which expresses itself "through penetration, analysis, and criticism—through individuality and the willingness not to conform—even through outright heresy and rebellion, but not through uncritical acceptance of prescribed policy, whether of corporation, church or government" (p. 44). (In judging the case of my dismissal from Lutheran, Professor Smith overlooked his criteria and did not censor Lutheran or demand my reinstatement.)

Professor Frank Underhill adopts the Socratic stance: "Modern universities constitutes a sort of collective Socrates in modern societies," he proclaims. Underhill believes in "the intellectual elite" or the Jeffersonian concept of democracy in which meritocracy dominates the common man whose range of experience is "not wide enough for him to be able to act wisely without the help of this leadership" (p. 64). (Professor Underhill was a staunch CCFer in his younger days. In the early sixties, he joined the Liberal Party and became one of his celebrated ideologues.)

Professor W. L. Norton inveighs against the external authority of the dictatorial and bureaucratic state of the university and characterizes it as "death to any kind of university work because it destroys that responsibility, not merely for professional competence, but for the whole life of the community, which is the essence of any free society and particularity of a university" (p. 97).

In sum, the professors, by and large, describe the existing conditions of the university accurately. Their professional bias is easily discernible. Like other professionals, they contend that their profession is "unique" and cannot be truly appreciated by people who had not devoted their lives to university teaching. They want self-government, but they make self-effacing and self-abnegating claims in seeking it for their profession. Professor Maxwell Cohen typifies this attitude. He is merely satisfied with a "reformation of monarchic-oligarchic character of the powers of the president-principal and of the lay Board, the upgrading of the

Senate as the highest academic body," and he advocates "overlapping membership of governors on the Senates and of Senators and staff on the Boards" (pp. 114–115).

Professor Murray Donnelly also writes in a reformist vein. He dismisses as "intransigent idealism" the proposal of abolishing the dualism of administrative and academic affairs and of making the professors the corporate body instead of the board or senate. That is, Donnelly opposes the notion of conferring legislative authority upon the teaching staff or the so-called university community—the students and teachers. He suggests that

"we accept the idea of dualism between academic and administrative matters and attempt to build a more adequate bridge between the two, to improve the decisions that will be made by both, and above all to ensure that administrative decisions are taken with full appreciation of their academic consequences. In short, the proposal is that both Senate and Board be maintained, but that changes be made in the structure of each, the Senate dominated by professors and the Board having a number of professors on it" (p. 146).

Professor George Whalley, the editor of *A Place of Liberty*, likens the university to an artist who "will always look a little strange in its self-possession" and its own "self-encroaching life." To maintain its "integrity," the university must be able to withstand demands made by society and "ignore threats by government, beguilings of industry and commerce, and the expostulations of ambitious and well-meaning citizens" (p. 166). To guarantee its "integrity," the university must be reformed in a way that makes it possible for the academic staff and the governing board to come into closer and more continuous relations. Moreover, the board must be altered to "include comprehensive representation of the academic community," and its functions and duties must be carefully defined and limited. Thirdly, the senate ought to become the center of gravity of university government and the principle of election of president, deans, and chairmen out to prevail. Lastly, all such reforms must be "codified and established by overt regulations" (pp. 172–175).

It is evident from our reproduction of the views articulated by the professors that their orientation is liberal, procedural, and somewhat "subversive," if taken seriously. They are spilling ink, not blood, to reach their objectives. They are seeking faculty power within the ambit of the university on the basis of meritorious argument and rational persuasion, the claptrap of professional liberalism. They make no ringing declarations. They exhort no one else to action, they search for no allies, they say absolutely nothing about the students' right for self-government. All this indicates that prescience and perspicacity are not professorial attributes, for their work was published in 1964 when students were merely regarded as children and professors as demi-gods. Therefore, the subversive bygone ideal of the university as being in the world but not of it can only be treated as another professional exposition worthy of "consideration." In other words, since the professors merely offer a reformist, legalistic blueprint, and plead with their employers to give them a little more recognition, and use their talents more effectively, we can only conclude that the professors are not interested in social transformation but social status—the poetry surrounding the republic of knowledge and the kingdom of learning notwithstanding. What is most extraordinary about the whole book is that the classical ideal the professors espouse cannot even be nostalgically resuscitated because it was never implemented on this continent, and none of them seems to be aware of the interrelations among institutions in advanced capitalist societies. Moreover, since the professors never attained a professional status and have no governing professional body that regulates their conduct and sets standards of admission into their ranks, it is not surprising that the businessmen who control the universities with their professional hirelings have not heeded the "rational" analysis of the professors. But those hard-nosed people will sooner or later discover what Columbia and Harvard did in 1969, namely, the use of professors and students as regulators of internal student life on campus. This discovery stifled rebellion and dissent and enabled the "university community" to maintain its sanity and sense of balance. The professors turned out to be much more vicious and effective than any combination of Fascist pigs, screaming editorial writers, beleaguered deans, and public vigilante committees put together.

Lastly, even if we take the democratic ideal to heart and give the professors self-government, assuming they are fit for it, what are they likely to do with it? They will probably do what they are doing presently as electors, i.e., vote or absent themselves from the political process and let the demagogues buy and sell their votes. You see, comrade professors, you are too busy with your research, teaching, CIA spying, business advising, cats and dogs, and families to be concerned about democracy and the fate of freedom. If you were, you would not abstract the university from its environment and treat it as a floating island on the high seas. On the contrary, if you were aware, you would become participants in the life of society and act as its beacons of light rather than continue as its gas station attendants! You would indeed curb your avarice and stop pandering and prostrating yourselves to the powers that be! That you will not do, nor are capable of doing so, the habit of servitude is too deeply ingrained to be overcome by liberal autism.

# Chapter 11

## The University Game

Social criticism in contradistinction to muckraking is a rare commodity in North America, and it is as alien to this culture generally as the hot dog and Coca-Cola are familiar to it.

One of the areas that social criticism has not penetrated is the university. But with the publication of the *University Game*,[11] this is no longer the case: the sacred cow is on the way to the slaughterhouse. However, we cannot be too sanguine. This is a beginning; and in characterizing it as such, Arab wisdom may be relevant: "Vague and nebulous is the beginning of all things, but not their end. And I fain would have you remember me as a beginning. Life, and all that lives, is conceived in the mist and not in the crystal. And who knows but a crystal is mist in decay?" If, therefore, we take the *University Game* as a beginning pregnant with ends, we must take into account what it is that the authors purport to tell us about the university, its purposes, functions, administration, staff, and students.

It is very clear at the outset that the university curriculum—a fact that determines the character of the university—reflects the needs of the society in which it operates. The subject matter studied, for instance, in historic universities such as Bologna and Paris and in the more recent proliferation and multiplication of North American universities clearly illustrates that the universities proclaimed and elaborated the doctrines of the church and provided clerks for the church and state in the medieval period. And in the closed societies that purport to be liberal and open, the universities have functioned as places of research whose

---

[11]  Lee and Adelman, *The University Game* (Toronto: House of Anansi, 1966).

findings contributed to the mutilation of nature and the mastery of man. Moreover, the "liberal arts" have served the bourgeois order as producers of symbol manipulators whose task it is to justify the system and inculcate its values, beliefs, and myths. The university, in brief, is not a "community of scholars," whose primary concern is the pursuit of truth, knowledge, and goodness. It is part of the political economy and a subsidiary adjunct at that. In other words, its much-flaunted autonomy, learning" excellence, and all that are no more than procrustean phantasmagorias that deceive only the "liberal" practitioners and their accomplices and victims, which is to say the university is a fraud in the guise of the immaculate virgin whose innocence is believed in by those who take the white garment for purity of heart when the heart and the mind are corrupt and corrupting, feeble and enfeebling, destroyed and destructive.

Thus, the university, irrespective of place and time, has been the training center for the powers that be; and all the talk about scholarship is no more than scholasticism, pedantry, and apologia. More specifically, the North American University is a place where the licensed doctors train apes in the values of capitalism, produce the unquestioning slaves to augment the economic system, and supply the high priests to expound the morality, religion, and manners of the bourgeois order. It is, therefore, no accident that there is no political philosophy in Canada, no political analysis, and no political reflection. All that political science does in this country is recite the operative rituals of the past and the political cup readers go about taking opinion polls to help their political masters, read the trends, and adjust accordingly. Politics, the queen of the social sciences in the body politic, is the whore of politicians seeking office for self-enrichment, aggrandizement, and recognition. With this, the human becomes inanimate, the vitals become inert, and the good becomes the appropriate. In all this degradation of life, the university plays a central role that is the negation of life and reason, and "the community of scholars" is the readiest of collaborators in this unholy enterprise. And this leads us to an examination of the functions of all the participants in this enervating agency of brutalization.

The participants in this holy of unholies are the professors who have nothing to profess, the students who have come to be molded, the administration who rule tyrannically with PR smiles. Let us begin with the administration, the most "noble" in the hierarchy of hierarchies. Those benefactors adopt the family model and treat the university "family" as if it were their exclusive preserve. They feel they know more and they know better, and in their exercise of "the living-death, false-nirvana ethic which dominates our society," they oppress professor and student and compress life into their neat files of reality. In their cooperation with absentee landlordism, they run the university in a businesslike, efficient manner and produce the "organization man" to man the citadel of monopoly capitalism. What they want is "responsible criticism"—that is, the kind of criticism that can be coopted and put into effect, the criticism that demonstrates one's agility, maneuvering, flexibility, and readiness to play in the game of the "circulation of the elite."

What administrators want is a smoothly run machine, a "happy" family whose members say yes to titanic dad, yes to injustice, yes to collaborative rationalizations of iniquity. Thanks for the recent increment, now you can crush my soul, my conscience, my all. What an essay in liberty for "professors" who fear that their skins may be burned if they say no to tyranny! Yes, professors, he who wears his morality as best garment would do better to walk naked for the sun and the snow will tear no holes in his bodies, for he is dead because he has stilled his tongue and thrown away his pen and in the process said farewell to life, to love, to liberty; and I, as a matter of rejoinder, say I am dead. Long live the dead, and may the gravediggers multiply!

As to the students, what is it that they need to do other than to recall and reproduce "the thoughts, feelings, imagining and concerns" of their "betters"? Are they not incidental to the schemes of things? Are they not transitional products destined for adolescence and supplanting by more numerous robots to come? How silly it is that they should even ask to be "decision makers" when "parents" have thought of every debilitating avenue to pulverize their thought and have charted every conceivable course to make them "happy." Ungrateful, petulant, unempancipated adolescents, do you not see how we programmed you for future "leadership" of our society? Do you not understand that administrating and professing are tasks beyond your capacity and we the doctors know what is best and good for you? Let no "agitators" disturb your peace, withdrawal, calm, and "happiness." Go and search for sex, alcohol, drugs, and foods so we can be left alone in our felicitous state of being.

Students! Your function is cram and recall. Care not about "student power"; that is a Communist conspiracy. Learn the rhetoric, not the practice of democracy. Groom yourself for anxiety, occupation, income, status. Just be like us. We are your archetypes. We understand; we too were a bit "radical" in the thirties and forties. Take it easy, baby. You will grow up. This is the treason of the intellect! This is it: condescension of the deed, the beginning of the beginning of freedom!

What does all this mean? It means simply that command relation prevails in every aspect of society, including the "university," or what McCulloch calls "unilaterality," which he defines as a "relationship of respect and constraint," and juxtaposes it to "mutuality," which is a relationship of "respect and cooperation."

McCulloch correctly observes that unilaterality comes "into being whenever two persons or groups come into sustained contact and potential conflict, perceive differences between themselves, define these differences as inequalities," accept this relationship as real, internalize the values of the dominant order (p. 25).

This kind of relationship cultivates worthlessness, self-deprecation, and status anxiety. And in this process, man becomes Caliban, submits to "authority" without question, surrenders his integrity to the powers that be, and perceives himself as "retaining some measure of personal control and mastery" in matter of sex, alcohol and passive entertainment (p. 51). In brief, the system that prevails produces the "hippy," the sex maniac, and the general unease felt by students. The students' "badness" comes from their elders and "betters"; the only difference there is between these two is that the latter can better absolve themselves of their guilt and hide behind their pedantry and irrelevance. They can better deceive themselves! The students are not as capable of such culpability. They still retain part of the innocence of obsolescence; they have not become callous and "practical men."

Now the problem is, can we replace unilaterality by mutuality and, if so, how? If mutuality means the perception of self and others in a state of becoming not being, it follows the interaction is the principal means of understanding; and if we predicate "differences as differences not as inequalities," we have the burden of constantly facing the unexpected, which generates a feeling of uncertainty about goals and outcomes. This is a dangerous enterprise from the point of view of command relations. It is dangerous because it requires initiative and creativity, whereas command relations regularize and stylize life in a way that is predictable and routine. In other words, if we were to assume that all a man wants is to "escape from freedom," the model of mutuality is unworkable; but if we assume that "man is born free and everywhere he is in chains," the question is, "how do we break the 'chains'," and do we dare break them throughout society or in some institutions such as the "university"?

Four of the nine authors who wrote the *University Game* seem to think that some kind of counter-university is required to overcome the "stuff-and-throttle philosophy" of the "schoolmen." Gonick, for instance, proposes the establishment of "true centres of learning, creativity, and scholarship" within the multiversity and with "no obligation to train useful citizens." The question we must ask of Gonick is, will the "power elite" foot the bill, and if they do, will the selection be on the basis of the "foundations scholars"? And if we persuade the gods to establish such "centers," will we not be merely used as experimentalists in the service of pluralism? The problem then is not the creation of such centers but the people who will man them, finance them, and use them.

The second approach is adumbrated by George Grant who embraces nostalgia as a means of escape and suggests "the reliving of buried memories" as essential therapy to renew our vision of excellence in the arid world of the technological tradition (p. 67). This may be good therapy, but it is no tool of social change. Lee, on the other hand, offers Rochdale and characterizes it as "an experiment in higher education and urban living" (p. 75), where it is assumed that those whom a decision affects are the decision makers and are responsible for carrying out the decisions once made. Here roles (teacher, student, etc.) do not exist, and we live in an "institutional vacuum"; everyone is a student. No *one* is a professor who has to rely on his authority rather than his reason to expound an idea; everyone is a learner in a society for intellectual growth, human communication, the sharing of life.

This model fulfills the needs of the "liberal" who still believes in liberalism as a revolutionary social goal. It can encompass the values of liberal education; it cannot overcome the dehumanization of North American liberal society. It could be a promising beginning; it can answer personal but not social questions. It is liberating in its "doctrinaire unwillingness to prescribe or proscribe any activity whatsoever." In this environment, the individual creates a "structure for oneself to embody one's own living necessities" (p. 71).[12]

---

12   Rochdale has become better known as Roachdale. The building has become a residence where "radicals" of all stripes congregate under the watchful and benevolent eyes of the RCMP. It is much easier to keep track of them this way. As

Lastly, we have the Adelman prescription for "radical scholars" who know that "rules and social conventions are arbitrary but they nevertheless must master them, and in so doing, acquire 'scorn and disrespect for the present society' by embracing the whole bundle of rules and subverting them thereby." Again, what we have here is a liberally individualized view, which applies to the select, the few, the accomplished, not the many, the majority, or the totality of mankind.

*University Game* as an essay in self-liberation is the work of a potentially strong radical hand. If they develop and broaden their foundation, which I doubt very much, we could have the beginning of university life; but should they remain primarily concerned with a limited aspect of society, their work could only be regarded as beginning and no more. If they expand their basis of analysis to other social institutions with the same skill they exhibited in *University Game*, they will become the pioneers of a new social movement in Canada. But things Canadian are mainstream, and no one dares walk more than a half step ahead of the crowd. Furthermore, since the starting point is liberal, return to the fold is all a matter of time. For this reason, genuine radicals and revolutionaries must not be diverted by such games and must proceed to create their own institutions.

---

an educational experiment, Rochdale has collapsed, and its "founders" are fighting among themselves to divide the remaining riches. Indeed, one or two of them have made a fortune in the process and are branching out into other enterprises such as real estate.

# Chapter 12

## The Thoughts of Comrade Bissell

Claude Bissell is one of the very few university presidents in a multiversity on this continent that has thus far escaped unscathed the tidal wave of student activism. Men of much greater distinction, stature, and ability have either been swept by the tide or their reputations suffered irreparable damage: from Berkeley's Kerr to Columbia's Kirk, to Cornell's Perkins, to City College's Gallecher, to the near ouster of Harvard's Pussey and Chicago's Lowi, to the bruising of Yale's Brewster and Princeton's Goheen. All those educational *entrepreneurs* and many of their confreres at the most prestigious institutions like Stanford, Wisconsin, Michigan, MIT, etc., have encountered some form of student rebellion that tarnished their reputations or caused their downfall. Claude Bissell is the exception. Why? Has revolt been averted at U of T because of the stodginess and inertia of its hierarchical structure, because of the deferential values inculcated by its teachers and imbibed by its students; or is it because of Bissell's nimbleness as a public relations agent, his clever salesmanship of bourgeois norms, his bland moral stances, his intellectual mediocrity (this will be shown in the book under review), his firmness and flexibility; or is it because of student fatalism and apathy, and faculty abdication and collaboration; and finally, is it because the U of T, the citadel of colonialism, and structural organic conservatism in Canada is impregnable to assault and impervious to the laws of contagion? What, indeed, is the secret of Claude Bissell, if there is one? Why had he survived?

Many reasons could be adduced to explain the durability of Mr. Bissell since he was appointed president of U of T in 1958. Bissell has had an excellent press that has celebrated his deeds however insignificant. He has been a faithful and loyal servant to his class by effectively carrying out its will and performing according to its dictates, a class that has rewarded him by giving him continued and sustained material and moral support. The ruling class has confidence in Bissell. It will not abandon him unless he commits irreversible blunders. If he does, his heavenly mandate will be terminated in a Canadian manner, not by dramatic action but by the slow dismantling of his authority, his eclipse, his almost-unannounced exit. Canadian confrontations are not vivacious, public encounters whose outcomes depend on the power and potency of individual contestants, but are vicious backstage knifings, conspiracies, plots and counterplots, intrigues, bribes. In brief, the intellectual and social conflicts of Canada are unadorned middle-age security-conscious combats. The next two or three years will test the Bissell-like style of university politics as student radicalism gathers momentum, the colonial mentality erodes, and the political culture disintegrates. Bissell could very well weather the oncoming storm, but he is not likely to come out undrenched. If he does so, he will have to be pronounced the most resilient, agile man of the age. That he and the U of T have survived is no reason to believe that they are invincible. For this reason, Dean Ernest Sirluck's "Opinion" (*Toronto Daily Star*, July 28, 1969, p. 7) is basically a lie.

After Sirluck conjures up a conspiracy that has allegedly been thwarted and makes a concession that the U of T is a "tradition-bound university, with an obsolete structure of governance and no means of fundamental reorganization other than provincial legislation," he points out why the U of T enjoyed "freedom from disruption" during the 1968–1969 academic year. He says that "the militants used faulty tactics"; that they "underestimated the critical intelligence" of student; that the university "has now genuinely accepted the need for very extensive change to bring it into harmony with current conditions, and it is moving in that direction with what, for it, is quite remarkable expedition"; that the university has persuaded the student body of the "reality and irreversibility of its commitment" to change and of "the effectiveness of the methods it has chosen for achieving them." The evidence for this deception abounds; for structural change, it is nil. Nevertheless, Sirluck and company have discovered that an "open" autocracy is more viable than a closed one, not realizing that the new generation of Canadians will not be assuaged by verbiage and liberal rhetoric but by the abolition of his "tradition-bound university," the dismissal of its high priests, and its restructuring. That regular liberals will forever *be* deceived by the likes of Sirluck, we can confidently predict, but we can also predict that a new age is dawning for Canada that will not encompass the Bissells and their mentors—*The Age of The Intellectual Worker* in a liberated Canada. Let us, therefore, return to an examination of the collected wisdom of comrade Bissell to refute Sirluck and expose Bissell.

One of the biggest lies propagated in *The Strength of the University*[13] by Bissell is that the university is a "primary institution" whose "primacy issues not alone from the university's success in preparing men and women for professional life and in uncovering new sources of material power, but from its nourishing of social and political ideas and its part in fashioning man, the creator and artist" (p. 3). Bissell does not offer a shred of evidence for these pseudo-poetic assertions. What social and political ideas did the U of T "nourish" under his stewardship and suzerainty or, indeed, in its history of one and a half centuries? Can Mr. Bissell, or any of his squires for that matter, point to a single Canadian idea or Canadian political philosopher? In fact, is there such a thing as a Canadian history of political philosophy and philosophers? If not, we must dismiss the university as sheer hypocrisy that does not "fashion man, the creator and artist" but distorts his perception and warps his thinking. That this is the case can be easily ascertained from the kind of contempt. Mr. Bissell manifests for ideas that challenge his empire building and his apologia for the bourgeois. He alludes to the university as finding itself "the centre of a bitter moral dispute that arises from an increasing sense of alienation from the goals of society" (p. 9) and deprecates "secular revivalism" as a cyclical minority movement. He professes to be a "democrat"; but instead of encouraging students and faculties to participate in decisions affecting their lives and fostering democracy, he goes on a tangent to attack students trained in "the Machiavellianism of the left" who, according to the Holy See, have discovered that the university is "sensitive to the use of force" and, being dedicated to the "rational reconciliation of conflicts," it is at the "mercy of those who choose to use the tactics of compulsion or of crude force" (p. 11). If the students were cleverer, they could take a leaf or two from Bissell's book of machinations and Machiavellianism, but some satraps like Bissell think that such "civilized" activities are the exclusive preserve of the ruling class especially since they possess police power to enforce their well and since there are enough fools to believe them. To soften this unscrupulous and scurrilous attack on the left, Bissell

---

[13]   University of Toronto Press, 1968.

returns to the time-honored liberal doctrine of shallow syncretism. He declared that "the university should maintain its traditional stance of watchful reservation" on the affairs of society as if the university ever did anything not assigned to it, then complacently announced that the university "should recognize and welcome the growing areas of common concern and the role of the university in providing the expert knowledge upon which political decisions must be based." To further illustrate his liberality, Mr. Bissell affirms that "the university must accord to faculty and to students an increasingly larger role." The role, of course, is not defined, and the gradualist posture is nullified by the proviso: "This does not mean, however, that the university should accept the naïve concepts taken over from political life by student movements and crudely applied to the university setting" (pp. 12–13). In case we failed to appreciate Mr. Bissell's bureaucratic elitism in the past, we should no longer do so: "Surely the university is the last place where quantitative political ideas should be given the dignity of doctrines" (p. 13).

If the university cannot be considered a bourgeois democracy, why should the corporation, political party, civil service, the military, newspaper, or any other institution be? Apparently, only those endowed with infinite wisdom like Bissell can lead; others cannot manage their affairs without his guardianship. Such anti-democratic sentiments are attenuated by Bissell's transparent cosmopolitanism. He approvingly quotes St. John Galbraith of the Liberal Order of Philistines to the effect that the university need not (as if it has not) "choose to become a subservient ally of the corporation" but "assert its independence and become a forge for skepticism, emancipation and pluralism." We mistakenly thought Harvard and her sister U of T where the two gentlemen occupy seats of learning had been doing precisely that all the time! Where has Mr. Bissell been? Furthermore, Bissell's worldliness takes on a pontifical-ecumenical physiognomy as he points to Canada's history as having been a search for a focal point for national life" and of Durham's idea of Canada as "the laboratory of the Empire, evolving ideal political patterns that could be transferred elsewhere" (p. 16). The clear implication of this pronouncement is, of course, that Canada should become the "umpire in the clash of principalities" with the "splendid synthesis" of two notions, which will be greatly strengthened by "the systematic support of our universities, and by the creation both in English-speaking and

French-speaking Canada of several internationally-recognized centres of scholarship" (p. 17).

Thus wrote Bissell in 1968 in his introduction to the *Strength of the University*. Let us now reproduce and evaluate, in fashion, the speeches Bissell considers the summation of his thought in the past decade or so.

The first section of the book deals with the students. Bissell flatters his students in a standard "opening address" by telling them that they are "indispensable" to his enterprise. "You are the raison d'être of the of the institutions," he fervently declares as he foxily concedes that "presidents are particularly subject to a form of myopia which makes it difficult to recognize individual students." Bissell informs his students that they are summoned as citizen "to roles of high responsibility and wider loyalty" (p. 23). He deplores student "immaturity" and proclaims: "In any country he students are passive and tractable, if passionate concern for the general good, enthusiasm for ideals, and zeal for reform are not to be found in academic halls, then that country is prey to a malignant disease" (p. 24). I wonder what country, if any, Mr. Bissell had in mind in this comment. Moreover, he advises his students not to be "spherical" but "angular": "During your university days you should emphasize concentration and intensity; you should not be in the least afraid of being angular or lop-sided" (p. 25). In this so-called voyage of self-discovery, the students are urged to do battle with "spiritual confusion" and fight for respect of the individual and "belief in the freedom of the human spirit" (p. 27). The gospel of angularity must have had some disturbing repercussions on U of T thinkers. Therefore, the stilted balance had to be restored, and Bissell (1959) expounded further the doctrine of "proper angularity," which must be based upon "a background of knowledge and upon submission to discipline." In other words, Bissell wants his audience to understand that angularity is "not the production of a race of angry young men and women" (p. 31) but, basically, nice and responsible people like himself! People who embody the "new mood" (civil rights) embrace the doctrine of "racial equality" and are prepared to "put their bodies on the line" (p. 31). Bissell welcomes this "increasing sophistication" of students but deplores "the old surliness and self-glorification" and the "new aggressiveness," which are "the after-effects of permissiveness" (p. 40). Angularity deteriorates further as Bissell confronts the "new radicalism" and begins to feel that he too could become its victim.

He pinpoints the radical assumptions of revolt against institutionalism, the demand for relevance, the democratization of life and condescendingly characterizes the militants as "romantics" who are "part of that recurring cycle of protest against reason, order, and selectivity that constitute the classical virtues" (p. 50). Bissell makes a disarming statement about the salutary effects of this radical propensity and flatulently declares: "But capitulation to these romantic assumptions would be more dangerous than stubborn opposition or indifference. For radical romanticism can lead to a denial of intelligence, to an emotional anarchy that in the past has been the prelude to political and social darkness" (p. 51): this emphatic inflexibility alone should dispel all illusionism about Bissell's suave reasonableness and adaptability and disqualify him and his class as being capable of making structural change and fathoming the new radical environment. Such romantic organic conservatism, however sacrosanct and firmly entrenched it may be, is a welcome enemy to confront and defect. Its sanctimonious posturing and repugnant orthodoxy are likely to enrage the vacillating radical rather than assuage him, thereby contributing to its own collapse.

In the second part of the *Strength of the University*, Bissell grapples with the issues of curricula and governance. He foresees two dangers that threaten the university: the onrushing wave of students and the tendency of business and industrial concepts "to take over in areas where they are irrelevant" (p. 75). Bissell proposes to obviate the first danger by not converting (as if he has not) his institution into a social agency "for the relief of the dull and the dim-witted" (p. 74). His university is opposed to "mass, mechanical education," and it is a place of "serenity and productive leisure" where the scholar is "king" (p. 76). Bissell's scholar could more accurately be depicted as vassal or knight to the only true king. On the second danger to the university, Bissell contrasts liberal education with professional education and accommodates both as a "good liberal businessman." He cites Newman, at length, to emphasize the "disinterested cultivation of the mind" and its "immersion in the philosophical habit" (p. 81) that would prepare "the individual for any of the professions" (p. 88). He explains that professionalism involves specialization, technique, utilitarianism (p. 93) and concludes by arguing that the "house of intellect" ought to be a place of coexistence for this technocratic and scientific biases and the "apocalyptic mode" of thought (pp. 122–125).

As to the government of the university, Mr. Bissell makes a "revolutionary" proposal he announced before a meeting of the Association of University and Colleges in 1966, a pronouncement that has not been fully appreciated by the radicals: he *advocates the abolition of the board of governors and the academic senate*. He discerns two major inadequacies in the present setup and labels a system of "double innocence": "He first one is the enormous waste of time involved in the maintenance of two supreme governing bodies with the consequent multiplication of staff. The second inadequacy is the intensification of the inherent suspicion between the academic and the lay" (p. 149). Without imputing any sinister motives to Mr. Bissell, we must point out that his advocacy of this unitary form of government amounts to the removal of the only two existing impediments there are to personal rule, to Gaullism. Indeed, to a voyeurist, Bissell's proposal is no less than a proclamation of unadulterated Caesaropapism. It involves neither a presidential nor a parliamentary system of accountability. It is a Fascist liberalism with style. It ought to be strenuously opposed as it stands unless the corollary of the proposal—electivity—accompanies it. As the proposal stands, Bissell will continue as U of T Caesar, his "impartial" retinue as pro-consuls, the chairmen as Roman senators, the faculty as couriers between presidents and provincial governments, and the students as subjects of the far-flung empire. The least that could be expected is that Bissell will be anointed prime minister for life. If this were not Bissell's intention and aspiration, what provisions, if any, did he provide for the election of president and executive committee? None! What kind of power did he plan to "delegate"? What kind of sovereign did he want to be? Surely, not a male Queen Elizabeth? But Bissell is intelligent; the U of T Commission on University Government adopted and proclaimed his proposal as its own, and the good Mr. Bissell did not stoop to sign the proclamation!

In the third part of the book, Bissell discusses the role and purpose of the university. As usual, Bissell begins by making obeisance to the value of non-conformity, then proceeds obtusely to cope with the subject at hand. The first issue is "business and the university." He states that "business has interpenetrated society, and in doing so it has been responsible for creating a dominant pattern" (p. 169). He criticizes business for having usurped "a dominating position in the undergraduate curriculum," but of course, he will make no effort to dislodge it" (p. 171). Therefore, he shifts his grounds and attacks advertising for substituting "mass instinct for thought" (p. 174) and pleads with the university not to "capitulate to shortsighted requests of business" (p. 175) without distinguishing between the short and farsighted requirements of business.

On the question of "moral values," Bissell makes a cursory examination of the religious, humanistic, and scientific traditions and asserts that "although the university is not a moral agent, although it is not a substitute for the church, it should never make the pursuit of its great goal, intellectual illumination, an excuse for ignoring or slighting moral values" (p. 210).

Lastly, on such issues as academic freedom, the independence of the university, power, and education, Bissell cannot be accused of novelty or imagination. He inveighs against the doctrine of "environmental appropriateness" under which the professor has the right "to roar like a lion in his own house, but outside he should mew like a kitten" (p. 214). He does not point out, however, that his university would not condone or appoint roaring lions but castrated liberal academics who "mew on the campus" but purr outside it! With reference to "independence," Bissell aims at absolute control over his bailiwick. He wants to be able to determine who shall teach, who shall be taught, what shall be taught and how the financial resources will be distributed (p. 236). On power, Bissell hopes to see the power of persuasion prevail because it is more conducive to university life though it "may not attract much contract research to the university" (p. 244), but he will unhesitatingly call on the power of compulsion to retain his power should anyone entertain the notion of overthrowing him or try to disrupt his bureaucratic empire.

In sum, Bissell is the consummate liberal administrator who displays liberality in the absence of civil war or the threat of it but absolute ruthlessness and arbitrariness should the barbarian hordes be seen at the gates of the empire. Will the Caesars forever prevail? Will the Huns be absorbed by the empire again? Will we have a new age of darkness or nuclear holocaust?

# Chapter 13

——◆◇◆——

# The American Model

The university, whether we regard it an irrelevant institution, a firehouse, a powerhouse, or a service station, is no more than a reflection of the society and social formation in which it operates. Moreover, like most institutions, it retains, in various mutations, its original animating principle, whether it be the training of the clerics in metaphysical and otherworldly values, the preparing of bourgeois clerks in the predatory tricks of self-advancement and aggrandizement, or the humanizing of man by instilling in him communal norms and social concerns. In brief, the university is a creature of its time. What functions it will assume, what projects it will embark upon, what issues it will take up or fail to touch will be determined not by its cloistered personnel but by the social forces at work in that particular society.

In North America, we are in the age of monopoly capitalism, advanced technology, counter-insurgency, general retreat of capitalism, and home entrenchment; and above all, we live in an epoch of imperialist disintegration, international civil war, the rise of the oppressed, the division of the socialist world, the floundering of the national colonial revolutions, the refocusing of world history. It is in this context that we must view the North American university, its direction, purposes, and the kind of services it will render and to whom. It is, therefore, palpable that the university is a bourgeois institution, and it must be examined in this milieu as such.

No serious revolutionary Socialist could fail to detect the conflicts—religious and metaphysical—that split the contending forces for supremacy in a capitalist university. There are those who appeal to the "idea of a university" propounded by John Henry Newman who was

175

instrumental in the founding of Dublin University in 1852. Newman's model was the Oxford of his idea—a university that manufactured the cultivated "gentlemen" and generalist that ruled his inferiors, expanded the empire, and trained its natives. Oxford was based on the Paris model, which was a medieval theological disputationist school. But in England, the spirit of nascent materialism as reflected in the rise of the bourgeois and its wars affected the nature of Oxford, where the spirit of feudalism fought strenuously to defeat the coming of capitalism. Finally, capitalism penetrated feudalism and overwhelmed its upholders. Nevertheless, its structural vestiges remained and remain to this day in all bourgeois universities, i.e., authoritarian hierarchy, metaphysical mysticism, the divine rights of rulers.

On the other hand, there are those who advocate the German model, *The Modern University*, best portrayed by Abraham Flexner and distilled from the *Berlin* experience of 1809, where "the emphasis was on philosophy and science, on research, on graduate instruction, on the freedom of professors and students." The Berlin model embodied science and nationalism. It reflected the rise of the bourgeois spirit in Germany. Then we have in this age "the idea of a multiversity," a phenomenon sketched by Clark Kerr in the Bodkin lectures at Harvard University in 1953. As a perceptive analyst, Kerr described what he was witnessing and implicitly promoting in the age of the "end of ideology" in America. One can hardly discern any overt ideological commitment on the part of Mr. Kerr until page 125 of his 126-page essay.[14] After his gratuitous advice that no theorist has ever been as "incorrect" as Marx yet "so influential," Kerr declared that "the wave of the future may more nearly be middle-class democracy, with all its freedoms, through its better use of intellect in all intellect's many dimensions, than "the dictatorship of the proletariat" (which, in fact, is the dictatorship of the single part).

The crucial point to understand in reviewing the work of Kerr and his ilk is that they look upon the multiversity as a non-ideological "knowledge industry" that will be the focal point of national growth in the second part of twentieth century in the same manner that the railroad was in the nineteenth century, and the car was in first half of this century (p. 88). Kerr, of course, like all liberal ideologues, accepts the status quo as his starting point without questioning its validity or legitimacy. He also pays lip service to liberalism and civil rights, but this tactic is merely

---

[14]   *The Uses of The University* (Cambridge, MA: Harvard University Press, 1963).

designed to disarm the gullible and those who enjoy being deceived. Put differently, the multiversity to him is some sort of an accident that just happened—that nobody planned, intended, or willed. It is like the Vietnam War; the United States just appeared to be there! In Kerr's words: "No man created it; in fact, no man visualized it" (p. 99).

If this were the case, how on earth did the penny-pinching state legislatures and federal government ever allocate literally billions of dollars ever annum? How did it come to pass that the United States is the greatest industrial giant of the world, with the best-trained labor force and the most docile working class? How was it possible for America to produce the bomb, to destroy its natural environment, to achieve world hegemony? Is it not because the United States has the most effective system of miseducation that creates the bourgeois automaton, the individual atom, the servile slave? Is it not because Kerr is an unconscious cog in the "knowledge industry" whose center is the university? Or should we merely regard the university as "a mechanism—a series of processes producing a series of results—a mechanism held together by administrative rules and powered by money" (p. 20)? But unluckily for Mr. Kerr, he gives away his cards in revealing that the students are "consumers" whose choices "guide university expansion and contraction" and who by their "patronage" determine the kind of teaching they will have and teachers who will teach them (p. 22). Kerr's ideology can now be clearly disclosed: he not only advocates consumerism and treats the multiversity as an overweening bureaucracy but also expounds corporate capitalism and predicts its inevitable and universal victory.

Kerr traces the historic strands of the multiversity to the models alluded to earlier but much more specifically to the land grand movement (the Morrill Land Grant Act of 1862) and its merger with German intellectualism. What he fails to underscore in his cursory remarks is the elementary fact that the American college is the mirror of American socioeconomic evolution and, indeed, a microcosm of U.S. social reality. However, such recognition of history will mar the liberal picture of reality and make the multiversity look like a center not only of industry but also of prescribed values and ideas. The most important aspect of the multiversity is the subjugation of science and its use to enhance capitalist growth and world dominion. Moreover, Kerr's smug and complacent liberalism assumes universal dimensions in his passive Quaker imperialism of the future. The multiversity will not only become pervasive in America, but it will become the universal model. Let Mr. Kerr speak for himself: "The university is being called upon to educate previously unimagined numbers of students; to respond to the expanding claims of national service; to merge its activities with industry as never before; to adapt to and rechannel new intellectual currents. By the end of this period, there will be a truly American university, an institution not looking to other models but serving, itself, as model for universities in other parts of the globe. This is not said in boast. It is simply that the imperatives that have molded the American university are at work around the world" (pp. 36–37).

It should be noted that the Kerr model is based on universal harmony. That is not to say that there will be no localized internal conflicts in the multiversity but to suggest that the multiversity is of this world of liberal illusionism where presidents like Kerr wield power without opposition and "educate" people in the "natural" doctrines of corporate capitalism. This false notion, of course, was dispelled in the autumn of 1964 at Berkeley when Mr. Kerr became the victim of his own illusions and lost his position: the consumers revolted against the producers and labeled the commodities shoddy and poisonous. The owners were appalled by this ungrateful act of rebellion and discovered a flaw not in the organization of production or the product and its nature but in the packaging and distribution of the product. Therefore, it was decided that the general manager and his subordinates be dismissed. Thus, the beginning of the Berkeley phenomenon was ushered into our era of student turbulence and campus confrontation. At Columbia, to the charges of impersonality and bureaucracy was added the charge of the imperialist university: territorial expansion into a neighboring colony and counter-insurgency services for the warlords. In Paris, an effort was made to create a worker-student alliance; and at Southern, in New Orleans, the blacks proclaimed their symbolic independence. The University, the world over is an occupied Palestine manned by the surrogates and the legions of world imperialism. The rebels everywhere are Palestinians in dispersion. Some have given up, others have recovered their sense of manhood and are girding up their loins for the day of battle, while the advanced cadres are striking terror in the hearts of Jerusalem, Tel Aviv, and Kaifa. The courageous among them are setting up models to emulate and paragons to follow—may they form a million Fatah!

According to Kerr, the multiversity is the wave of the future. He is probably right. But in the halls of Ivy, nostalgic spirits have emerged to challenge the multiversity idea and attack its welfarism and societal involvement in the name of "liberal education." The attackers offer no alternative. Their attacks, however, are a brake, a retarding force, a diversionary tactic that will slow down rather than alter the course of events. Of these, Barzun[15] of Columbia is the most eminent.

Barzun is an unrepentant bourgeois gentleman who for twelve years presided with Grayson Kirk over the disintegration of Columbia and found "no reason to change or add to the substance of what I had written" as a result of a student upheaval at Columbia on April 23, 1963. He, like his Bourbon predecessors, "learned nothing and forgot nothing"! At any rate, his book attacks the university as a residual (welfare) institution and deplores its openness. To Barzun, the university ought to be selective; it "should be and remain One, not Many, singular not plural, a republic, not an empire; and that no matter how old, large, rich, or conceited, it should from time to time join with other universities to introduce ripened innovations" (p. 246). While Barzun does not call for the revocation of the multiversity, he calls for continued tight controls by administrators and reviles students and faculty for desiring to degrade democracy by insisting on participation in university government. He favors the traditional lecture method and expects the university to "watch over the public's intellectual diet and interpose a corrective when called for!" (p. 281)

As a further gesture of liberality, Barzun concedes that "the ever-present sense of arrangement" is the result of "the computered life" of the student, "the new assumptions and multiplied relationships of the university that have destroyed the old calm" (p. 17). But on closer examination, we find that Barzun inveighs against the "new Christianity" of students and dubs them "rebels without a cause" bent on destruction (pp. 74–77). Without reproducing the hackneyed arguments of this literary liberal, we ought to point out that he thinks students "fight on slight pretexts" (p. 64) because they are young and have "social and individual resentments" (p. 65). So much for Pope Barzun and his pseudo-Freudian psychologism! We also find a speck of Freudian Marxism in Barzun. He contends that society is the "villain" because it requires a "mandarin system" of qualifications (p. 65). Yet with inevitable Freudian pessimism, Barzun expects the present trends to continue because society

15   *The American University* (NY: Harper and Row, 1968).

does not want to detechnify and deprofessionalize its structures. What is most striking, however, is that Barzun opposes faculty participation in university governments on the ground that professors prefer naked generalities, fear finality, lack concrete imaginations, and are timid. Besides, they cannot be trusted with the secret affairs of the university, and they are indecisive and impatient with niggling routines (pp. 125–130). Barzun's opposition to student participation is based on the idea that they are at the university to learn, not to govern, and the "veritable student" is one who is there to be taught, not one who "presumes to teach" (pp. 90–91). Campus agitators, he contends, "are only enlarging the tactics of the *enfant terrible*, whose chief trait is that he does not quite know what he wants, though his desire to "see how far he can push" is shrewd and strong" (pp. 88–89). Furthermore, students do not have the time or knowledge to administer or are reliable enough to be privy to the secrets of administration, and in a most damning summation, Barzun states that "it is not likely that as policymakers students would concentrate on dispatch, or regard as binding the seal of confidence in matters touching rank, salary, or susceptibilities. They would honestly not see why anybody should care" (p. 85).

Faced with aristocratic and outdated grandiloquence, need we probe further into the causes of the Columbia uprising? Need we ask any more questions? Need we wonder why it was inevitable? Oh, how the sage of Columbia wished his students to eat cake rather than storm Columbia's Bastille!

# PART 4

# Chapter 14

## Rousseau's Emile: Education for Enlightenment

This essay is designed to praise and defend mankind and slander our sacred institutions. In it, I hope to defend man's essence against his existence, man's core against his surface, man's reality against his appearance. And that is in essence the significance of the question, "Education for what?" Education for servitude or for liberty? But before we enter into the substance of the question, I ought to underscore the motivation and the significance of Emile and the meaning of morality, which underpin the Rousseauist hypothesis. To Rousseau, morality has something to do with character evaluation; it is a judgement about what is wrong and what is right, what is good and what is bad, what is ugly and what is beautiful, etc., that is the subject matter of morality. As to its components, it consists of an instrumentalist or utilitarian ethic, which refers to the ways and means of carrying out practical reason into effect. The second component is a transcendentalist ethic, which by and large looks to a heteronomous source as the ultimate fount of its authority. Moreover, Rousseau begins with a teleological view of nature, which is the source of his moral outrage against technological civilization, which homogenizes us and undermines our search for the question "Who am I?" and therefore underlines the absence of self and community in our life. By this type of analysis, we discover the fundamental task of education and its moral function. If we regard education as something essentially vocational, then we have negated the character of man and community. If we regard it as instruction to habituate us in the good, then we have a different type of education, and this is the kind Rousseau advocates. He does because ape training, appearance glossing, market orientation, and other features of "education" are a negation of man. This type of education is valueless because it merely trains the child to become a trader. This does not imply that Rousseau does not want to train the child to learn to acquire a livelihood. On the contrary, in a technological society, this is an essential prerequisite, and Rousseau recognizes it but wants to stress liberal education and values, not vocationalism and professionalism, as the supreme goals of education.

With this normative posture, Rousseau takes a child who is no prodigy or genius, and he tries to teach him life from infancy to manhood, and he supervises his entire training from childhood to marriage, which is the entire story of *Emile*.

As an eighteenth-century man, Rousseau was revolting against the evolving cult of efficiency, which replaces the human value of liberation. To him, education is "nurture"—the nurture of the mind, its cultivation and liberation by its development. In this process of development, the man, the citizen, the lover are created. Therefore, the purpose of education is intellectual and emotional growth; if education is not intellectual and emotional growth, it is not education. It is the destruction and suppression of all that is human in man. And this is why contemporary education is no more than an adjunct to technological civilization where artificiality and superfluity replace need and luxury becomes necessity. This process, of course, makes man a slave to things, a slave to his car, to his furniture, to his friends, and indeed a victim to superfluity and to social pressure. He loses his autonomy, his self, his being; he is dehumanized, and education eases the burden of transition from potential freedom to absolute slavery.

Thus, all that is holy in man dies; he becomes victim of the machine, victim of change for the sake of change, victim of what is called the "marginal man," a man whose business is the multiplication of wants, the manufacturing of wants, the sale of unnecessary and spurious goods. Here then in a nutshell the problem in *Emile*: how to overcome uniformity and its ugliness, and avoid victimization, and how to create an autonomous man in a debilitating and enervating social environment. The problem of alienation or incipient alienation begins here also. That is why Rousseau declares that man is born free and is everywhere in chains. And his first comment in *Emile*: God makes all things good; man meddles with them, and they become evil. He forces one soil to yield the products of another, one tree to bear another's fruit; he confuses and confounds time, place, and natural condition. He mutilates his dog, his horse, and his slave, etc. You see, man has alienated himself, nature, and his species. Alienation begins with the first gift we give the child, which is fetters. We deform and torture him. We give him clothes. The first symbols of civilization, or what is called civilization. And in so doing, this socialization process of a given particular "civilization" commences by cultivating in the child the values we uphold and the environment we subjugate and are subjugated by—things that are considered sacrosanct by us, holy, beautiful, and sublime. This is the essence of dehumanization. Our peculiar civilization is being imposed by making the child or creating him in our own image and producing our own replica, which is the antithesis of civilization and, of course, the antithesis of man and his negation. If we can recognize this problem, we can begin to nurture the child to create the man, the good man. If not, our philosophy of education is conceived and born in falsehood. Moreover, we have the problem of educating the "educator," and here the question is, can the slave train you to be free? The answer is self-evident; and the "educator" must first be educated himself, which is a much more difficult process of unaided self-liberation. With our educator, we go back and trace our steps, and walk step by step with Emile to determine how growth develops and how his nature unfolds.

If we aim to cultivate feeling and humaneness in the child, we must train him in one habit, namely, to have no habits. This is basic, but Rousseau does not offer us ways and means of training people how to have no habits. The only thing he advises is not to allow a child or make a child habituated in doing routine or aggrandized things. Rousseau understands that life has its aspects of creativity, as well as its aspects of routine and regularity; and he is aware of the laws of biology, which cannot be tampered with. This is the "law of necessity," which is the only natural law, and all other laws are man-made and designed to suppress man and to destroy him.

Thus, we begin with the child as a biological entity whose nature requires physical nurture and whose human potential requires a mother to help actualize it. According to Rousseau, the mother has to look after her child herself and forget about society, appearance, and substitute mothers. Without motherhood, he contends there can be no development of feeling, and a child cannot develop feeling if every other day there is a babysitter whose function it is to merely service his physical needs. He needs love, and only a mother can give that. Moreover, to develop feelings and sensibilities, the pyschosocial environment must be conducive to growth. Surroundings, care, and affection are particularly essential in his formative years; and these are crucial years—the first two or three years of the child's life—and determine the character of the emotional and intellectual growth of the child. If his emotions are developed, a life of balance and proportion will ensue. If they are thwarted and suppressed, the slave is in the making. He will learn to lie and smile and play the game of artificiality. He becomes an automaton, a plaything for anyone to manipulate and buy for a price. He becomes the salesman with the pleasant solicitude of the slave.

We therefore must avoid the conventional "teachers" who only know how to produce hypocrites. They are slaves and capable only of producing their likes. So are the doctors and the nurses vis-à-vis the child's physical nature; both are corrupters, spiritual and physical. But the teacher is the worst. He preaches and moralizes; he is a pedant. He is not a man. He corrupts the students. If he is to help the child grow, the teacher must be the model, the example of the student. It is the deed and the action of the teacher that matter, not his words, which are the tools of tyrants to wheedle us into believing in lies and cleverness. Such a corrupter thinks of advantages to himself first and then to his pupils. He provides them with goods, which can be readily displayed in the shop windows of the marketplace, not the temple of life and its social intercourse of virtue.

Thus, the first lesson in hypocrisy, in inauthenticity, in immorality comes from the teacher. But this can be reversed by the good teacher whose art turns the child's attention from trivial details and guides his thoughts continually toward relations of importance, which he one day may need to know that he may judge rightly of good and evil in human society. Hence, the function of the teacher is to turn the child's inner light toward the true light, to bring him to the threshold of his mind, to teach him reason so that he can learn to compare, evaluate, and examine relations. And therefore, the babble of teachers and their employers about order, discipline, authority, and taxpayers, etc., is the negation of education, the obliteration of the desire to learn, the annihilation of the child. We then must pose the question of method: what is the method of good teaching? If the teacher's function is so crucial, his deeds and his actions are much more important than his words, his pedantry, and his footnotes. We are training people for manhood, not automatons for personnel. Therefore, the method must depend on man's powers at different ages and the choice of occupations adapted to those powers. In other words, Rousseau says, fit man's education to his real self, not to what is no part of him. The method of education must be designed to help the person realize his potential and develop his sensibilities and powers as a human being. Education is then for freedom, to liberate man from the tyranny of public opinion, to liberate him from impulsive and compulsive behaviour, and to teach him the laws of morality. In brief, it is a training for civility, not for executive positions in the political economy of the marketplace. If that is the purpose and value of education, and if that is the way we educate people for the good life, then the schools of society are schools of falsehood and the academies are places for chatter and illusionism and the teachers are the chatterboxes—the source of hypocrisy and evil and the world of make believe. Our objective here is not to teach callousness and money making but suffering—the suffering of humanity. Emile will be trained not to become an ape but a human being, sensitive to the cries of mankind. And he will be trained to distinguish falsehood from truth, appearance from reality, vice from virtue, and in the process learn why he holds beliefs so that he will lead the examined, not the unexamined life. In sum, Emile will be educated in temperance, patience, steadfastness, courage, imagination, and humaneness.

To traverse this arduous path of education, Emile's tutor will live with him from age one to twenty-four, approximately. Rousseau is not specific about age because exposure to various aspects of life is related to one's emotional and intellectual maturity, and the teaching of standard school subjects is related to the readiness and eagerness of the child to acquire much information. As Rousseau sees it, the real problem in education is that the child is taught to ask theological and metaphysical questions when neither he nor his parents or teachers know the answers. Education in theology will be introduced in early adulthood, not in infancy when the child possesses only sensation that can develop into perception. Therefore, education must start with physical objects that are visible to the naked eye and teach him introductory geography and things related to his immediate environment. At about twelve, we must expose him to sex education not by stimulating his curiosity but by treating sex as a natural subject, without mystery or confusion or suggestive smiles. On the question of sex, the emphasis, Rousseau believes, should be placed on childbearing, which inspires repugnance, fear of death, not "romantic" love and the joys of sexual escapism. The idea here is to teach Emile through experience and not to mystify the sex relationship, which conduces curiosity and impels him to pose more and more questions that will be embarrassing to teacher and pupil. But if he insists, the answers must be forthcoming and expressed as plainly and as simply and as clearly as possible with this provision, that complete respect for the human body and the human relationship is maintained. Emile only knows by experience and not from books; he has to be shown but with reverent awe before the creation of nature. And Rousseau asserts if we have no respect for physical nature, we cannot have respect for the biological.

At twelve, Emile's adolescence launches him on an emotional and social consciousness, which compounds his problems and those of his tutor. He has reached a turbulent age when intimacy, trust, and confidence are required for his further development. He and his tutor must exercise mutual reciprocity. And the tutor's authority must rest on the authority of his reason, his ability to instruct in the good life, not on his office. If this is the case, and if the teacher understands his function as that of activating the pupil's mind and teaching him to develop as a human being, he is a good teacher; if not, he is not worthy of the title.

If we can understand the need for this kind of relationship, we must ask, what is man, and is such relationship possible? Is man capable of being human as we defined humanity? If the answer is in the affirmative, obviously, it is possible to create an alternative system. If not, our effort is an exercise in futility.

Rousseau begins with the Greek premise that man is pliable and plastic, and therefore, he rejects the fixed nature idea. He sees man not as good or evil by nature but as a potentiality, capable of either good or evil. Evil, as he understands it, is acquired in society—the fetters of civilization and its masks, which make us bad. The question is then how we can overcome civilization, or can we? If so, how and when? Before the age of twelve, the only book we introduced to Emile was the book of life. The next book is *Robinson Crusoe*.

Our aim is to teach him the value of independence, which is necessary to unleashing his own initiative and creativity. In other words, here we introduce liberal values: the value of independence, of self, of personal integrity, and the right to exist as a human being capable of love, of manhood, and of citizenship. Self-love—that is the concern for one's well-being. It is the only innate passion man possesses. It must not be allowed to degenerate into selfishness, exploitation of others, and the use of others for our own purposes, which in part is the negation of self-love. It must not become greed. It must develop into a fellow feeling, which will enhance the growth of self and society and expand itself into a concern for others. Only self-love and conscience are inborn; reason and other passions are acquired. Conscience, however, is a feeble feeling. It cannot regulate our life without the development of reason. And reason, if not internalized as a value, cannot protect us. Thus, we have two internal attributes—the value of self-love and conscience—and reason to reinforce them. The problem in society, Rousseau says, is that self-love degenerates into selfishness, selfishness into greed, and a train of vices follow; and finally, we reach the level of pride and vanity, which are the most destructive of passions. Having attained this state of alienation, we define man as greedy and evil by nature so that our commercial, industrial economy can function and prosper. And in the final analysis, social Darwinism replaces liberalism as the greatest good of civilization, and the corporation becomes the source of ethics. To overcome commercialism, Emile is taught craftsmanship and workmanship to help him develop his independence, individuality and self-reliance. He is also taught history to discover the heart of men. Emile, at the age of fourteen, is studying about the deeds of man and their goodness, not evilness and rascality. He is taught history as a story of mankind, as development and evolution of civilization, as mastery of nature, and as conquests and glories of man.

At a later age, he will be introduced to the relapses in civilization. Meanwhile, ancient historians who write as spectators, not as sycophants, are to be studied for the moral lessons to be derived from their works. Moreover, to sharpen Emile's evaluative power, we next introduce him to philosophy because he has a need and a wish to know, and he must obtain an impartiality to judge by developing his reasoning faculty. This philosophy cannot be barefaced sophistry or systems of non-systems; it must be an inculcation of reason and virtue. Otherwise, Emile will not be able to unmask theology—which is prejudice triumphant, pride, and dishonesty—and expose the theologians, the liars of mankind, the parasites of civilization. He will also be taught that religion is a matter of geography and the only true religion is that of the heart, the love of our creator, nature, and fellow man.

Emile's curriculum from geography to religion completes his studies of himself, environment, and manhood. In becoming a man and an individual in society, Emile has obligations as a citizen and a husband; and more importantly, he needs to develop his consciousness of his species and enlarge it. He is introduced to a sweetheart of comparable tastes, talents, and background but of less learning and worldliness. Then he is sent off on a two-year travel scheme to acquaint him with the world and increase his knowledge of social and human geography, thereby lessening his ethnocentricity and teaching his respect for other cultures. Upon completion of the journey, Emile plunges into the study of political science and citizenship; and at twenty-four, he marries Sophie, the model of simple humaneness, lovingness and cooperation. Sophy is a good woman who complements rather than rivals Emile. His reasoning and physical powers are greater than hers, but such weaknesses are compensated for by the natural art of cunning inborn in women. Emile marries Sophie, and the tutor is informed that she will be giving birth to a child. Thereupon, he ceases being the instructor, and Emile and his beloved are able to function on their own in a self-regulating conjugal society and not leading the life of "other-directedness."

We have an organic body politic. The individual is not only to be disinterred and enhanced, but he is part of the new universe; he is a citizen and has moral obligations as a citizen. And our Emile is not only part obligation, but he is part white, and he knows what his rights are as a citizen and as a man. Then the only inherent rights are the rights to liberty and the rights to property, and that is why society and institutions are created. There is no reason why Emile or you or I should enter society and let society free to protect liberty and property and to actualize our potentiality. And if it does not do that, it is not a society but a babble of tongues and a forgery that destroys men. And so that is the real crucial problem in teaching him about religion, philosophy, history, and all the subjects you and I have to learn. And so we have Emile taught the things that attain nature and develop his potential. At ten, he says, Emile will seek kicks; at twenty, a mistress; at thirty, pleasure; at forty, ambition; at fifty, avarice. And the question is posed, when will he seek good?

At this juncture, we confront two issues: the upbringing of Sophie and society where they must live. Now, how are we to train a female? Well, we are to train her in needlework, dressmaking, and other things (p. 163). He says the weak, feeble timid man is condemned by nature to a sedentary life. He is fit to live among women or in their fashion. The first outburst on artificial woman. Well, society women, what do they do? You saw the mannequins who were chattering aimlessly. The woman is to be taught to be self-sufficient. She has got to do the things that are proper to women, he says, and needlework and dressmaking are necessary for women. Now we have to guard Emile, you see, from wanton and insolent women; and therefore, we have to create a woman that will be worthy of him and he of her. So we have to develop a woman who will be trained in grace (p. 329). And now he begins really talking about the greatness of women. The function of a woman is to train a man in childhood and to tend him in manhood. That is the noblest of functions for a woman, he says—the most creative, the most noble function. She trains you in childhood and tends you in manhood. A woman, in other words, is not only the better of the man but the maker. Now our little Sophie is also going to be trained by Emile to develop her feelings and her affections. And this is where Emile slips into the medieval notion of women. A woman is supposed to live in the home. She stays in the home. Sophie isn't going to be trained by her granny because if she was she is going to be a ten-year-old kid who lives and thinks like granny. Away with grannies and the business of going and grabbing her so we can go away for a vacation. The kids go along. And the kids have to be trained in virtue and live among the vigorous and the eager. Because childhood is a stage of vigor and eagerness (p. 306). Once we have Sophie developed into a woman, he says, consult woman's opinion in bodily matters and all that concerns the senses. Consult man in matters that concern morality and understanding. What does that mean? He is saying that man has reason as a regulator of his life. Now, he is not saying that women do not have reason, but he is saying that women have less reasoning power. That's why I say that he lapses into the medieval concept of the woman. Rousseau does not think that women are as capable as men in the art of reasoning. No woman has contributed to truths, he says. But he says women with blue stockings— that's what regulated parents. That's why we have to keep Emile from these women. And so we have a situation here in which, although he does not think that women are as intelligent in terms of reason, he thinks that women have something that is powerful. That is, the art of cunning. The art of cunning is something that women have, and that is what they use to subjugate man. They know how to play the game. He says the woman is by nature a professional coquette (p. 347). That is what women possess, and that is how they control man (p. 324). He says the woman reigns; and he cites how Hercules, Sampson, and all the rest of those characters were compelled to spin on the feet of woman. And more than that, he pays the highest to woman when he introduces woman in history, how women, in fact, liberated the Roman Republic. And he begins his adulation of women. Funny, you say, that not too long ago he said that women had no reason. Now he has given them cunning, he has them subjugating us, he has them ruling. Well, that is Rousseau. That's why he thinks in fact that men and women are complementary by nature and necessary, and that is his justification of marriage. If there were no such thing, if woman had reason as much as man, what is reason? Reason compares, evaluates, criticizes. And if you had two reasoning animals, what do you have? Two bitchy people. And so you see, you have to have the man who is a reasoning animal and a woman who nods without understanding yet she reads. Who rules here? The people who have written on Rousseau and on his analysis of woman I think are mistaken because they stop reading when they have gotten to the point where Rousseau, in fact, says that women must be confined within four walls. They don't read after that and this art of cunning and the business about how women rule.

Now, how are we going to introduce the two people together? Sophie is a young lady. She was raised in a small town. And so was he. She goes to Paris, and she is really shocked. She returns home after six months. Our friend Emile also goes to Paris, and he is introduced into society and its artificiality. Both are shocked by abominable in Paris and its artificiality, and they return to their little villages to live a simple elementary life in towns. Rousseau wants people to live in towns and villages, not in cities of millions. That is where anonymity and indifference grow up. So we get him going uphill there with his little tutor. They wander into a valley, and he goes through the entire process. They get to know each other, and one of the most interesting things; when she comes to visit them, they play the races, etc. The thing that I cannot figure out quite yet is that he and Emile and Sophie get into someplace where a woman is having a birth, and they perform the service. I really can't figure out anything unless he wants to show Emile the problems of life, the problems of birth. He's got a man with a broken back, and his wife is having a baby, and there is no doctor. And Rousseau himself in the story performs. Now, that's the only value I can see in that scene: he wants to instruct them again in suffering and what life is likely to be like.

Sophie is learning the art of loving, and Emile is responding. He takes them away. He says the time has come to travel and see the world. He sends them on a two-year trip. You see, when he began to learn about love, he was twenty. At twenty-two, he is fully enveloped as a human being, he loves, he knows what is the value of love. Love is really care, respect, recognition, mutuality. You see, her appeal, although essentially maybe physical, without a relationship of love, it cannot be physical because sooner or later your physique is going to decay, and you're in trouble. And so it's got to be based on something much more profound: mutuality and, above all, on what he called on extended self-love (p. 215). Extended self-love means that you have to learn to love your beloved in the same fashion that you had an innate feeling for self-love. And that extended self-love is also for humanity. This is how you relate morally. You relate your beloved as the first man or woman you choose. We said choose; we didn't say convenience. You choose. And you define yourself by choosing and leading the examined life. You don't accept convention or tradition or anything. If that is love, Emile is capable of loving whether he is physically close or absent. So is she. So Emile is sent on a two-year trip to see the world, to learn about his fellow man, and to find out about all the good things. And that's where he introduces the races. He attacks the French language as obscene, the study of languages as a study of lumber. A waste of time. He attacks taste and food. The French are the only people who do not know what good food is since they require such a special art to make their dishes edible (pp. 116–17). The French and all the people who pretend to be French have no taste (pp. 305, 335). What is taste, an evaluation? And on style (p. 330). So food, taste, and style are also introduced in this context; but they are scattered passages. So we have a situation here. He is away, he gets back, he marries Sophie, but he lacks political science before he marries Sophie. Finally, Sophie has a child. And Emile says to Rousseau, "No, sir, you are not going to be her teacher." He is not going to allow him to become the tutor of his child. And this brings me to the final piece I have to say.

In political science, the man is taught what is citizenship. On page 421, he says, in commenting on the citizen soldier, the more cringing, mean, and degraded you are, the more honor you will attain. If you have decided to take your profession seriously, you will be despised, you will be hated, you will very possibly be driven out of the service or at least fall a victim to favoritism and perhaps be supplanted by your comrades because you have been doing your duty in the trenches while they have been attending to their toilets.

Finally, the value of *Emile* as a model is that it teaches us that human possibilities are what we make them out to be within circumscribed historic and social milieus. There is nothing absolutely "given," but the prospects of liberation from the established shackles of society are much less promising than the ease with which one is socialized and integrated into white whiteness, civilization, and the pursuit of self-enrichment in an environment of social Darwinism. *Emile* offers a glimmer of light, a sign of hope, and a promise that all is not lost if we proceed with intelligence, care, and affection in our effort to salvage a few children before they are ruined by "education." While we need not be awed by the grandiosity of the plan or frightened by the cost of one tutor per student or repelled by the eccentricities of Rousseau, we need a starting point, and I think Rousseau's view of man as a potentiality neither good nor bad but inclining in either direction is the most accurate and humanely relevant premise. Without such conception, we cannot hope to rescue people caught up in the system. We cannot until we put an end to metaphysics and theology; we cannot hope to enthrone man as self-determining or expect to overcome command relations in society and the world about us unless we reverse the entire system. If we want man, we must make him; if we want freedom, we must seize it; if we want a world community, we must build it; if we want love, we must be loving; if we want life, we must seek it; if not, Calibans we are shall continue to be; and no sophistry can gloss over our dehumanization, alienation, and loneliness.

## Appendix

1. Intellectuals of All Countries, Unite!
2. On Student Radicalism
3. The Non-intellective Consciousness: Apocalypse versus Revolution
4. Letter on Religion and the Future of Man
5. Why Waterloo Lutheran Wants to fire Dr. Haggar
6. Human Rights but for Whom? Haggar: a Professor without a Classroom

2) On Student Radicalism, June 3, 1968

To the editor of the *Globe*:

Oliver Clausen's article, "Tantrums and Sex," and Harvey Simmons' "Roots of Revolt in Academe" (*Globe*, June 1, 1968) are a patent example of the reflexive reaction of an outraged conservative and a liberal-minded professor in tune with the surface but not the core of life. Mr. Clausen alleges that students desire perfection and as advocates and practitioners of nihilism, anarchy and mindless romanticism, are out to destroy the "democratic" institutions we have. He is annoyed by the shibboleth and idealization of alien tyrannies yet he concedes there is something wrong somewhere in the West. Mr. Simmons seems to think that the students are revolting against university bureaucracy and power structure because they are suffering from the student-as-nigger syndrome and by implication, he suggests that 'democratization' is desirable. The basic facts of the matter are: (a) in the past decade, a significant amount of footwork has been carried out, the purpose of which was not only to examine the university structure but also government, business, religion, labour and the mass media. Most of these studies were undertaken by socialists and communists and some by liberal intellectuals, and each study was done so meticulously that very few scholars dare challenge any of its findings. These studies, in the light of the revolutionary movements— domestic and international—and the dogmatic centrisms which prevail in the Western world, have become the well-springs of thought for liberals who demand that their parents and governors live up to the democratic tradition and its professed ideals, and sign-posts for socialists who aspire to restructure the foundations of society. (b) The authoritarianism, hypocrisy and bureaucratization of life which characterize not only the social, economic and religious institutions but a university education as well. The universities are operated as "investment" outlets whose aim it is to fashion, knead and mould youngsters to fit the industrial and commercial requirements of a tyrannical and obscurantist middle class who pass as freedom-lovers according to the gospel of Mr. Clauson, but who are in fact little czars in their compartmentalized pursuits of life and more importantly, obnoxiously self-righteous and extremely smug in their just and complacent ways. Think-tank has become the function of the university now that the community colleges can train lower echelon clerks for middle-size businesses. (c) The abjuration of radicalism by the traditional champions of reform—the unions, the Social Democrat and Communist parties, the intellectuals—has left an enormous gap which has to be filled by someone. The students who are claiming this role are not only the precursors of a new order but the founders and the children of the future. The students (approximately 40% in North America and from working-class backgrounds) have grasped the fundamental issues confronting the age—technology, cybernation and their uses—and have rediscovered the humanist values which underpinned liberalism and socialism in their revolutionary stages. Therefore, they have to either create their own models for the new society or borrow from abroad in order to create it, and it is clear that the two approaches are being fused. What is perturbing from a liberal point of view is that the liberals are refusing to account for liberal abdicationism and apply the democratic process—a course they refuse to follow in any sector of life, i.e. the church, the economy, the university, the state, the union and indeed the newspaper. (d) The students' primary concern is not a change of personnel in the university or the co-option of a student or two to some peripheral university agency, but the participation in decisions affecting their lives and environment, and the ability to express unhindered their views about the quality of their life, the work of their demi-god instructors and the manipulation of university bureaucrats. Indeed, they are out to establish democracy and convert the formal democracy we have into a functioning and viable democratic community of citizens, not subjects, of free men, not bondsmen, of equals, not of masters and slaves. That is the essence of democracy and that is why the students are the democrats and their opponents the autocrats and authoritarians, irrespective of what Mr. Clausen and his like would like us to believe. (e) As the struggle for restructuring the various aspects of our society develops, proponents of social change are appearing in each sector and the convergence of their interests is beginning to take shape in such a manner that what we have seen thus far is only a glimpse of the coming reality and not a full moon of the new society. Therefore, the mass media, including the *Globe*, have a choice of debasement, as they have been doing, or analysis and projection, as they ought to do, in reporting and writing articles on this historic movement. It is obvious that no facile approach such as the student-as-nigger viewpoint can explain the depths, the dynamics and the direction of the new order. The student-as-nigger explanation is a psychologism that befits a middle-class temporary anarchist looking for self-discovery and waiting for prospective co-option. It is not a multi-faceted approach that takes cognizance of the domestic upheaval, the international setting and the seeds of the new order in the midst of the dying old one. (f) Lastly, the disintegration of traditional structures, the decay of its values and the subsequent disharmonies that trouble the conservative-liberal mind should not stupefy us into inaction, escape or surrender. We have to face reality and it is revolutionary. Revolutionary one must be in an age of revolution or join the counter-revolution and blaspheme the present and the future, romanticizing an idyllic non-existent past. It is the burgeoning of life and the high epiphany of the future. It is ours not to plead for but to seize and claim. We will not lay prostrate before the editors of the *Globe*, begging permission to be free. We shall be free!

## 3) The Non-intellective Consciousness: Apocalypse versus Revolution

George Haggar

The deadening effects of the cold war, the madness of McCarthyism, and the quietism of academe produced the now-famous "silent generation." But something in the late fifties set in motion a significant movement that began to break the silence of the night and challenge the armies of bureaucrats that undergird it: it was the forces of counter-culture.

The proponents of the new culture, the Beatniks, and their followers were not and have not become a coherent whole and are they not likely to, whatever their successors may be called. As a cultural uprising that ridiculed the way of life of the middle classes, it caught on and turned into sporadic upheavals that plagued the European and American continents in the sixties and continues somewhat haphazardly. The most demonstrative outbursts occurred in 1968 at Columbia and the Sorbonne, but since, the "movement" seems to have disintegrated and lost momentum. Indeed, it could be cogently argued that such anarchism reached its acme, and now it is on the decline; and it is not likely to recover in the visible future except as a periodic, episodic "happening" in reaction to some outrageous governmental or bureaucratic act. It is also crucial to record the esprit de corps, the elan, and the bonds that united those romantic student revolutionaries. And it is essential to remember that counter-culture was intended as a substitute to the prevailing myths of industrial society, its mores, morals, and manners. Moreover, its counter-thesis was that technology and organization were the root causes of alienation in society, in human relations, in family relations. The "experts" in social control, such as Lewis Feuer, regarded the conflict as generational and held it was fraught with dangerous Nazi propensities, whereas others such as Theodore Roszak held that the conflict had nothing to do with any given ism such as capitalism or Socialism but was a wholesome humanist uprising against the pervasive character of the "scientific" cultural ethos—a cultural construct that had ignored human feelings, passion, love, tenderness or simple humanity. The enemy was thus identified and the means of overcoming him elucidated. The enemy was the machine. The things that flowed therefrom, the bureaucratic structures created to maintain it, and the personnel recruited to enshrine the reign of the "scientific" terror.

Within the counter-culture outlook, hordes of prophets offered their revealed "visions" of the new order to come and called upon the alienated to accept their prognostications and to partake in the new "sacraments" of redemptions. Cults emerged, tribes flourished, mystics roamed the land as some of the children of the affluent and other aspirants responded with enthusiasm and seized the opportunity to either make personalist history or withdraw from society to find a life of simplicity and contemplativeness. Other youngsters and their "mature" parents watched the parade sometimes with indifference, sometimes with hostility as the spoiled rich kids confronted the "pigs" and got maced by the protectors of their parents' privilege of power wielding. Those were the days of revolutionary festivals and feasts of joy!

Technocracy or technique is understood as a "social form in which an industrial society reaches the peak of its organizational integration," according to Theodore Roszak in his book *The Making of a Counter-Culture*. Technocracy not only devotes structure, mode of operation, and high discipline but also reflects an attitude of mind and a habit of thought—a cultural octopus that is compulsively modernizing, updating, rationalizing, planning, etc. It is an apparatus that is continuously preoccupied with a self-image of perpetual growth, conquest, expansion. As an all-embracing cultural machine and malaise, technocracy dominates the industrial barons, the financial magnates, the workers. Hence, we are all the potential victims of the machine however unconscious we may be of its awesome power and organizational degradation. Moreover, we not only worship the machine, we also abide by outmoded ideologies designed to sustain it; and the "oppressed" not only admire this mechanical juggernaut but also compete for the procurement of its products and jostle for favor to sell their labor to its managers. In this kind of analysis, Roszak excludes class conflict and regards the conflict a struggle between man and machine in an environment conducive to the programmed victory of the latter and the continued "alienation" of the former. The struggle then is not over institutions or power and what party or class shall govern and in the name of whom and for whom. The struggle is Moloch versus the people; but the "people" have no historic agent, class mission, or a vanguard party to emancipate them. They are left alone to face Moloch and his countless legions. However, since Roszak sees the conflict as "generational," we can derive some psychic satisfaction if by accident we were bourgeois. Roszak informs us that "the bourgeois, instead of discovering the class enemy in its factories, finds it across the breakfast table in the person of its own pampered children." The generational conflict is thus revealed and the resultant tolerance of bourgeois society is patently clear. Furthermore, the disaffiliation to be underscored is not that of the dispossessed, the disinherited, and the disadvantaged but of the "pampered children" subsidized by their guilt-ridden parents, the sponsors of hippiedom, the financiers of the occult, the participants in the "sacraments."

Roszak discerns some undesirable features in the new counter-culture, psychedelia, for instance. But that is not his principal target: the myth of objective consciousness is. Therefore, he offers us a substitute myth: shamanism-Quakerism. However, before Roszak expounds his theory of salvation, which is thoroughgoing pacifism, the kind of ideology the ruling classes enjoy publishing treatises about and admire at cocktail parties, he introduces us to the dialectics of liberation according to the apostles Marcuse and Norman Brown; and he traces the rising crescendo of counter-culture to Allen Ginsberg and the journeys to the East. He also gives us a glimpse of the "mystic revolution," "the beatific illumination," the "ethereal quest" as he leads us into the visionary land of Paul Goodman and his Gestalt therapy. On the way to paradise, Roszak tramples over the counterfeit infinity of Timothy Leary, bulldozes the objective consciousness of scientism, and counterposes the vision of the non-intellective consciousness to this human wreckage. The new tribalism of the global pillage embraces "libidinal liberation" as the raison d'etre of the revolt and overlooks the central issue of our times: the liberation of the oppressed from the yoke of imperialism. Thus, instead of attempting to liberate the immense majority of mankind, we are urged to imitate a handful of corpulent American-style merchants living in a nation whose population is less than 7 percent of the world and consumes 70 percent of its products. The new consumerism of expanded consciousness seems to have distorted the vision of Mr. Roszak; and its accoutrements seem to have blinded him by their ritual, magic, sacraments, metaphysics, organic foods.

In the dialectics of liberation, we are offered a melange of biologism and a bit of social determinism. The key that unlocks the mystery of life is the psyche, according to both Marcuse and Brown. With such a starting point, the differences among the saints become minimal as they deluge us with their mystifications, obfuscations, and bastardizations of man and society. Both reveal alienation as psychic; it is not a sociological phenomenon. If this were the case, it follows that all we have to do is to alter our consciousness to overcome "alienation." The question is how, by what means, and under whose leadership. If alienation is a personal psychic matter, the "alienated" person can find relief in a multitude of ways in a hierarchical, descending medieval order of knighted wealth. The super rich can visit psychoanalysts; the less rich, psychiatrists; the semi-rich, psychologists; the pseudo-rich, chiropractors; the semi-poor, social workers; the less poor, priests; the truly poor, the cops; the oppressively poor, themselves. Such are the means of salvation implicitly prescribed by the ideological stance of Marcuse and Brown. As to obfuscatory dialectics, here is a set of undecipherable terms: repressive sublimation, repressive desublimation, basic repression, surplus repression, repressive tolerance, etc. By the end of the liberation process, Marcuse and his followers are so overcome by repression that their liberation climaxes and the poor practice without guilt, fanfare, status anxiety, or CIA mission, Marcusian style. However, if the aim is a secure academic career and an adulating coterie of sycophants, this area of fashionable post-industrial philosophy can be an inexhaustible source of power, glory, achievement. In the meantime, such utter disregard and contempt for the life of mankind, on the part of the aesthetic entrepreneurs, can be cloaked under the guise of romantic sensibility, paradox, madness, ecstasy, spiritual striving. And in a swinging society, academic respectability can be easily conferred on those who partake in the apocalyptic illumination and propound "libidinal rationality" and its "Dionysian ego." Because of the absorptive capacity of bourgeois society, the lifestyle, the ideology, and the personal preoccupations of the disaffiliated young rich and their imitators, counter-culture has become the central topic of our time. In other words, upper-class tolerance, professional hucksterism, and academic support have made counter-culture the most important development of the past decade. Thus, we have reached the stage where middle-class solipsism is predicated as a given and projected on the screen of history as a means of divulging the secrets of eternity; and it is issued from on high, in pontifical tones that repression and alienation are the primordial conditions of the life of man. The titanic disputants of counter-culture are thus revealed. On the one hand, we have Norman Brown who contends that alienation and repression are coeval with the emergence of man and therefore cannot be eradicated; on the other, we have Marcus who declares that they are interrelated biologically and sociologically and therefore can be mitigated. According to Marcuse's scarcity-abundance theory, authority and its growth relate to scarcity; but as abundance increases, authority ought to decline until "surplus repression" is eliminated. Now why authority has multiplied instead of declining, Marcuse seems unprepared to explain. But that is to be expected from a celebrated philosopher who thinks that everything is digestible and co-optable in America, including himself perhaps. What we should point out, however, is that the positions of both Brown and Marcuse ultimately lead to political quietism, a life of acquiescence, and an obsession with the self—propositions quite compatible with the "individualism" and self-reliance of bourgeois society. Thus, to sum up, it must be said that since repression and alienation are innate characteristics of man, we cannot abolish them. The only thing we can do is to modify and minimize their impact by some kind of individualist communitarianism and heroic histrionics. By this method, social strife, social class, and social structure are not placed on the agenda; and the dehumanization, depersonalization, and degradation of man are not the central project of liberation. We therefore can only have periodic personalist outbursts and spontaneous anarchic student upheavals that, in the final analysis, reinforce the ruling class, cushion its moral stance, and justify its repression, retrenchment, retribution. The vision, the imagination, the apocalypse of counter-culture thus culminate in a despondent despair that impels the practitioners either to retreat to a primitive rural asceticism or withdraw to a life of psychedelia, succumbing to the inevitable by returning to the family business or accept co-optation into the higher clerisy. The elect of counter-culture are thus obliterated, and the chiliastic movement must await a new generation to revive it.

If, indeed, Marcuse and Brown offer us the politics of joyous despair and social impotence rather than the politics of liberation, what can we say about the more flamboyant politics of the spells, incantations, and chantings of the Ginsberg ilk? Exotic clutter, desperado whimperings, bravado posturings. That is precisely how the ruling class sees this genre of politics; and that is why they have turned the Ginsbergs into heroes, demi-gods, and demiurges. Moreover, to ward off revolution, the ruling class imparts all sorts of charlatans, quacks, and spurious social critics for the purpose of cultivating a social penchant of the occult, the magic, the exotic ritual. From the point of the exploiter, why not invoke divine fire and call for mediation? Why not proclaim the adolescentization of life and disseminate the euphoric phantasmagoria of religiosity? Why not appeal to Jungian racialism in search of good vibrations? All these diversions are promoted and become profit-producing instruments as soon as the ruling class recognizes their exchange value. This has happened because of the inauthenticity of counter-culture, especially its saints, Abbie Hoffman and Jerry Rubin (who have become the most highly paid entertainers of the seventies) and because the commercial hucksters are now at the head of the caravan. This is why we have such an effete cultural heroes like Ginsberg and his groovy crowd of American color in Canada, and that is why a new repressive liberation is absurd as noted "scholars" advocate the legalization of cannabis and the enlargement of the realm of pluralism to encompass community groups such as tenants, women's lib, ethnic minorities, and the poor. The reason the new liberalism is growing is easy to determine: new weapons, systems of social control, are needed to maintain the arsenal of bourgeois freedom. Since religion has lost its grip on the people, a new opinion has to be invented, and what better opium than opium itself? Moreover, the middle class and its children will be able to share in the "sacraments," but the poor, as usual, will get the crumbs, and they will not share the wealth. Thus, counter-culture inexorably leads us to the league of spiritual discovery and its cultic swarm, Timothy Leary, where "neurological politics" or "the politics of the nervous system" occupy center stage. On the new stage, we embark on a new pilgrimage and "groove to the music of God is great song," not to the music of revolutionary violence. In the kingdom of freedom, "personal salvation and social revolution are packed in a capsule" as Roszak puts it. But Roszak does not see its ineluctable ascent of the elect from Ginsberg to Leary. Therefore, he assails psychedelia and cites its absurdities to enhance the status of his shamanism-Quakerism. However, before we are to turn to Roszak's utopian sociology, he has a dragon to slay: the myth of objective consciousness.

To Roszak, the regime of expertise is not only an infidel secular god; it is a god of subliminal destruction, cultural enervation, dessicated psyches. He is at his best in inveighing against the predominance of scientism and technologism in our era. His critiques pinpoint these abhorrent characteristic of scientism. The alienative dichotomy, the invidious hierarchy, the mechanistic imperative. The crucial point here is the separation of feeling from project and the reduction of the participant to the status of observer or spectator. The best scientist according to the prevailing cultural ethos is the least involved or committed; the most reliable knowledge is the least emotionally colored; the greatest scientific undertaking is the nomothetic project. To Roszak, such scientism is anthems because reality is divided between the in here and the out there, a situation that produces insensitivity and "a cool curiosity untouched by love, tenderness, or passionate wonder"—in turn, creating a contempt for the "drift, unpredictability and stupidity" of the out there. Since the "scientist" can only reach "the behavioral surface" of the observed, "an invidious hierarchy is established, which reduces the observed to a lower status. But such human hubris is frustrated by the claims of the irrational, intruding itself "in behalf of sensuous contact, fantasy, spontaneity, and concern for the person." Objective consciousness, in other words, cannot subdue man; but it can mutilate and warp his passion, life, love, and anything that "degrades visionary experience commits the sin of diminishing our existence." Scientism is thus to be combatted because it does not accept "the beauty of the fully illuminated person as our standard of truth"; it only accepts the logic of domination, conquest, war. Thus, we must accept counter-culture as an alternative to technocracy and the "isms" associated with it. If mankind is to be served, which is to say we must proclaim a new heaven and new earth were technical expertise is subordinate, where the consciousness of life entails opening ourselves to visionary imagination, where the rhapsodic report of enchanted seers are appreciated.

With the above summary of counter-culture, we arrive at shamanism and Quakerism. The shaman, according to Roszak, is "ambushed by the divine and called forth by surprise." He communes with the "transcendent power" and possesses a "talented uniqueness" rather than a trance-inducing repertory of practices. He knows there is more to be seen of reality than the waking eye sees, and in his "superconsciousness," all things of this earth are "swayed by sacred meanings." From this vision of man and environment, Roszak informs us that there is "a symbiotic relationship between man and not-man in which there is a dignity, a gracefulness, an intelligence that powerfully challenges our own strenuous project of conquering and counterfeiting nature." What Roszak calls an overwhelming sense of mystery in his unfolding shamanism must be called an overbearing sense of mysticism propounded by a celestial-bound man uninspired by the blighted lives of the masses and unaffected by the plight of the oppressed. Moreover, in this Olympian mysticism, Roszak appears like a Brahmin who refuses to commune with the untouchables and a social eunuch in the court of capitalism. But such a verdict cannot be maintained because Roszak is a shaman-Quaker who advocates utopian communities in the Goodman style. Here is an illustration of his Quakerism in which he advises that we ought "to stand still in the light, confident that only such a stillness possesses the eloquence to draw man away from lives we must believe they inwardly loathe, but which misplaced pride will goad them to defend under aggressive pressure to the very death—their death and ours."

If Roszak can approach the enemy with song, festival, and love, most people cannot, though most would sympathize with his idea of communalism not in a capitalist but in a non-capitalist society. While the shaman scientist of our age displays his magic, robotizes man, and uses his "science" to serve the Pentagon and the financial houses of America, it is refreshing to see an occasional challenge to the power of militarism and regimentation. But the Roszak prescription for ending alienation and the subjugation of man is purely a personalist solution that cannot alter the direction of history nor restructure society. Roszak misidentifies the enemy: it is the owners, managers, and bureaucrats of technocracy that must be overthrown, not technocracy itself. At this juncture, in human history, it is foolish if not downright treasonous to speak of Goodmanian spontaneity, self-regulation, and animal impulsiveness. The question we must address ourselves to is how to overcome the present social order and what are the most effective ways of mobilizing the working class to become a class for itself and attain power. Thus, the utopian communities that are being organized only solve temporarily individual, not social, problems; and in a few years, new fads will have overtaken them. Therefore, we cannot share the optimism of Roszak who appears to think that the new counter-culture is a prelude to a new order that will replace the technocratic regime in the same fashion that Christianity replaced the Hellenistic-Roman would view, and science and enlightenment dislocated Christianity in the modern period and became the mistress of mankind. Thus, we must conclude that the Roszak analysis scratches the power of technocracy and its perverters; it cannot abolish the reign of privilege! The issue is not Apollo versus Centaur; it is not machine versus man; it is not the technocratic man versus the manipulated peasant; it is not man to recover his humanity and/or naively conceive utopian schemes in the shamanistic style of Roszak, which cannot solve the social problems of our time!

4) March 26, '69

Letter on Religion and the Future of Man

To: Darrol Bryant

Let me at the outset deal with what you termed "ironic comment" in your letter of March 14, 1969, which stemmed from my use of Christian imagery in depicting your personal plight and how it might overcome you or overcome it yourself.

Since I regard Christianity and other world religions as part of the human heritage and as significant historic manifestations that reflected man's consciousness of himself in his adolescent stage, I find it convenient and helpful at times to use religious symbolism as a means of communication. That's not to say that I accept religion as a valid hypothesis to be promoted, disseminated or fought for. I am not a member of the anthropomorphic race of rulers, tyrants, bureaucrats and apologists who need to rely on religious mystifications to justify capitalist treachery and barbarity and defend it as divinely or naturally ordained.

Thus I object to Christianity not only because of its destructive, delusionary otherworldliness, but also because of its worldliness as an historic institutional instrument put in the service of every detestable dictatorship: Roman slavery, Christian feudalism, Protestant capitalism, pseudo-rationalist laborism. In short, I am opposed to religion as theology, church, activity, idea. I find it a repugnant system of priestly manipulated thought and an abdication of reason; but I am prepared to study it in an effort to understand historic systems and how religiously motivated people perceive themselves, think, and act. In our era religion is ancillary to capital and as such it stifles human progress by masking capitalism robbery and snobbery and by helping socialize people into becoming docile slaves. Therefore radicals must attack the socio-economic functions of religion and fight for the secularization of life and the abolition of the oligarchies that man its institutions.

It is my considered opinion that North American radicals engage themselves and get bogged down in revolutionary rhetoric and polemics within the religious-metaphysical or within the moralistic-psychological rather than within the historic-scientific context. In other words, instead of starting with the actual and existential; radicals start with the religious esthetic or ethical angles of vision and get mired up in the verbal process of self-identification—a condition that forecloses the prospect of social revolutionary action. Under such conditions and with such perspectives a revolution cannot be conceived, let alone carried out. Put briefly, the road from the "personal god of love" to revolutionary social violence and total personal commitment to the human community is long and steep and very few of us will ever traverse that road and reach the summit of the mountain. Thus we ought to, but do not seem to know that to avow the emancipation of man is not commensurate with going to the Sierra Maestra or the Caves of Hunan, or transporting weapons on the Ho Chi Minh trail or fighting American Marines in Vietnam, to exploring the Andes and dying heroically in Bolivia, to combatting imperial Zionism in the Judean hills or Tel Aviv. To affirm personal liberation and be a subsidized radical is not to feel the scorching sun of the desert and the debilitating diet of the Palestinian Arab. To implore people to abide by Christian principles is not tantamount to living with worm-infested stomachs or dying of malnutrition or waiting in hopelessness for the hand of death to snatch you from the midst of your beloved. To make "revolutionary" pronouncements or issue manifestoes before T.V. cameras is not equivalent to facing nobly instant death before American B52 saturation bombing, napalm and other nefarious forms of gunpowder. To give press conferences, do your "thing," stage "peaceful" demonstrations, organize teach-ins and walk-outs is infantile indifference compared to falling to the music of machine guns and the thunderous roars of American bombers. To build "resurrection or soul cities," operate counter-institutions, mobilize the poor and shed tears for foreign martyrs is not half as sacred as making the revolution right here in North America—the bastion of world imperialism.

Darrol, I have no illusions that my analysis is the last word in human wisdom. I believe as you do that Marxist methodology and social analysis are superior to the abdicationist doctrine of the Liberal-Conservative procrustean matrix of reality. For this reason, I rejected and strenuously assailed liberal academic politics and was proscribed as a result. Therefore, the answer to the question you pose—Do I expect "some kind of apocalypse" to replace a caste-ridden world by a classless society—is self-evident. To make it crystal clear, I believe revolutionary warfare is the only weapon worth considering at the juncture of human history and radicals must prepare themselves for prolonged struggle in North America. They must discard—but not completely—such outmoded methods as legal channels, parliamentary parties, counter-institutions, non-violence, direct action and other methods and tactics of liberal radicalism and moralistic reformism. These and other methods have not borne the fruits of liberation but repression they have forced the system to contrive subtler methods of co-optation, isolation and proscription. They have not produced revolutionaries or radicalized the masses. They have deluded people into believing that this marginal and trivial acts were meaningful and significant when they were not. They have simply demonstrated the meaning and effectiveness of bourgeois dissent and shown how dissent, moderate agitation and "responsible leadership." Pay and open avenues of ascent to Anglo-Saxon society. To ascertain the validity of this assertion one must study closely the careers of the successful practitioners of Jewish liberalism, protestant moralism, and academic agnosticism in both the U.S. and Canada. On this evidence it is not unfair to contend that the *Movement* exists only in the headline, the editorial page and the kitchen of romantic liberals, and utopian conservatives whose supreme goal is the suppression of true revolution.

In sum, I am saying radicalism on this continent is a liberal fraud perpetrated as a means of social control and repression and "leftists" must stop deceiving themselves and thinking that they are making the "revolution" when they are the making of practicing psycho-therapy. The test of radicalism is revolution, and radicals will show their mettle when they plan and propose for the seizure of power and the smashing of the bourgeois state. If this were not their aim, let us then stop the fraudulence and sophistry of liberalism and reorganize on the basis of "revolutionary perspective" and goals and find the cadres and the masses to carry it out. Therefore, first and foremost, we must organize a revolutionary party and arm it with revolutionary theory and the strategy of guerilla warfare. And we must not confuse the anomic riots of Watts, Newark, Detroit etc. and the "police riot" of Chicago with revolution. If we do, we will not be able to understand that what passes for ubiquitous radicalism is a sponsored goat of the establishment and a pampered child of "liberal" society and a miscreant to justify further repressive measures.

Lastly, let me return to the intellectual error that I discern in your work and which I find suffuses your present article with the spirit of modern Christianity: your view of man as an "ambiguous possibility" as opposed to the traditional notion of man as being born in sin and iniquity. I believe this concept is the root-cause of much obfuscation and deflection among "Christian radicals" because it raises relevant, fundamental existential question without answering it! At this point, clever ideologists and religious escapists in consonance with the spirit of bourgeois liberalism recognize the problem and speculate about it endlessly instead of coalescing with progressive forces to work for the abolition of "ambiguity" and capitalist slavery. If by "ambiguity" you mean man's inability to foresee the future with absolute clarity then you are right. If, however, "ambiguity" means a new metaphysic, then it is a "pipe-dream." Comrades of the revolutionary persuasion therefore begin with man not as an ambiguity but a potentiality capable of doing either ill or good. Which of these antagonistic hypotheses prevails depends of course, on the kind of social environment man inhabits, and the kind of social institutions that rear, educate, and socialize him and the kind of values he imbibes and internalizes as operational and ethical norms. Therefore, revolutionaries conclude that sin and iniquity and its modern variant ambiguity are not inborn to man but are immanent in the social institutions of capitalism and all system based on human exploitation whatever the espoused ism may be.

Thus we proceed to construct an environment that actualizes man is potential for good, which is the creation of social relations based on human interaction and social processes underpinned by a co-operative ethic. From this local arrangement we build a national and an international system not on abstract brotherhood but on a brotherhood undergirded by the equitable distribution and sharing of wealth and power nationally and internationally and predicated on the principle of individual participation in decision-making affecting one's life and destiny and the communal life of mankind. This type of society presupposes the replacement of

Caliban by man, the abolition of the Kingdom and Want, the institution of the realm of freedom, the extinction of the state system, the creation of an international federal polity. Then and only then can we speak of the coming of man and the unfolding of freedom. Then and only then can we speak of human growth, happiness, love. Then and only then can we speak of co-operative labor, social commitment and rule by man. Then and only then can we speak of voluntary, spontaneous and willed action. Meanwhile the party of men must plan and prepare the overthrow of capitalism which is our most immediate and urgent task!

# APPENDIX

The new Intellective Consciousness: Apocalypsis
Revolution
George Hoggar

    The deadening effects of the cold war, the madness of McCarthyism and the quietism of academe produced the now famous "silent generation". But something in the late 50's set in motion a significant movement that began to break the silence of the right and challenge the armies of bureaucrats that undergird it; it was the forces of counter-culture.    The proponents of the new culture, the Beatniks and their followers were not and have not become a coherent whole, nor are they likely to; whatever their successors may be called. As a cultural uprising that ridiculed the way of life of the middle classes, it caught on and turned into sporadic upheavals that plagued the European and American continents in the 60's and continues somewhat haphazardly. The most demonstrative outbursts occurred in 1968 at Columbia and the Sorbonne but since the "movement" seems to have disintegrated and lost momentum. Indeed, it could be cogently argued that such anarchism reached its acme and now it is on the decline and it is not likely to recover in the visible future except as a periodic, episodic "happening" in reaction to some outrageous governmental or bureaucratic act. It is also crucial to record the esprit de corps, the elan and the bonds that united those romantic student revolutionaries. And it is essential to remember that counter-culture was intended

211

as a substitute to the prevailing myths of industrial society, its mores, morals and manners. Moreover, its counter-thesis was that technocracy and organization) were the root causes of alienation in society, in human relations, in family relations. The "experts in social control," such as Lewin Feuer and ~~Seymour~~ Lipset regarded the conflict as generational and held it was ~~fraught~~ with ~~dangerous~~ Nazi propensities, whereas others such as Theodore Roszak held that the conflict had nothing to do with any given ~~issue~~ such as capitalism or socialism, but was a wholesome humanist uprising against the pervasive character of the "scientific" cultural ethos — a cultural construct that had ignored human feelings, passions, love, tenderness or simple humanity. The enemy was thus identified and the means of overcoming him elucidated: the enemy was the machine, the things that flowed therefrom, the bureaucratic structures created to maintain it and the personnel recruited to enshrine the reign of the "scientific" terror.

Within the counter-culture outlook, hordes of prophets offered their revealed "visions" of the new order to come and called upon the alienated to accept their prognostications and to partake in the new "sacraments" of redemption. Cults emerged, tribes flourished, mystics roamed the land as some of the children of the affluent and other aspirants responded with enthusiasm and seized the opportunity to either make personalist history or withdraw from society to lead a life of simplicity and contemplativeness. Other youngsters and their "mature" parents watched the parade with indifference, sometimes with hostility as the

3

spoiled rich kids confronted the 'pigs' and got maced by the protectors of their parents' privilege of power-wielding. Those were the days of revolutionary festivals and feasts of joy.'

Technocracy or technique is understood as 'a social form in which an industrial society reaches the peak of its organizational integration', according to Theodore Roszak in his book, The Making Of A Counter-Culture. Technocracy denotes not only structures, modes of operation and high discipline, but also reflects an attitude of mind and a habit of thought — a cultural octopus that is compulsively modernizing, updating, rationalizing, planning etc. It is an apparatus that is continuously preoccupied with a self-image of perpetual growth, conquest, expansion. As an all-embracing cultural machine and malaise, technocracy dominates the industrial barons, the financial magnates, the workers. Hence we are all the potential victims of the machine however unconscious we may-be of its awesome power and organizational degradation. Moreover, we not only worship the machine, we also abide by outmoded ideologies designed to sustain it and the 'oppressed' not only admire this mechanical juggernaut, but also compete for the procurement of its products and jostle for favor to sell their labor to its managers. In this kind of analysis, Roszak excludes class conflict and regards the conflict a struggle between man and machine in an environment conducive to the programmed victory of the latter and the continued 'alienation' of the former. The struggle then

-4-

is not over institutions or power and what party or class shall govern and in the name of whom and for whom. The struggle is Moloch vs the people; but the "people" have no historic agent, class mission or a vanguard party to emancipate them. They are left alone to face Moloch and his countless legions. ~~However~~, since Roszak sees the conflict as "generational", we can derive some psychic satisfaction if by accident we were bourgeois. Roszak informs us that "the bourgeoisie, instead of discovering the class enemy in its factories, finds it across the breakfast table in the person of its own pampered children". The generational conflict is thus revealed and the resultant tolerance of bourgeois society is patently clear. Furthermore, the disaffiliation to be underscored is not that of the dispossessed, the disinherited and the disadvantaged, but of the "pampered children" subsidized by their guilt-ridden parents, the sponsors of hippiedom, the financiers of the occult, the participants in the "sacraments".

Roszak discusses some undesirable features in the new counter-culture, psychedelia for instance. But that is not his principal target. The myth of objective consciousness is therefore he offers us a substitute myth: shamanism - Quakerism. However, before Roszak expounds his theory of salvation which is thoroughgoing pacifism — the kind of ideology the ruling classes enjoy publishing treatises about and admire at cocktail parties — he introduces us to the dialectics of liberation according to

214

the apostles Marcuse and Norman Brown and he traces the
rising crescendo of counter-culture to Allen Ginsberg and the
journeys to the east. He also gives us a glimpse of the
"mystic revolution", the "beatific illumination", the "ethereal quest" as
he leads us into the "visionary" land of Paul Goodman and
his Gestalt therapy. On the way to paradise, Roszak tramples over
the counterfeit infinity of Timothy Leary, bulldozes the objective
consciousness of scientism and counterposes the vision of the
non-intellective consciousness to this human wreckage. The
new tribalism of the global pillage embraces "libidinal liberation"
as the raison d'être of the revolt and overlooks the central
issue of our times : the liberation of the oppressed from the yoke
of imperialism. Thus instead of attempting to liberate the immense
majority of mankind, we are urged to imitate a handful of corpulent American style merchants living in a nation whose population
is less than 7% of the world and consumes 70% of its products.
The new consumerism of expanded consciousness seems to have
distorted the vision of Mr. Roszak and its accoutrements seem
to have blinded him by their ritual, magic, sacraments,
metaphysics, organic foods.

In the dialectics of liberation, we are offered a
mélange of biologism and a bit of social determinism. The key
that unlocks the mystery of life is the psyche, according to both
Marcuse and Brown. with such a starting-point the differences
between the saints become minimal as they deluge us

with their mystifications, obfuscations and bastardizations of ?
man and society. Alienation as psychic (both reveal), it is
not a sociological phenomenon. If this were the case, it follows
that all we have to do is to alter our consciousness to
overcome "alienation." The question is how, by what means, and
under whose leadership. Now if alienation is a personal psychic matter,
the "alienated" person can find relief in a multitude of ways in
a hierarchical, descending, medieval order of knighted wealth; The super-rich can
visit psychoanalysts; The less rich psychiatrists; The semi-rich
psychologists; The pseudo rich chiropractors; The semi poor
social workers; the less poor priests; The truly poor the cops;
The oppressively poor themselves. Such are the means of salvation
implicitly prescribed by the ideological stance of Marcuse and
Brown. As to the obfuscatory dialectics here is a set of
undecipherable terms: repressive sublimation, repressive desublimation, basic repression, surplus repression, repressive tolerance
etc. etc. by the end of this liberation process, Marcuse
and his followers are
too overcome by repression that their liberation climaxes
in masturbation — a discovery infants instinctively make
and the poor practice without guilt, fanfare, status anxiety,
or CIA mission, Marcusian style. However, if the aim
is a secure academic career and an adulating coterie of psycho-
phants sychophants, this area of fashionable, post-industrial philosophy
can be an inexhaustible source of power, glory ...

216

In the meantime, such utter disregard and contempt for the life of mankind, on the part of the academic entrepreneurs ~~especially the intellectuals of the hinterlands of metropolitan imperialism,~~ can be cloaked under the guise of Romantic sensibility, paradox, madness, ecstasy, spiritual striving. And in a swinging society, academic respectability can be easily conferred on ~~those~~ those who partake in the apocalyptic illumination and propound "libidinal rationality" and its "Dionysian ego". Because of the absorptive capacity of bourgeois society, the life style, the ideology, and the personal preoccupations of the disaffiliated young richos, their imitators, Counter-culture has become the central topic of our time. In other words, upper class tolerance, professional hucksterism and academic support have made counter-culture the most important development of the past decade. Thus we have reached the stage where middle class solipsism is predicated as a given and projected on the screen of history as a means of divulging the secrets of eternity, and it is issued from on high, in pontifical tones that repression and alienation are the "primordial conditions of the life of man." The titanic disputants of counter-culture are thus ~~clarified~~ revealed. On the one hand, we have Norman Brown who contends that alienation and repression are coeval with the emergence of man and therefore cannot be eradicated; on the other, we have Marcuse who declares that they are interrelated biologically and sociologically and therefore, can be mitigated. According to Marcuse's scarcity-abundance theory, authority and its growth relate to scarcity, but as abundance increases, authority

8

to decline until "surplus repression" is eliminated. Now why authority has multiplied instead of declining, Marcuse seems unprepared to explain. But that is to be expected from a celebrated philosopher who thinks that everything is digestible and co-optable in America, including himself perhaps. What we should point out however, is that the positions of both Brown and Marcuse ultimately lead to political quietism, a life of acquiescence, and an obsession with the self—propositions quite compatible with the "individualism" and self-reliance of bourgeois society. Thus to sum up, it must be said that since repression and alienation are innate characteristics of man, we can not abolish them. The only thing we can do is to modify and minimize their impact by some kind of individualist communitarianism and heroic histrionics. By this method, social strife, social class, and social structure are not placed on the agenda and the dehumanization, depersonalization and degradation of man are not the central project of liberation. We therefore can only have periodic personalist outbursts and spontaneous, anarchic student upheavals that in the final analysis, reinforce the ruling class, cushion its moral stance and justify its repression, retrenchment, retribution. The vision, the imagination, the apocalypse of counter-culture thus culminate in a despondent despair that impels the practitioners either to retreat to a primitive, rural asceticism, or to withdraw to a life of

*· 8·*

to decline until "surplus repression" is eliminated. Now
why authority has multiplied instead of declining, Marcuse
seems unprepared to explain. But that is to be expected
from a celebrated philosopher who thinks that everything is
digestible and co-optable in America, including himself perhaps.
What we should point out however, is that the positions of
both Brown and Marcuse ultimately lead to political quietism,
a life of acquiescence, and an obsession with the self—
propositions quite compatible with the "individualism" and self-
reliance of bourgeois society. Thus to sum up, it must be
said that since repression and alienation are innate characteristics
of man, we can not abolish them. The only thing we can do is
to modify and minimize their impact by some kind of communitarianism and heroic historicism. ~~the best by proudest~~ ~~revolution-
ary of examples, rather than the general body of the proletariat~~
By this method, social strife, social class, and social structure
are not placed on the agenda and the "dehumanization, depersonalization
and degradation of man are not the central project of liberation."
We therefore can only have periodic personalist outbursts and spontaneous, anarchic student upheavals that in the final analyses, reinforce
the ruling class, cushion its moral stance, and justify its repression,
retrenchment, retribution. The vision, the imagination, the
apocalypse of counter-culture thus culminate in a despondent
despair that impels the practitioners either to retreat to a
primitive, rural asceticism, or to withdraw to a life of

219

Commercial hucksters are now at the head of the caravan. This is why we have such an effete cultural heroes like Ginsberg and his groovy crowd of American colons in Canada and that is why a new "repressive liberation" as absurd as noted "scholars" advocate the legalization of cannabis and the enlargement of the realm of liberation to encompass community groups such as tenants, women's lib, ethnic minorities, and the poor. The reason the new liberation is growing is easy to determine: new weapons systems of social control are needed to maintain the arsenal of bourgeois freedom. Since religion has lost its grip on the people, a new opium has to be invented and what better opium than opium itself? Moreover, the middle class and its children will be able to share in the "sacraments", but the poor as usual, will get the crumbs and they will not share the wealth. Thus counter-culture inexorably leads us to the League of Spiritual Discovery and its cultic swami, Timothy Leary, where "neurological politics" or "the politics of the nervous system" occupy center stage. On the new stage, we embark on a new pilgrimage and "groove to the music of God's great song", not to the music of revolutionary violence. In this kingdom of freedom, "personal salvation and social revolution are packed in a capsule" as Roszak puts it. But Roszak does not see the ineluctable ascent of the elect from Ginsberg to Leary. Therefore, he assails psychedelia and cites its absurdities to enhance the status of his

-11-

Shamanism — Quakerism. However, before we are taken to Roszak,'s utopian sociology, he has a dragon to slay: the myth of objective consciousness.

-11-  To Roszak, the regime of expertise is not only an infidel god; it is a god of subliminal destruction, cultural enervation, desiccated psyches. Roszak is at his best in inveighing against the predominance of scientism and technologism in our era. His critiques pinpoint three abhorrent characteristics of scientism: the alienative dichotomy, the invidious hierarchy, the mechanistic imperative. The crucial point here is the separation of feeling from project and the reduction of the participant to the status of observer or spectator. The best scientist according to the prevailing cultural ethos is the least involved or committed; the most reliable knowledge is the least emotionally colored; the greatest scientific undertaking is the nomothetic project. To Roszak such scientism is anthema because reality is divided between the in-here and the out-there, a situation that produces insensitivity and "a cool curiosity untouched by love, tenderness or passionate wonder" and in turn creates a contempt for the "drift, unpredictability and stupidity" of the out-there. Since the "scientist" can only reach "the behavioral surface" of the observed "an invidious hierarchy is established which reduces the observed to a lower status." But such human hubris is frustrated by the charisma of the irrational intruding itself "in behalf of sensuous contact, fantasy, spontaneity, and concern for the person". Objective consciousness in other words, cannot subdue man, but it can mutilate and warp his passion, life, love and anything that "degrades visionary experience commits the sin of diminishing our existence". Scientism is thus to be combatted because it does not accept "the beauty of the fully illuminated person as our standard of truth", it only accepts the logic of domination, conquest, war. Thus we must accept counter-culture as an alternative to technocracy and the "isms" associated with it, if mankind is to be served, which is to say we must proclaim a new heaven and new earth where technical expertise is subordinate, where the consciousness of life entails opening ourselves to visionary imagination, where the rhapsodic reports of enchanted seers are appreciated.

With the above summary of counter-culture we arrive at shamanism and Quakerism. The shaman according to Roszak is "ambushed by the divine and called forth by surprise". He communes with the "transcendent powers" and possesses a "talented uniqueness", rather than a trance-inducing repertory of practices. He knows there is

- ji -

Shamancism ~ Quakerism. However, before we are taken to
Roszak's utopian sociology, he has a dragon to slay: The
myth of objective consciousness.

- II -

To Roszak, the regime of expertise is not only an
infidel god; it is a god of subliminal destruction, cultural enervation,
desiccated psyches. Roszak is at his best in
inveighing against the predominance of the scientism and technologism
in our era. His critiques pinpoint three abhorrent
characteristics of Scientism. The alienative dichotomy, the
invidious hierarchy, the mechanistic imperative. The
crucial point here is the separation of feeling from
project and the reduction of the participant to the
status of observer or spectator. The best scientist
according to the prevailing cultural ethos is the least
involved or committed; the most reliable knowledge is
the least emotionally colored; the greatest scientific undertaking is the nomothetic project. To Roszak, such
scientism is anthema because humanity is divided between

more to be seen of reality than the waking eye sees, and in his "superconsciousness", all things of this earth are "swayed by sacred meanings". From this vision of man and environment, Roszak informs us that there is a symbiotic relationship between man and not-man in which there is a dignity, a gracefulness, an intelligence that powerfully challenges our own strenuous project of conquering and counterfeiting nature. What Roszak calls an overwhelming sense of mystery in his unfolding shamanism must be called an overbearing sense of mysticism propounded by a celestial-bound man uninspired by the blighted lives of the masses and unaffected by the plight of the oppressed. Moreover, in this Olympian mysticism, Roszak appears like a brahmin who refuses to commune with the untouchables and a social eunuch in the court of capitalism. But such a verdict cannot be maintained because Roszak is a shaman-Quaker who advocates utopian communities in the Goodman style. Here is his Quakerism in which he advises that we ought to stand still in the light, confident that only such a stillness possesses the eloquence to draw man away from lives we must believe they inwardly loathe, but which misplaced pride will goad them to defend under aggressive pressure to the very death — their death and ours.

If Roszak can approach the enemy with song, festival, and love, most people cannot though most would sympathize with his idea of communalism not in a capitalist, but in a post-capitalist society. While the shaman-scientist of our age displays his magic, robotizes man, and uses his "science" to serve the pentagon and the financial houses of America, it is refreshing to see an occasional challenge to the power of militarism and regimentation. But the Roszak prescription for ending alienation and the subjugation of man is merely a personalist solution that cannot alter the direction of history nor ~~restructure society~~ ^restructure society^ ~~abolish imperialism~~. Roszak misidentifies the enemy; it is the owners, ~~and~~ mongers and bureaucrats of ~~the~~ Technocracy that must be overthrown, not technocracy itself. At this juncture in human history, it is foolish if not downright treasonous to speak of ~~Goodmanian~~ ^Goodmanian^ spontaneity, self-regulation, and animal impulsiveness. The question we must address ourselves to is how to overcome the present social order, and ^what^ ~~are~~ the most effective ways of mobilizing the working class to become a class-for-itself and attain power. Thus the utopian communities that are being organized only solve temporarily individual not social problems and in a few years new fads will have overtaken them. Therefore we cannot share the optimism of Roszak who appears to think that the new counter-culture is a prelude to a new order that will replace the technocratic regime in the same fashion that christianity replaced the Hellenistic-Roman world view and science ~~and~~ enlightenment dislocated christianity in the modern ~~world~~ period and became the mistress of mankind. Thus we must conclude that the Roszak analysis scratches the power of technocracy and its perversities; it cannot abolish the reign of privilege. The issue is not ~~not~~ ~~Trolls~~ VS centaurs; it is not machine VS ~~man~~ man; →

it is not The Technocratic man vs the manipulated peasant; it is not man to recover his
humanity; and naively conceived utopian schemes
in The Shamanistic style of Rozak which can
not solve the Social problems of our time!

DEPARTMENT OF POLITICAL SCIENCE

Letter on Religion and the future
of man

To: Darrel Bryant,

Let me at the outset deal with what you termed "ironic comment" in your letter of March 14, 1969, which stemmed from my use of christian imagery in depicting your personal plight and how it might overcome you or overcome it yourself.

Since I regard christianity and other world religions as part of the human heritage and as significant historic manifestations that reflected man's consciousness of himself in his adolescent stage, I find it convenient and helpful at times to use religious symbolism as a means of communication. That is not to say that I accept religion as a valid hypothesis to be promoted, disseminated or fought for. I am not a member of the anthropomorphic race of rulers, tyrants, bureaucrats and apologists who need to rely on religious mystifications to justify capitalist treachery and barbarity and defend it as divinely or naturally ordained.

Thus I object to christianity not only because of its destructive, delusionary other-worldliness,

227

2

**Southern University in New Orleans**
6400 PRESS DRIVE
NEW ORLEANS, LOUISIANA 70126

DEPARTMENT OF POLITICAL SCIENCE

but also because of its worldliness as an historic institutional instrument put in the service of every detestable dictatorship: Roman slavery, christian feudalism, protestant capitalism, pseudo-rationalist laborism. In short, I am opposed to religion as theology, church, activity, idea. I find it a repugnant system of priestly manipulated thought and an abdication of reason; but I am prepared to study it in an effort to understand historic systems and how religiously motivated people perceive themselves, think and act. In our era religion is ancillary to capital and as such it stifles human progress by masking capitalist robbery and snobbery and by helping socialize people into becoming docile slaves. Therefore radicals must attack the socio-economic functions of religion and fight for the secularization of life and the abolition of the oligarchies that man its institutions.

It is my considered opinion that North American radicals engage themselves and get bogged down in revolutionary rhetoric and polemics within the religious-metaphysical or within the moralistic-psychological rather than within the historic-scientific context. In other words, instead of starting with the actual and existential, radicals start with the religious esthetic or ethical angles of vision and get mired up in the

228

~~in the~~ verbal process of self identification — a
condition that forecloses the prospect of social
revolutionary action. under such conditions and with
such perspectives a revolution cannot be conceived, let
alone carried out. Put briefly, the road from the
'personal god of love' to revolutionary social violence
and total personal commitment to the human community
is long and steep and very few of us will ever
traverse that road and reach the summit of the
mountain. Thus we ought, but do not seem to know
that to avow the emancipation of man is not commensurate with going to the Sierra Maestra or the caves of
Hunan, to transporting weapons on the Ho chi Minh
trail or fighting American marines in Vietnam, to exploring
the Andes and dying heroically in Bolivia, to combatting
imperial Zionism in the Judean hills or Tel Aviv. To
affirm personal liberation and be a subsidized radical
is not to feel the scorching sun of the desert and the
debilitating diet of the palestinian Arab. To implore
people to abide by christian principles is not tantamount
to living with worm-infested stomachs or dying of
malnutrition or waiting in hopelessness for the hand of
death to snatch you from the midst of your beloved.
To make 'revolutionary' pronouncements or issue manifestoes
before T.V. cameras is not equivalent to facing nobly

229

**SOUTHERN UNIVERSITY IN NEW ORLEANS**
6400 PRESS DRIVE
NEW ORLEANS, LOUISIANA 70126

DEPARTMENT OF POLITICAL SCIENCE

instant death before American B 52 saturation bombing, napalm and other nefarious forms of gunpowder. To give press conferences, do fout "thing", stage "peaceful" demonstrations, organize teach-ins and walk-outs is infantile indifference compared to falling to the music of machine guns and the thunderous roars of American bombers. To build "resurrection cities", or soul, ~~suppress~~ operate counter-institutions, mobilize the poor and shed tears for foreign martyrs is not ~~important~~ half as urgent as making the revolution right here in North America — the bastion of World imperialism.

Darrol, I have no illusions that my analysis is the last word in human wisdom. I believe as you do, that Marxist methodology and social analysis are superior to the abdicationist doctrine of the liberal-conservative procrustean matrix of reality. For this reason, I rejected and strenuously assailed liberal academic politics and was proscribed as a result. Therefore, the answer to the 1st question you pose — Do I expect "some kind of apocalypse" to replace a caste-ridden World by a classless society — is self-evident. To make it crystal clear, I believe revolutionary warfare is the only weapon worth considering at this juncture of human

230

history and radicals must prepare themselves for prolonged struggle in North America. They must discard—but not completely—such outmoded methods as legal channels, parliamentary parties, counter-institutions, non-violence, direct action and other methods and tactics of liberal radicalism and moralistic reformism. These and other methods have not borne the fruits of liberation but suppression. they have forced the system to contrive subtler methods of co-optation, isolation and proscription. They have not produced revolutionaries or radicalized the masses. They have deluded people into believing that their marginal and trivial acts were meaningful and significant when they were not. They have simply demonstrated the meaning and effectiveness of bourgeois dissent and shown how dissent, moderate agitation and "responsible leadership" pay and open avenues of ascent to Anglo-Saxon society. To ascertain the validity of this assertion one must study closely the careers of the successful practitioners of Jewish liberalism, protestant moralism, and academic agnosticism in both the US and Canada. On this evidence it is not unfair to contend that the Movement exists only on the headline, the editorial page and the kitchen of romantic liberals, and utopian conservatives whose supreme goal is the suppression of true revolution.

231

In sum,

I am saying radicalism on this continent is a liberal fraud perpetuated as a means of social control and repression and "leftists" must stop deceiving themselves and thinking that they are making the "revolution" when they are the making for practicing psycho-therapy. The test of radicalism is revolution. Our "Radicals" will show their mettle when they plan and prepare for the seizure of power and the smashing of the bourgeois state. If this were not their aims, let us the they stop the fraudulence and sophistry of liberalism and reorganize on the basis of a revolutionary perspective and goals and find the cadres and the masses to carry it out. Therefore, first and foremost, we must organize a revolutionary party and arm it with revolutionary theory and the strategy of guerrilla warfare. And we must not confuse the anomie riots of Watts, Newark, Detroit etc. and the "police riot" of Chicago with revolution. If we do, we will not be able to understand that what passes for ubiquitous radicalism is a sponsored goat of the establishment and a pampered child of "liberal" society and a miscreant to justify further repressive measures.

232

SOUTHERN UNIVERSITY IN NEW ORLEANS
6400 PRESS DRIVE
NEW ORLEANS, LOUISIANA 70126

DEPARTMENT OF POLITICAL SCIENCE

Lastly, let me return to the intellectual error that I discern in your work and which I find suffuses your present article with the spirit of modern christianity: your view of man as an "ambiguous possibility" as opposed to the traditional notion of man as being born in sin and iniquity. I believe this concept is the root-cause of much obfuscation and deflection among "christian radicals" because it raises the relevant fundamental existential question without answering it. At this point, clever idologists and religious escapists in consonance with the spirit of bourgeois liberalism recognize the problem and speculate about it endlessly instead of coalescing with progressive forces to work for the abolition of "ambiguity" and capitalist slavery. If by "ambiguity" you mean man's inability to foresee the future with absolute clarity then you are right. If however, "ambiguity" means a new metaphysic, then it is a "pipe-dream". Comrades of the revolutionary persuasion therefore begin with man not as an ambiguity but a potentiality capable of doing either ill or good. Which of these antagonistic hypotheses prevails depends of course on the kind of

social environment man inhabits, and the kind of
social institutions that rear, educate, and socialize
him and the kind of values he imbibes and
internalizes as operational and ethical norms.
Therefore, revolutionaries conclude that sin and
iniquity and its modern variant ambiguity are
not inborn to man but are immanent in the social
institutions of capitalism and all system based on
human exploitation whatever the espoused ism may
be.

Thus we proceed to construct an environment that actualizes man's potential for good,
which is the creation of social relations based
on human interaction and social processes
underpinned by a co-operative ethic. From this local
arrangement we build a national and an international
system not on abstract brotherhood but on a brotherhood undergirded by the equitable distribution of and
sharing of wealth and power nationally and internationally and predicated on the principle of
individual participation in decision-making affecting
one's life and destiny and the communal life of
mankind. This type of society presupposes the

DEPARTMENT OF POLITICAL SCIENCE

replacement of caliban by man, the abolition of the Kingdom of Want, the institution of the realm of freedom, the extinction of the state system, the creation of an international federal polity. Then and only then can we speak of the coming of man and the unfolding of freedom. Then and only then can we speak of human growth, happiness, love. Then and only then can we speak of co-operative labor, social commitment and rule by man. Then and only then can we speak of voluntary, spontaneous and willed action. Meanwhile the party of man must plan the overthrow of capitalism which is our most immediate and urgent task!

To the editor of the Globe:

Oliver Clausen's article,"Tantrums and Sex",and Harvey
Simmons' "Roots of Revolt in Academe " (Globe,June 1st,1968)
are a patent example of the reflexive reaction of an outraged
conservative and a liberal-minded professor in tune with the
surface but not the core of life.Mr.Clausen alleges that students
desire perfection and as advocates and practitioners of nihilism,
anarchy and mindless romanticism,are out to destroy the 'democratic'
institutions we have.He is annoyed by the shibboleth and the
idealization of alien tyrannies yet he concedes there is something
wrong somewhere in the West.Mr. Simmons seems to think that the
students are revolting against university bureaucracy and power
structure because they are suffering from the student-as-nigger
syndrome and by implication,he suggests that 'democratization'
is desirable.The basic facts of the matter are:(a)in the past
decade,a significant amount of footwork has been carried out,
the purpose of which was not only to examine the university
structure but also government,business,religion ,labour and the
mass media.Most of these studies were undertaken by socialists
and communists and some by liberal intellectuals, and each
study was done so meticulously that very few scholars dare challenge
any of its findings.These studies,in the light of the revolutionary movements-domestic and international-and the dogmatic
centrisms which prevail in the Western world,have become the well-
springs of thought for liberals who demand that their parents and
governors live up to the democratic tradition and its professed
ideals , and sign-posts for socialists who aspire to restructure
the foundations of society. (b)The authoritarianism,hypocrisy
and bureaucratization of life which characterize not only the

236

social,economic and religious institutions but a university education as well.The universities are operated as 'investment'outlets
whose aim it is to fashion,knead and mould youngsters to fit the
industrial and commercial requirements of a tyrannical and obscurantist middle class who pass as freedom-lovers according to the
gospel of Mr Clausen , but who are in fact little czars in their
compartmentalized pursuits of life and more importantly,obno-
xiously self-righteous and extremely smug in their just and complacent ways.Think-tank has become the function of the university
now that the community colleges can train lower echelon clerks
for middle-size businesses.(c)The abjuration of radicalism by the
traditional champions of reform-the unions,the Social Democrat and
Communist parties ,the intellectuals-has left an enormous gap
which has to be filled by someone.The students who are claiming
this role are not only the precursors of a new order but the
founders and the children of the future.The students (approximately 40% in North America come from working-class backgrounds)
have grasped the fundamental issues confronting the age-tech-
nology,cybernation and their uses-and have rediscovered the
humanist values which underpin$^{ned}$ liberalism and socialism in their
revolutionary stages.Therefore,they have to either create their
own models for the new society or borrow from abroad in order to
create it,and it is clear that the two approaches are being fused.
What is perturbing from a liberal point of view is that the liberals
are refusing to account for liberal abdicationism and apply the
democratic process-a course they refuse to apply$^{following}$ to any sector
of life,i.e. the church,the economy,the university,the state,
the union and indeed the newspaper.

f) Lastly,the disintegration of traditional structures,the decay of its values and the disharmonies that trouble the conservative-liberal mind should not stupefy us into inaction,escape or surrender.We have to face the reality and that is revolutionary.Revolutionary one must be in an age of revolution or join the counter-revolution and blaspheme the present and the future , romanticizing an idyllic non-existent past.It is the burgeoning of life and the high epiphany of the future.It is ours not to plead for but to seize and claim.We will not lay prostrate before the editors of the Globe , begging permission to be free. We shall be free !

# Index

## A

academic freedom, 38, 40–42, 48, 62, 71–73, 78, 87, 90, 93–96, 103, 138, 149, 174

alienation, 24–25, 81, 122, 169, 184, 189, 194, 197–98, 200–201, 204

American imperialism, 18, 37, 85, 116, 140

Aptheker, Herbert, 46

Arab–Israeli conflict, 18, 85

Arab revolution, 16, 18, 85

Arabs, 16, 59, 85, 116

Aun (faculty member), 73, 75, 77–85, 87–89, 94, 96–97

## B

Bains, Hardial, 145, 152–53

Barzun, Jacques, 179–80

Benello, George, 150–52

Bissell, Claude, 42, 49, 167–74

black community, 101, 105, 111, 117, 127, 130

black consciousness, 110–11

black faculty, 110

Black Liberation, flag of, 107, 111, 113, 116, 124

black revolution, 99, 109, 112, 117, 128

Brown, Norman, 4, 93–94, 199–201

## C

Caliban, v, 22–25, 28, 164, 194, 209

Canadian Association of University Teachers (CAUT), 38, 42, 58–59, 71, 77–79, 81, 87–88, 91, 93–94, 98, 154

capitalism, ix–x, 11, 13, 18, 22, 24–28, 35, 37, 79–80, 137–38, 140, 162–63, 175–78, 204–6, 208–9

  monopoly, 11, 18, 25, 37, 59, 76, 80, 137, 163, 175

Carrigan (principal), 96–97

Catholicism, 147–48

Chomsky, Noam, 150–51

crime, 106, 131, 133

Cronkite, Walter, 130

## D

Darwinism, social, 189, 194

Davis (minister of university affairs), 57, 59

Dawson (faculty member), 94–95, 98

dictatorship, 76, 116–17, 176

Downing, Peter, 95

Durst, George, 97

## E

Emile (fictional character), 184–85, 187–93

*Emile* (Rousseau), vii, 183–84, 193–94

Endress, Henry, 55, 71–73, 75, 78, 85–86, 88, 90, 93

## F

fascism, 147–48, 152
Ferdinand, Valerie, 115, 119, 121
Flexner, Abraham, 176
Ford, Gerald, 112
Forman, James, 109
French, Lynn, 111–12, 118, 121
Friddle (faculty member), 96

## G

Ginsberg, Allen, 199
Goodman, Paul, 150–51, 199, 204
Graham, Billy, 131
Grebb (chairman of the board of governors), 56, 75, 85, 93

## H

Haggar, George, 59, 71, 74–79, 85, 93–98, 108, 111–12, 114, 116, 131, 133, 194, 197
Halleck, S. L., 145
Harding, James, 146
Hauge (faculty member), 81–82, 84
Hellyer (faculty member), 75, 78, 87–90, 93
Humphrey, Hubert, 127

## I

ideology, 3, 31, 34–35, 80, 108, 145, 147–48, 199–200
immigration, 131–32
individualism, 27, 201

## J

Jewish professors, 86
justice, ix–x, 11, 53, 56, 59, 61, 63, 66–67, 73, 75, 90, 102, 116, 129, 131–34

## K

Kelly, Neil, 148, 150
Kerr, Clark, 167, 176–79

Kirk, Grayson, 179
Kitchen (faculty member), 27, 94, 96

## L

Lane-Brown, Mary Kay, 93–94
Langen (faculty member), 94–95, 97
language, 32–34, 96, 193
La Touche, Daniel, 146–48
Leary, Timothy, 199, 202
Lee, Dennis, 150–51, 161, 165
Little, Fred, 97
Lutheranism, 53, 57–58
Lutherans, 42–44, 46–47, 53–55, 57–59, 75, 85–86, 88, 91, 93–95, 145, 157

## M

Maoism, 33, 153
Marcuse, Herbert, 200–201
Marx, Karl, 80, 176
Marxism, 37, 151, 153, 179
May Day, 124, 129
McGuigan, G. F., v, 144–45, 148–53
Miljan (faculty member), 79
Milner (professor), v, 87–88, 91
Mitchell, Lansing L., 133
multiversity, 165, 167, 176–79
Murray, Hugh, Jr., 132
mystic revolution, 199

## N

nationalism, 37, 107, 121, 176
Negro colleges, 100, 103, 106, 110
Newman, John Henry, 172, 175–76
New Orleans, 99–100, 102, 109, 112, 124, 128, 131, 178
niggerness, 106–7, 110, 123, 125
Nixon, Dick, 126–28

## O

oligarchies, 11, 15–16, 54, 206

oppression, xi, 13, 30–31, 116, 122, 124, 145–46

Overgaard (faculty member), 79–81, 84–85, 93–94, 96–98

**P**

Paape (faculty member), 95, 97

pacifism, 62, 148, 199

Payerle, George, 153

Peters, Frank Cornelius, 73, 75, 87, 89

poetry, xiii, 12–16, 18, 25, 159

**R**

racism, 101, 110, 112–13, 116, 120, 123, 127, 129–30

radicalism, x, 6, 9, 18–19, 29, 33–35, 37–38, 46–47, 79, 82, 137, 145–48, 150, 168, 207–8

religion, xiii, 5, 7, 9, 12–18, 40, 57–58, 141–42, 162, 189–90, 194–95, 202, 205–6

repression, 6, 11, 24, 47, 49, 56, 108, 112, 125, 137, 200–201, 207

Rochdale, 151, 165–66

Roszak, Theodore, 197–99, 202–5

Rousseau, Jean-Jacques, vii, 183–89, 191–94

**S**

scholarships, v, 28, 43–44, 46, 48, 60, 74, 76, 78, 92, 108–9, 128, 138–39, 156, 162

scientism, 14, 25, 199, 203

self-love, 188–89, 193

slavery, vii, 22, 25–27, 48, 50, 56, 104, 116, 119, 125, 131

Smith, Percy, 39, 88–90, 157

society
    Afro-American, 106, 111, 114–15, 118–19
    bourgeois, ix, 24, 26, 199–201

Caliban, 25
    industrial, 197–98
    liberal, 22, 24, 44, 50, 165, 208
    racist, 118, 128–29
    Western, 22, 145, 151
    white, 101, 104, 110–11, 122

Sophie (wife of Emile), 190–93

Southern University New Orleans (SUNO), 100–101, 103, 105, 109–10, 112–13, 115–16, 118, 120–21, 128–29

Southern University New Orleans (SUNO) upheaval, 99

*Strength of the University, The* (Bissell), 169

Strickler, George, 131–33

student boycott, 115, 117

student movements, 48, 144–45, 147, 170

student power, 34–36, 146–47, 163

*Student Protest* (McGuigan), 144–45, 148–53

student radicalism, v, 29, 34–35, 145, 147, 168, 194

students
    black, 104, 111, 117, 129, 134
    radical, 48, 149

syndicalism, 35, 147–48

systems
    educational, 22, 46
    political, 3, 5–6, 10
    social, v, ix–x, 3, 10, 15, 26, 139–40
    socioeconomic, xiii, 3, 22
    university, vii, 38–40, 46, 49, 57

**T**

technocracy, 198, 203–5

technology, xiii, 3, 9, 12–13, 15–18, 22–23, 196–97

totalitarianism, 3–5, 126

**U**

Underhill, Frank, 157

universities
  American, 121, 155, 178–79
  Canadian, 40, 47, 76
  private, 57, 59
university administrators, 34, 146
university autonomy, 41, 49, 103
university education, 42, 82, 195
*University Game, The* (Lee and Adelman),
    vi, 38, 151, 161, 165–66
university government, 34–35, 39, 49,
    158, 173, 179–80
university life, 27, 42, 166, 174
university structure, 32, 34, 36, 195
university teachers, 58, 87, 92, 138, 154

**V**

Vietnam War, 108, 177
Villaume (faculty member), 81, 83–85,
    97–98
violence, 7, 9, 11, 24, 46, 108, 126, 128
virtue, 23, 43, 61, 76, 90, 92, 186–87, 189,
    191
vulgarity, 61–62

**W**

Wilfrid Laurier University (WLU), 57–
    59, 74, 79, 81, 87, 89, 95, 97
Williams, Charles, 118, 121
Woodcock, George, 148
world history, 11–12, 28, 175
world revolution, 17, 19, 112

**Z**

Zionism, 59, 85, 112, 206
Zirnhelt, David, 150–51

Friday, November 24, 1967

# Faculty: intellectuals or clerks

by Dr. George Haggar
Department of Political Science

The fundamental issue facing university faculties in Canada is whether our "intellectuals" will continue to act as sales clerks or begin to act as intellectuals. Doubtless, most of them as "liberal-minded-people" consider the question before us irrelevant as a social issue, but significant as an academic exercise in this world of liberal harmony and "fellowship".

The exponents of harmony in this country have of late discovered that students in fact have passions and those untutored minds are people.

What is amazing, however, is that those consumers are raising questions about the quality of the sold products and sometimes the manufacturing skill of the producers. And most irritating of all, is the fact that the students are asking the higher clerks — the administrators — about the conditions of work for the producers, the environment in which they are shopping and above all, they are demanding a share in the management of the factory system.

As catalysts of the coming revolution, the students are the harbingers and the heralds of a new civilization — a civilization that asserts that man is not a speck in the cosmic dust, nor a chattel to be bargained about, nor a child to be assuaged by a pacifier. They are saying no to dehumanization, no to pleasant platitudes, no to programmed education; they are proclaiming their humanity in a debauched milieu and they know who is responsible for this monstrosity.

In their quest for self-discovery, human committment and social emacipation, the students have put their seniors on the defensive and the latter have reacted in a typical ruling-class manner.

They have either withdrawn into their shells hoping that this "generational gap" is a temporary phenomenon; but having noticed the mounting tide of the

onslaught, they tried to harness it so as to reinforce the existing order and demonstrate their liberality. Thus the new "public relations" in the universities, the commissions, the joint committees and the new "fellowship." But all this utilitarian activity and this "humanism" seem to have whetted the appetites of the consumers who are no longer satisfied with "joint partnership" and are seeking the substance of power, not its shadow.

Here, I think, is the crux of the matter The students have learned here and elsewhere that in fact, the supporters of the status quo have no intention of sharing in the government of the university and do not plan to abdicate or surrender. Moreover, the faculties have become the Girondists in "this best of all possible worlds." And since they do not want any basic change; they simply want to be "in" on the secrets of empire and to achieve this "historic mission" some of them would like to have a united front for the students. Though most professors are contemptuous of "student power", they think that the "radicals" are a small but a useful minority whose immense energies could best be channeled to advance professiorial interests.

Put bluntly, professors have no regard for student radicalism and have not examined its contents. But they want to use it as an instrument to club the administrators with rather than use it as a means of opening new fields of student-faculty relations or broadening the existing sources of co-operation and communications. This opportunism is being slowly detected by the students but as accredited clerks and members of the new priesthood the professors will go on demanding a role commensurate with their functions in the eternal design of the contemporary university, thinking that they can call in the troops if the occasion requires them. Meanwhile they will rely on "reason" to persuade the administration that the "ma-

chine" can be operated more productively and more efficiently if they sat in on more non-accountable and non-functioning committees.

To illustrate this principle, let us cite our campus—the best of all possible campuses. Here we have no social community. We merely have an ecological community—a personalized environment of monads linked together by a physical plant and a "benign" administration whose members prepare and distribute the monthly "diet" and hope to bridge the lagging two-year gap between the national and local diets. The faculties protest and they grumble in their "palatial" faculty lounge and they even talk about "power," but the moment someone has access to power, his information becomes privileged and it cannot be divulged, etc., etc., etc.

The difficulties of the professors are compounded by their lack of collective consciousness as a group and thus their relationships with the students cannot be any more than transactional. For these reasons, the faculties are half-victims, half-accomplices and therefore half-human beings. And this leads me to say: unless the intellectual replaces the clerk, both the administrator and the teacher will become superfluous clerks in this great private enterprise of ours. Therefore, it follows that the intellectual as the interpreter of the "tradition" must become the author of the tradition and if he does not, or refuses to, he, like his predecessors, must be consigned to the dustbin of history.

Knowledge is pain and the demands of virtue are onerous And only the great create great needs And this epoch is a time of greatness, a time of quest, and a time of love; a time of spring and a time of passions; a time of brotherhood and a time of integrity; a time of choice and a time of authenticity; a time of man becoming man and a time of freedom and her majestic unfolding.

It is a time of revolution!

السعر ٣٠٠٠ ل.ل.

Printed in the United States
By Bookmasters